Also by Constantine FitzGibbon

Fiction

THE ARABIAN BIRD
THE IRON HOOP
COUSIN EMILY
THE HOLIDAY
PARADISE LOST AND MORE
WHEN THE KISSING HAD TO STOP
GOING TO THE RIVER

Non-fiction

MISS FINNIGAN'S FAULT
THE LITTLE TOUR (WITH GILES PLAYFAIR)
THE SHIRT OF NESSUS
THE MAXIMS OF LA ROCHEFOUCAULD
NORMAN DOUGLAS
THE BLITZ
RANDOM THOUGHTS OF A FASCIST HYENA
THE LIFE OF DYLAN THOMAS
SELECTED LETTERS OF DYLAN THOMAS
THROUGH THE MINE FIELD

Constantine FitzGibbon

Denazification

NORTON

First published in Great Britain by
Michael Joseph Ltd.
26 Bloomsbury Street,
London W.C.1
1969

© *1969 by Constantine FitzGibbon*

7181 0668 7

PRINTED IN GREAT BRITAIN BY
NORTHUMBERLAND PRESS LIMITED
GATESHEAD

writing to W. M. Fullerton on November 15th 1886, said: 'Since their most noble closing of Civil War, I have looked to them as the hope of our civilization.'

On the lower, or local, political level, it was a different story. By law, every man was disfranchised who had 'participated in the rebellion', and all such were debarred from holding public office of any kind. This immediately raised the question of what was implied by 'participation'. It caused great confusion and the answer varied from one military district to another, but it was generally assumed to mean all who had held Confederate commissions and all who had served in the Confederate or Southern States' administrations. In the State of Missouri an attempt was made to apply this law to the professions, and to exclude former 'rebels' from the bar. This, however, was defeated by a Supreme Court Ruling (*Cummings v. Missouri*, January 14th, 1867). President Andrew Johnson also disfranchised all Southerners who had participated in the Rebellion and who possessed a taxable fortune of over $20,000.

It is not the intention here to tell in capsule form the long and intensely complex story of Reconstruction which extended over some four or five years. (It is coincidence that this is almost exactly the same space of time as that which separated the surrender of Hitler's forces from the creation of the German Federal Republic.) But the preceding paragraph does, I think, show that the political intention of the United States Government and of the Congress was to drive out of public life the whole governing élite of the smashed Confederacy. To this must be added the fact that the democratic process was only to be restored to the Southern States on a basis of universal suffrage (minus the disfranchised rebels), which meant that some 700,000 Negroes were to get the vote. It was thus the obvious hope of the Northern politicians that the South could be remodelled after the Northern image, just as it was to be the American hope that Germany could be remodelled in the American image. Congressman Thaddeus Stevens of Pennsylvania had written: 'The whole fabric of Southern Society must be changed.' Substituting the word German for Southern, this sentiment was to be re-echoed a thousand times during and after the Second World War.

In the South, this policy was only a very partial success. In the short run, that is to say during the Reconstruction period, even the

'Mississippi was now without a state government of any kind. The Governor was in prison charged with treason; the legislature was forbidden to meet, the archives and public property were in the hands of the military; the writ of habeas corpus was still suspended, the President had not yet officially announced the end of the war; martial law was supreme throughout the state. What would come next no one could foresee. This was a period of anxious uncertainty. Many expected wholesale confiscation, proscription and the reign of the scaffold. People were thrown into more or less terror.'

The four years' slaughter had left a legacy of hatred and great bitterness behind it. These emotions were much aggravated, at least in the North, by the murder of Abraham Lincoln immediately after hostilities had ceased. With his death, the South lost the one man who might have played the part of a Charles II or a Louis XVIII. Whether he could have in fact mastered the intricate problems of the day will, of course, never be known. That his overriding wish was to recreate a more perfect union and not to exact vengeance upon the Union's enemies is, however, certain. He had wished, he said, 'to bind up the nation's wounds' and to do this 'with malice towards none, with charity for all'. Winston Churchill, himself the greatest advocate of moderation in dealing with the defeated Germans after the Second World War, wrote in his chapter on *The American Civil War*:

'With him (Lincoln) vanished the only protector of the prostrate South. Others might try to emulate his magnanimity; none but he could control the bitter political hatreds which were rife. The assassin's bullet had wrought more evil to the United States than all the Confederate cannonade. Even in their fury, the Northerners made no reprisals upon the Southern chiefs. Jefferson Davis and a few others were, indeed, confined in fortresses for some time, but afterwards all were suffered to dwell in peace. But the death of Lincoln deprived the Union of the guiding hand which alone could have solved the problems of reconstruction and added to the triumph of armies those lasting victories which are gained over the hearts of men.'

Indeed, the moderation, at the highest political level, of the North in its treatment of the South immediately after the war was remarkable. 'Nobody was hanged for a political crime, no land of the vanquished Confederates confiscated.'[1] And George Meredith,

---

[1] James F. Rhodes: *Lectures on the American Civil War*.

So it is apparent that while the events of 1660 provide only a very slim precedent for those of 1945, there are certain resemblances: the trials of the regicides dimly foreshadow the war crimes trials; the indemnities paid to some of the Royalists were, in principle, not dissimilar to the restitution made to some of Hitler's victims; and the expulsion from power of those Cromwellian ideologues, the preachers, was motivated by the same intense dislike of their ideas that the Nazis also inspired. What is perhaps more important is that all this was done, in theory at least, legally, even though new laws had to be passed to deal with an unprecedented stituation. There was no counter-revolutionary terror. Among other great institutions restored in 1660, one of the most important, and most attractive to the English people, was the old legal system and methods, constitutional, criminal and civil, which the Cromwellians had so frequently twisted or ignored. And one of the major war aims of the British between 1939 and 1945 was to restore law and order, as they understood it, to the European continent as a whole after the ravages of Hitler's war. If the British had simply shot captive Nazis without trial or after a brief and foredestined court-martial—a course which was frequently advocated, though more in private than in public—they would have been betraying their own war effort, their own dead, and their own history, just as surely as if they had collaborated with Hitler's people.

The situation in the United States in 1865 was very different from that which had prevailed in England in 1660. The Confederacy had been totally defeated after a bloody war that cost some 750,000 lives. The Confederate leaders had accepted the Union's terms, which were, significantly, that same 'unconditional surrender' that President Roosevelt was to demand of the Union's enemies in 1943. And in large parts of the South, particularly the deep South, conditions immediately after the surrender closely resembled those in Germany eighty years later, with freed slaves roaming the countryside much as bands of freed slave labourers were to walk home across Central Europe. In the State of Mississippi, to give but one example, Governor Clarke was arrested, the State legislature forbidden to meet, and the civil officers of the State and of the Confederacy ordered to submit any public papers or property in their possession and then to remain in their homes. As J. W. Garner has written in his *Reconstruction in Mississippi*:

the most emotional and ideological forces of the age. The Cavalier Parliament, *plus royaliste que le roi*, overruled the King himself. Some two thousand clerics who had sided with the Cromwellians were expelled from their livings in the harshest manner. The so-called Clarendon Code, which Lord Clarendon deplored, introduced cruel legislation against Nonconformist ministers of all denominations, including the Presbyterians. Charles II's hope of religious tolerance for all, including the Roman Catholics to whom he himself inclined, was smashed for over a century and a half. A particularly mean clause in this series of legislation provided that a Nonconformist convicted of preaching and sentenced to transportation was not to be sent to New England where he would be among his own people. Thus were the Nonconformists forced out of society and, for many years, into illegality, where they were to find their following largely among the dispossessed and uprooted of the first Industrial Revolution, while the Church of England became increasingly the faith of the prosperous. It would be an oversimplification to say that this profound religious split in England, Scotland and Wales caused the creation of those two nations which Disraeli described, but it was certainly a contributory factor to that dichotomy in British society which the early Marxists misinterpreted as being of purely economic origin. The Clarendon Code was passed in a spirit of vengeance perhaps, but by men who believed it their duty to protect the people against lies and wickedness. And in this respect it does bear some resemblance to the concept of denazification.

As for the writers, a handful were punished. Milton's story is too well known to bear repetition here. None was executed nor even effectively silenced, as was attempted, with some considerable success, in the case of the preachers. John Bunyan, imprisoned because he refused to renounce preaching, had little trouble in having his work printed, even from prison. English literature was neither then nor ever again muzzled as effectively as it had been under the Commonwealth or as it was in the more devout Roman Catholic countries during the Counter-Reformation, not to speak of the totalitarian states in our century. Perhaps the glories of English literature can in part be ascribed to this tradition of freedom. Here again the personality and tastes of Charles II are relevant: he liked going to the theatre to see new plays, he liked ideas, and he never took himself seriously enough to equate criticism with treason.

weakening the King's former enemies. In particular, all royal property and all Church lands were returned. However, Charles, like Louis XVIII, wished to be sovereign of all his people and therefore did not spoliate his defeated foes to the extent that Cromwell had done. Of course, the redistribution of wealth caused resentment and from the ranks of those who felt ill-treated there was eventually to spring the Whig Party and hence the English two-party system. But just as the Civil War had never been essentially a class war, so the two-party system did not, for many generations, represent two classes. Indeed, throughout the eighteenth and nineteenth centuries the Whig aristocracy regarded itself, perhaps correctly, as considerably more 'aristocratic' than its Tory opponents.

When we come to the purification of the administrative machine —had our ancestors been more barbarous in their use of the English language, they might have coined the word 'decromwellization' —we are on less secure ground. Certainly the great offices of State had passed to Royalists or to men who had been active in arranging the Restoration. As for the lesser offices, the *State Papers* of June and July 1660 reveal that numerous office-holders were dismissed because of their political past. Thus the Postmaster of Staines, the Overseer of His Majesty's Iron Works in the Forest of Dean, the Master Locksmith at Whitehall, the Prothonotary of South Wales, several officials of the Central Post Office, the King's Printer and many more were dismissed. How many I would not venture to say, but to judge by the evidence of the *State Papers* the number could not have been very large. Furthermore, the reason for dismissal was usually that the man had been an active Cromwellian and had been appointed during the Commonwealth as a reward for services rendered, and not that he had merely served under the Protector. Indeed, the tiny civil service of the age—if that term is applicable to seventeenth-century officials—seems to have maintained a remarkable continuity throughout all the troubles. Charles I had needed these men, so had Cromwell, and now they carried on their functions under Charles II. That amiable if indolent monarch was surely the least revengeful of men and neither he nor Clarendon wished to persecute a class of persons who had merely carried out their duties in circumstances of great difficulty.

When we come to the clergy, however, it is a different story. Charles II would undoubtedly have liked his Act of Indemnity and Oblivion to apply to them as well, but here he came up against might be subdivided into five. First, there were the major criminals, as they were regarded, that is to say the regicides who had actually signed the death warrant and their closest associates. Forty-one of these persons were named and a dozen executed, the remainder either fleeing abroad or suffering imprisonment. These trials might be compared to the trial of the major German war criminals at Nuremberg, and seem to have been carried out with a conspicuous and surprising fairness. Historians are generally agreed in regarding only the trial of Sir Harry Vane as an act of political expediency and injustice. Secondly, there was the question of how, and how much of, the previous administrative and juridical system should be restored. The Cavalier equivalent of Louis XVIII's *ultras* would have liked to see it all back including the Court of Star Chamber, but Charles II was well aware of the dangers that this would entail and he and his Chancellor, Lord Clarendon, restrained the extremists. Thirdly, there was the property question. Much Cavalier property had been confiscated by the Cromwellian régime and much had been sold to pay that régime's fines imposed upon its enemies. Here a compromise was reached: confiscated property was restored, sold property was not. This obvious precedent for the France of 1815 caused considerable bitterness among loyal Cavaliers. Fourthly, there was the matter of public officials with known Cromwellian views or of Cromwellian appointment. And finally, to come to the real purpose of this rather lengthy parallel, there was the question of what to do with the restored Monarchy's ideological enemies, which in that age meant principally the clergymen and the preachers who were inimical to the Church of England, and those writers, such as John Milton, who had vocally supported the Republican régime. It is in these two categories that a certain precedent to the process of denazification can be found. Although by no means a close precedent, it is the closest in 'modern' British history known to me. On the other hand, whether it consciously influenced the British and Americans three hundred years later would seem extremely problematic. On a less conscious level, however, it may well have had a certain bearing on their belief as to how an extremely complex problem might best be solved.

In a society such as that which prevailed in the England of 1660, where land was the principal source of wealth and therefore of power, the restitution of confiscated property to its rightful owners was the most important administrative step in the process of

As F. Maitland has written in his *Constitutional History of England*: 'On 29th May, 1660, the King began to enjoy his own again, but it already was his own and he had been reigning for eleven years and more. All the Acts of the Long Parliament which had not obtained the King's assent were simply void. At the Restoration, no statute was passed to declare them void; they were obviously void as having been made without the royal assent, and no repeal was necessary. In 1702, no lawyer would have appealed to them as law, and no lawyer would do so at the present day: they have no place in our statute book.' Here again a comparison can be drawn with Hitler's Germany. The Government of the Third Reich was almost certainly a 'legal' government in that its authority derived from Hitler's appointment as Chancellor by President Hindenburg on January 30th 1933, from the General Election of March of that year which gave the National Socialist German Workers' Party a majority that became absolute with the exclusion of the Communist Party delegates, and from the Enabling Act of March 23rd 1933, which entitled the Chancellor to govern by decree; but it was also and quite obviously a criminal government. It was for this reason that it was abolished, root and, it was hoped, branch, by the victorious Allies in 1945. It was declared, *ex post facto*, an illegal government, and the legality of this declaration, whilst interesting no doubt to lawyers, is of purely academic interest. England had in fact no legal government from 1649 to 1660: it was pronounced by the Western Allies, and later accepted by the Germans themselves, that Germany had had no legal government between 1933 and 1945, or maybe 1949.

Here any constitutional parallels must end. No lawyer could or would dispute that once the Cavalier Parliament had been elected in 1661 England was again a legal state, a *Rechtsstaat*, to use the convenient German word. Even from the point of view of the still unborn theorists of democracy, Charles II had been recalled by the will of the overwhelming majority of his people who were delighted to see the moribund apparatus of the Commonwealth dismantled and the old order, so far as possible, restored. Charles II was greeted with immense enthusiasm and his progress to London was indeed a victory parade.

Once the celebrations were over, the problem arose as to how the State should be re-organized—or, rather, restored—and how the Cromwellians should be punished or removed. This problem precedents provided by the aftermath of the English and American Civil Wars.

The emotions aroused by the English Civil War and above all by the execution of King Charles I were not dissimilar, both in Britain and abroad, to those feelings of horror which swept the world when the truth about the Nazi crimes was finally and loathsomely revealed. The fact that the two acts of murder were so vastly different in scope as to make them different in nature is here irrelevant. Charles I, the Lord's Anointed, was beheaded in an age which was, in general, profoundly religious and in which the doctrine of Divine Kingship was, also in general, accepted. In cutting off their King's head the English had performed a crime against God, man and the 'natural' order of society. C. V. Wedgwood in the last chapter of her book *The Trial of Charles I* has described the thrill of disgust that passed across Europe. There were demands for a sort of crusade against the wicked English. 'Royalist exiles in France', she states, 'were frequently insulted in the streets because they were English and thought therefore to be responsible for the murder of their King'.

If the foreigners felt this way it is not hard to imagine how much deeper were the emotions of the English Royalists. The King's execution was repeatedly compared to the Crucifixion and Charles became a Martyr, even a Saint, in the eyes of many people for whom such similes and epithets had a very real meaning indeed. To them, in 1660, the regicides seemed evil personified much as the Nazi bosses and concentration camp commandants did to us in 1945, while smaller Cromwellians, like smaller Nazis, were deeply implicated and suspect. Nor is the parallel all that far-fetched. Though the Cromwellians showed a certain measure of restraint in their own country, as did some Germans in theirs, that their behaviour in Ireland was less lethal than that of the Nazis in Poland cannot be ascribed to warmer hearts but only to the absence of technological facilities. Their slogan for the Irish Roman Catholics—'Hell or Connaught!'—was the most effective programme for genocide available three centuries before Zyklon B.

Furthermore Cromwell's government was completely illegal. When Charles I died, on January 30th 1649, his son, Charles II, automatically became king, even though in exile. During the eleven and a half years that were to pass before the Restoration, England had a Parliament of sorts, but one which could legally pass no Acts.

be created. Far more than the War of Independence, the Civil War has magical properties and to Americans the names that stir the blood are still Lincoln, Stonewall Jackson, Lee and Grant, Gettysburg and Bull Run, and Johnny will still come marching home and Sherman will march to the sea. It may be deplored, but these great military events and names are what are remembered by a nation, particularly in time of war: Drake, Nelson, Agincourt, Waterloo; Fontenoy, Austerlitz, Turenne, Napoleon; Barbarossa, Leipzig, Moltke, Frederick the Great, and so on. For Americans, the Civil War was, for some three generations, quite simply 'the War' and all other wars in which their country was involved were therefore assumed to be, in some measure, modelled upon the unique events of the 1860s. It is not altogether irrelevant that the greatest American best-selling novel of the 1930s was Margaret Mitchell's Civil War novel, *Gone with the Wind*, and that the movie of the same name filled the cinemas almost throughout the 1940s. And that novel dealt, in large measure, with the problem of the post-Civil War period of Reconstruction. It would not be an oversimplification to say that for Americans all wars are to some extent civil wars—the diversity of racial origin makes, to United States citizens, Wendell Wilkie's concept of 'One World' far more easily acceptable than it is to the citizens of France or China—and furthermore that the problems which the victorious Americans face after any war are those of 'reconstruction' and the creation of a more perfect union between victor and vanquished. The great historic nations tend to run remarkably true to form, and particularly if they are democracies. They learn from their mistakes occasionally, but history, like so many of the very best teachers, can also bewilder her pupils with her parallels. However that may be, the American attitude, like the general British attitude in 1945, was based upon the premise that the recently concluded war was in large measure a civil war between member states of the same industrialized 'Western' world, with the same cultural and spiritual background; that the defeated Nazis were grand-scale delinquents from values which were generally accepted by the whole of that world; and that therefore the elimination of these deplorable people from German public life would, almost automatically, ensure the return of the German people to civilization and the Concert of the Nations. Whether or not this concept was correct will be discussed in the next chapter. Meanwhile it may be of some interest to examine the matters in 1945, and the two great Western powers which did, Britain and the United States, had a tradition of civil war which surely had a marked effect on their policies when it came to what was hoped would be a final pacification of Europe.

Despite what the Marxists have written and despite the fact that true revolutionary elements such as the Levellers were active in England in the 1640s and 1650s, the English Civil War was primarily political, to a considerable extent religious, and hardly at all social in motivation. And from the actions of that war, from Cromwell's Commonwealth and Charles II's Restoration, there emerged slowly at last the two-party democratic system and government-by-consent which the English regard, probably rightly, as their greatest contribution to the history of mankind. Indeed, to the overwhelming majority of Englishmen alive in 1945 it seemed quite self-evident that their method of governing themselves was not only the best in the world, but was also a high-grade export product which needed only slight modification in order to function equally well in India or Egypt, in Germany or Ghana. The fact that this belief may seem naïve today, only twenty odd years later, did not invalidate the arguments of those who held it then. They were pragmatists and the facts they knew best were those concerning the self-governing white Dominions and the United States. The modifications needed by other societies, in order that they too might enjoy the blessings of British-style democracy, were education and training. The blessed oil that permitted the democratic system to function was tolerance. And there can be little dispute that the British tradition of political, as opposed to social, tolerance dates from the Restoration of Charles II in 1660, after a civil war and interregnum that had been political, not social, in its main origins. A brief examination of the events of 1660 will follow later in this chapter.

If the English Civil War lay deep in the British unconscious during the period of the Second World War and its aftermath, the American Civil War (or the War between the States, as some prefer to call it) was in the very forefront of the American collective conscience since, to continue in the psychologist's jargon, it is the great traumatic experience of American history. It was not only the great tragedy, the bloodiest of all American wars, but also the great triumph—at least for the greater part of the nation—in that the Union was preserved and only thus could the modern United States

Chapter Two

Civil wars in modern times are usually—though by no means invariably—the outcome of social revolution and perhaps of 'revolutionary' war. The war of the Commune, the Russian Civil War, the Irish Civil War in some measure, and the Spanish Civil War have certain qualities in common. In each case a revolutionary group had previously overthrown the established political authority: in each case, the heirs to that authority had reacted and had attempted to regain power by the use of force: and though both sides might and did appeal to legality, what was really at stake was power and not the rule of law. True, revolutionary governments are essentially interested in the destruction of the old society and part of that society is almost inevitably the old legal system. It follows that until their own new legal system is estabished, they can hardly avail themselves, in honesty, of the old. Trials may be held, but the verdict is seldom in doubt. Enemies of the revolution are shot or locked away in camps. And when those enemies' opponents reappear upon the scene with guns in their hands, it is hardly probable that they will treat the revolutionaries with greater equity. The bloodbaths that take place during revolutionary and counter-revolutionary civil wars are too well known to bear recapitulation. Furthermore, they are scarcely relevant to the theme of this book save in so far as they provide the country in question with a new governing élite. The avowed purpose of the Western Allies in Germany was to achieve this same end by legal means. Whether or not this was, or is in fact, possible is the kernel of the whole subject.

Because there have been civil wars which were not essentially, or were only peripherally, revolutionary wars. Only in a part of Ireland, for instance, was the civil war one of social revolution and the Italian wars of the Risorgimento did little to hasten social change in the more developed parts of the Italian peninsula. However, neither the Irish nor the Italians had any say in German

'I do not understand your passion, your relentless hatreds. I pass every day by the house which belonged to my forebears. I see their property in other hands. I behold in museums the treasures which were theirs. It is a sad sight: but it does not rouse in me feelings either of despair or revenge.'

Thus though the scars left by the Revolution were visible throughout the nineteenth century and are even discernible today, there was as yet no real counter-revolution further to bedevil the division between Frenchmen. As de Maistre, who can hardly be described as a liberal, remarked at the time: Louis XVIII was not the heir to Louis XVI but the successor to Napoleon.

It can therefore be stated that the events which followed the overthrow of the Revolutionary and Napoleonic régimes provide no sort of precedent for what was to be called denazification. No more did the events following the German defeat in 1918. In any case, the First World War was not by any means a revolutionary war and there was little to choose between the combatants from an ideological point of view before the Bolsheviks seized power in Russia. Somewhat futile attempts were made to have certain German officers tried as war criminals: these foundered on the fact that Germany remained a sovereign state and that the German courts, not unnaturally, saw no reason why they should punish their own nationals in this way, and at the very time when the British Auxiliary Forces were scarcely observing the highest standards of military chivalry in their war with the Irish.

In fact in order to find any, even remote, parallels to what was attempted in Germany by the Allies after 1945, it is necessary to look at the aftermath of civil, as opposed to national, wars.

that Minister Ferrard's proposal of indemnities to the *émigrés* ensured his return from Elba to Paris on a wave of liberal and democratic enthusiasm. Certain excesses, such as a people's persecution of the Protestants in the South of France, also increased the unpopularity of the restored government. Napoleon was back, for one hundred days, and immediately issued decrees more liberal than those promulgated during the first Restoration.

The Hundred Days had much increased the atmosphere of bitterness in France when Louis XVIII returned for the second time after the Battle of Waterloo. There were two directly contrary interpretations of recent events; the *ultras* maintained that the King had adopted too liberal a policy in the previous year, while the Liberals thought he had not been liberal enough. The immediate result was White Terror in the South where several hundred persons were murdered. This in some ways resembled what was to happen in France in 1944 after the expulsion of the Germans, when men of the Resistance and others took the law into their own hands. Defectors to Napoleon during the Hundred Days were explicitly excluded from the earlier Act of Amnesty and a few were executed, including Marshal Ney. However, if it was a persecution, it was remarkably half-hearted and this for two reasons. The first was that the Duke of Wellington was, in fact, the master of France immediately after Waterloo. He insisted that the King not only recall Talleyrand, who had been totally compromised by his close links with Napoleon and by his atheism, but also appoint Fouché as his Minister of Police. Fouché had filled the same post during the Empire and, more important, he had been a very prominent Jacobin and had voted for the execution of Louis XVI. Thus his appointment made nonsense of the fact that the regicides were also excluded from the Act of Amnesty. It was rather as if General Eisenhower in 1945 had ordered a German democratic government to re-appoint Heinrich Himmler as Chief of Police. Wellington, in fact, deliberately obviated the dangers of an official White Terror and, probably, of a French civil war. Secondly, the new French Government contained some very level-headed men. When the *ultras* in the Chamber demanded extremely harsh legislation against some 1,200 named revolutionaries, threatening them with exile and confiscation of property, the Duc de Richelieu, who was the King's First Minister, spoke some sober words, nor was he a man who had in any way compromised with the previous régimes. He said:

so was most of the organization bequeathed by the Revolution, and in particular the principle of equality before the law. France was not, and never then had been, a democracy, but the Charter enabled advanced liberals, such as the aged Marquis de Lafayette, and even republicans, such as General Carnot, to accept the Restoration. The first Restoration rested on the assumption that men of all parties would be summoned round the Throne, a visible testimony to the unity of a free and pacified nation. Under these conditions, men who did not believe in the Divine Right of Kings were to be induced, both by motives of providence and by necessity, to accept the Monarch.[1]

However, among the *émigrés* who returned with the King, there were many who held no such views. They had been spoliated, their estates stolen and sold, their closest relatives executed, they themselves forced for twenty and more years to eat the dry bread of charity in exile from their native land. Their leader was the King's brother, who later succeeded him as Charles X. They wanted revenge and they wanted the restitution of their property and, if possible, of their pre-revolutionary feudal rights. They had little love for the French people, and that people none for them. They returned as conquerors, though brought back by the armies of other powers, and they often behaved as such. The *ultras*, as they were called, resembled in many ways some of those German refugees who returned to what had once been their country, in 1945, in American and British uniform. They will appear later in this book. The attitude of the *ultras* was foolish perhaps, but surely comprehensible.

They demanded and were promised indemnities, and here a problem arose which was also to exist in Germany in the post-war period. After property has been confiscated or stolen by revolutionaries, whether French in 1792 or German in 1938, within a few years the estate or business may well pass through many hands. The present owner bought it, quite legally, perhaps even unaware of its past history. It would surely be gross injustice simply to seize it and return it to its rightful and original owner. On the other hand, for the state to indemnify either the original or the present holder means, in effect, that the whole nation is being asked to pay for the revolutionary deeds, which many will not regard as misdeeds, of a previous régime. This is more or less the course that the German Government has followed and is following. But Napoleon stated

[1] See Cambridge Modern History, Vol. X: 'The Restoration'.

might loathe the Frenchness of the French, but it never occurred to them in the eighteenth century to try and make them less French.

The French Revolutionary War, and its continuation, the Napoleonic Wars, were in some ways the first international ideological wars of modern times. The leading men of the French Revolution, after destroying the remnants of feudalism in their own country by methods of terror and mass execution which horrified almost all Europe's governing class, proceeded to export these doctrines by force to other countries where they were sometimes greeted as liberators by the people (as in Northern Italy or Poland), sometimes as hated invaders (as in Russia and Spain). The revolutionary *levée en masse* and, later, Napoleon's introduction of conscription added a new dimension to warfare. This was not a war fought by the professional armies and navies of rival princes but a war between nations, the first of the People's wars.

However, it was not a People's peace. The sovereigns and statesmen who assembled in Vienna in 1815 were men of an earlier age, and though their detestation of revolution and democracy led them to restore as best they could the old order in France and throughout Europe, it never occurred to these aristocrats that they, as foreign conquerors, could or should use mass methods against the French or even against their leaders. True, the Duke of Wellington was ordered in 1814 to arrest Marshal Soult for war crimes committed by his armies in Spain, but he blandly ignored this and invited his defeated enemy to dinner instead. As for punishment for the instigators and perpetrators of the Terror, twenty years and an empire had come and gone since then and this was regarded as a purely French internal matter, to be dealt with by the restored King and his ministers. Many of these, who like Fouché and Talleyrand were recalled after the second Restoration, had been completely identified with the Napoleonic régime.

There is little doubt that when Louis XVIII returned to France he brought back within his breast the traditional concept of French monarchy: he wished to be king of all his people, not merely leader of the aristocracy. His principal ministers, Blacas and the Duc de Richelieu, encouraged him in this view of his function. The Charter promulgated during the first Restoration, that is to say before Napoleon's Hundred Days, affirmed the intention of the restored monarchy not to re-create the *ancien régime*. The centralized administrative organization created by Napoleon was retained and showed a certain scepticism about this, the French considerably more, whilst the Russians were quite uninterested. Moreover, the Western Allies were immediately confronted with the fact that almost every man of authority in Germany in 1945—unless he were in a concentration camp, and even this did not invariably apply— was likely to be politically compromised in at least some measure. It was decided that denazification of the Germans, and in appearance at least *by* the Germans, was the solution. And this was attempted. Before describing why and how this took place, it might be as well to look at the scanty historical precedents for this massive operation.

Wars are of course fought for innumerable reasons, and the motives which inspired the Western Allies in the Second World War were intensely complex and various. But what concerns us, in the context of the denazification which was intended to follow the Allied victory, is in essence the ideological content of Western war aims rather than the economic or the purely political, *Realpolitik*, in the old-fashioned sense. And here there are very few precedents in even comparatively modern times. The great religious wars of the sixteenth and seventeenth centuries offer perhaps a remote analogy in that spiritual values were certainly involved and each side was convinced of the other's wickedness. However, since these wars were fought on the principle *cujus regio ejus religio*, it was the consciences of the German princes rather than their subjects that were at stake. And since the Treaty of Westphalia, which ended the atrocious war in 1648, promised complete and unconditional amnesty to all, there could clearly be neither punishment nor re-education. The constitutional reforms embodied in that treaty did indeed effectively contribute to the destruction of the moribund German First Reich; but this was done for reasons of *Realpolitik*, for the greater glory of the Bourbons and the weakening of the Habsburgs, and morality was not at all involved.

During the century and a half of comparative social stability that followed the Peace of Westphalia, many international wars were fought but not for ideological, or even for purely religious, causes. Almost invariably the objective of one or both combatants was to gain land, and thus wealth, in Europe or overseas at the expense of the enemy. These wars were ended by formal treaties between the warring governments, political and territorial adjustments were made, and conditions returned to normal. The English at this time. They also left a lot of half-American babies behind, for that is another form of loot. All this is quite normal post-war practice and perhaps taught the Germans one of the stern lessons that they had apparently failed to learn after the First World War, namely, that it is excessively foolish to fight a war and lose it.

Individual punishment varied from the petty infliction of humiliation on men and women who had for some reason aroused the hostility of the occupying armies, or their individual members, to the gigantic international spectacle of the Nuremberg Trials, and particularly of the first trial, that of the Nazi leaders, which in many cases reached its climax with the gallows. Since the subject of war crimes trials is germane to denazification—though, as I hope to show, the two concepts are quite distinct—I shall be returning to this.

This was punishment. Re-education was to follow, though the two processes in some measure overlapped. The Germans had to be shown the horrors for which they had been so recently responsible. Their noses were rubbed in the Nazi filth. In some places, the occupying soldiers physically compelled them to visit the Nazi concentration camps and even to exhume the rotting corpses of Buchenwald and Belsen. The newspapers were filled with horror stories of Nazi atrocities, and there is every evidence that this had an entirely beneficial effect which has endured, at least until today. The West Germans have shown a healthy distaste for totalitarianism of any sort.

Attempts to educate the German people by means of books and films were less successful. No great German writer emerged from hiding to excoriate the Nazis, while what the conqueror writes on such a subject is invariably suspect to the conquered. The propaganda lies of the Allies' yellow press during the First World War and after were remembered. Furthermore, the fact that for four years the Soviets were numbered among the virtuous victors did little to convince the Germans—millions of whom had been in Russia as soldiers—that the Second World War was a simple story of political virtue's triumph over political vice.

Beyond and above this policy of punishment and re-education, there lay an Allied policy, which was essentially an American policy, of turning the Germans into good democrats before allowing them to resume their former rôle as a major power. The British cupation of half Germany by British and American armies was not politically feasible: neither the British nor the American electorate would have accepted so expensive a version of colonization indefinitely. Furthermore, the corollary of a permanent Russian frontier along the Elbe was becoming increasingly unattractive as Soviet intentions in Eastern Europe became clearer. So here a compromise was reached: Germany would remain fully occupied and without a government until such time as in the opinion of Washington, London, Paris and Moscow, the Germans had somehow proved that they were fit to govern themselves again. Moscow, in fact, never has reached that conclusion and continues to occupy the Eastern Zone, though this is of course inextricably implicated with Cold War policies, which are not the subject of this book.

This indefinite period of total occupation was to be used by the Allies for two main purposes. One was to punish the Germans, both collectively and individually, for their crimes; the other was, very roughly, re-education. Punishment took numerous forms. Collective punishment consisted in part of extreme moral pressure, from the original order against 'fraternization' to the proclamation of the quasi-theological, though certainly un-Christian, doctrine of 'collective guilt'. Berthold Brecht had written in his version of *The Beggar's Opera*: 'Erst kommt das Fressen, dann kommt die Moral' ('First the grub: morality comes later'). The Western Allies reversed this process. The Germans, who until the collapse of their Armies, were living fairly comfortably on their own industrial and agricultural produce (in large measure the produce of many millions of slave labourers) occasionally supplemented by luxuries looted from other countries, now became themselves the victims of an enormous looting operation. Apart from the Russians, who took almost everything movable, including railway track, the French set about this most thoroughly. They even cut down large sections of the Black Forest, which gloomy tourist attraction lay within their zone, for pit props. The British systematically dismantled many of the factories in their highly industrialized zone, though their motive was ostensibly demilitarization rather than loot. The Americans also went in for dismantling, though on a somewhat smaller scale. Being devoted to the free enterprise system, they looted individually. The kitbags of the G.I.s who returned from occupation duty in Germany immediately after the war contained many curious items, and some American officers made small fortunes particularly as it was precisely to prevent such horrors that the British and American peoples had made enormous sacrifices in the about-to-be-concluded war. For quite another reason the Russians were opposed to the immediate destruction of industrial Germany. They needed, for their own purposes, both German industrial equipment and German technical skills, and they set about at once transporting machines and men from their zone to the Soviet Union. Their ideology also told them, in those distant days, that Germany must soon become a Communist state and so a part of Stalin's empire. Thus pastoralization was a non-starter.

If the Germans were not to be pastoralized, what then was to be done with them? The victorious Allies were, on the whole, convinced that the Peace Settlement of 1919 had been a failure and that the failure was in large measure responsible for the triumph of the Nazis and the resumption of hostilities in 1939. It was felt that the Treaty of Versailles had been both too harsh, in that it had temporarily impoverished Germany, and simultaneously not harsh enough, in that it had left a German government in being, and had allowed a resentful and revengeful German nation the means to achieve wealth and power once again with very great speed. This was interpreted to mean that a traditional type armistice with any German government, whether that of Hitler's successor as Chancellor of the Reich, Admiral Doenitz, or with some puppet régime of Allied choosing, was ruled out. The Western Allies did not want a German Pétain, since they wished, for the time being, no successor state to the Third Reich with the legal rights that must in international law be vested in such a state. For the time being, Germany was to cease to exist. (The Soviets, who had had nothing to do with Versailles, held very different views. They immediately imported their own 'German government', in the form of Herr Ulbricht and his colleagues, as part of the Red Army's baggage train. As will be seen, this in some measure conditioned their whole attitude towards the Nazis and the problems of what the West called denazification. To this day, Ulbricht's soldiers wear Hitler's uniform less swastikas.)

The Western Allies being in general agreement (a) that Germany should not be annihilated and (b) that she must never again be allowed to threaten her neighbours, were faced with the immediate problem of how these two, by no means compatible, ends could be achieved. Experience had shown that a permanent military oc-

Chapter One

When, in January of 1943, Dr Joseph Goebbels proclaimed that National Socialist Germany would henceforth fight a 'total war' and when in the same month President Roosevelt, in the presence of Prime Minister Churchill, issued his demand for the 'unconditional surrender' of Germany and her allies, these two phrases, though semantically almost meaningless, indicated that the war must be fought through to the very end. And so it was, until indeed the defeat of Germany was itself 'total'. The condition of that country, in the summer of 1945, was awful to behold: its cities in ruin, almost all its youthful and middle-aged men dead or in prisoner-of-war camps, its civilians close to starvation, every square yard of its territory occupied by its enemies, without a government of any sort while local administrative bodies functioned spasmodically or not at all, and, finally, itself an object of almost universal and fully justified detestation for the crimes that had been committed at Auschwitz and elsewhere by the Nazi rulers and by so many of their subjects. Perhaps not since the Third Punic War had any great country of the West been so utterly smashed, militarily, economically and morally.

And indeed certain Western voices, notably that of Mr Henry Morgenthau, President Roosevelt's Secretary of the Treasury, even before the end, in late 1944, came out in favour of a Carthaginian peace. The polite name for this was the pastoralization of Germany, that is to say the almost complete destruction of German industry and the reduction of Germany to an essentially agricultural community with presumably a much reduced population living at subsistence level. However, it was soon realized that such a policy, if it was to be enforced, would involve a harsh and endlessly prolonged reign of terror not dissimilar to that employed by the Nazis in their former occupied territories. It was doubtful if British and American public opinion would support such a policy for long,

ACKNOWLEDGEMENTS

Deutsch Ltd., London W.C.1.; *The Future of Germany* by Karl Jaspers and *Forced To Be Free* by John D. Montgomery, The University Of Chicago Press, Chicago; *American Jewish Year Book, volume 55*, edited by American Jewish Committee and published by Jewish Publication Society, New York; *Article in The Times of 20th January, 1960*, The Most Reverend Archbishop Lord Fisher of Lambeth.

ACKNOWLEDGEMENTS

I would like to thank the following for their unfailing and invaluable help: the John Simon Guggenheim Memorial Foundation, whose generosity made the book possible; Herr Herwarth von Bittenfeld; Peter Bielenberg; the Wiener Library; Mrs. Joan Saunders of Writers' and Speakers' Research; and above all Mrs. Margot Pottlitzer, whose help both in research and advice has been invaluable.

I would also like to thank the following for permission to reproduce extracts from works in which they control the copyright: *The Trial of Charles I* by C. V. Wedgwood, and *Memoirs of Field-Marshal Montgomery*, William Collins Sons & Co. Ltd., London S.W.1.; *Constitioanl History of England* by F. Maitland, Cambridge University Press, London N.W.1.; *Reconstruction in Mississippi* by J. W. Garner, Peter Smith Publisher Inc., Magnolia, Mass.; *The American Civil War* by Winston S. Churchill, *The Second World War* by Winston S. Churchill, and *Before The Colours Fade* by Fred Ayer, Cassell and Company Ltd., London W.C.1.; *Essays On The Civil War And Reconstruction* by W. A. Dunning, Harper & Row, New York; *The Nazi Seizure of Power* by William Sheridan Allen, Eyre & Spottiswoode (Publishers) Ltd., London E.C.4.; *Commandant of Auschwitz* by Rudolph Hoess, Weidenfeld & Nicolson Ltd., London W.1.; *The Burden Of Our Time* (*The Origins Of Totalitarianism*) by Hannah Arendt, George Allen & Unwin Ltd., London W.C.1.; *The Answers* by Ernst von Salomon, Rowohlt Verlag Gmbh., Hamburg; *Documents On Germany Under Occupation* by Beate Ruhm von Oppen, published by Oxford University Press, London W.1. for the Royal Institute of International Affairs; *Psychologist in Germany* by Saul K. Padover, Duell Sloan and Pearce Inc., New York; *Berlin '45: The Grey City* by Richard Brett-Smith, Macmillan & Co. Ltd., London W.C.2.; *The Hidden Damage* by James Stern, the author; *Die Geburt Eines Neuen Deutschland* by Stefan Doernberg, VEB Deutscher Verlag Der Wissenschaften, Berlin; *The French In Germany 1945-1949* by Roy Willis, Stanford University Press, California; *Article 43 Conv. IV of 1907 respecting the laws and customs of war on land*. James Scott edition. *The Hague Conventions and Declaration of 1899 and 1907*, Oxford University Press, Inc., New York; *Memoirs* by Franz von Papen, André

For my friend
JOHNNY HERWARTH
with thanks

military governors found it impossible to carry on government if they fulfilled to the letter the new regulations, excluding from public life all who had served in the Confederacy. 'General Schofield (in Virginia) and other officers declared that the adoption of this policy would render government impossible, as there were not available enough competent persons to fill the places vacated . . . Until reconstruction was nearly completed, therefore, the Commanders were permitted to retain their discretion in the matter . . .'[2] General Schofield's complaint from Richmond was to be echoed by General Patton from Munich.

Economically, the old governing class in the South, drawn principally from the plantation-owners, was already almost, if not entirely, bankrupt when the Civil War ended. The more patriotic had invested in now valueless Confederate Bonds, their sons were dead and their plantations in ruin, their mansions not infrequently burned or plundered. Yet they still had to pay very heavy taxes. The emancipation of their slaves either deprived them of the labour force that they needed to reconstruct their properties or inflicted a further financial burden in the form of wages that few could meet. The plantations were broken up and sold to pay the taxes. The old Southern aristocracy was in fact destroyed by the war and the Thirteenth Amendment. Such was the quite deliberate intention of the Washington government. This is again a parallel to the decision in 1945, that the great German industrial combines be broken up.

However, the spirit of white supremacy was not broken, even though the Southern aristocrats who were its only, and only faint, justification disappeared. Just as the English conquerors of Ireland in bygone centuries either returned home or rapidly became more Irish than the Irish, so the carpet-baggers, the war profiteers and those other white heirs to the plantation-owners rapidly became at least as racialist—perhaps more violently and coarsely so—as the class that had vanished. One hundred years and more after the passage of the Civil Rights Bill of 1866 its provisions have only been very incompletely applied.

Yet despite the partial failure of the Americans to enforce the ideal American-type democracy on a large percentage of their own people by legal methods, the ideal remains very vital indeed. And if my point is taken—I realize that it is open to considerable dispute

[2] W. A. Dunning. *Essays on the Civil War and Reconstruction.*

—that the Americans and British regarded the Second World War as, in great measure, a civil war of the Western World, then it is surely almost inevitable that they should have tried to end it along much the same lines as they had ended, or thought to have ended, their own, applying the same principles and avoiding, if possible, the same mistakes.

But was the Second World War Europe's Civil War? Who were the Nazis who had rebelled and with whom the Western Allies decided to deal by a mixture of punishment, coercion and re-education within a legal framework?

Chapter Three

Once it had been decided that Germany should be denazified, a question of great complexity arose immediately and one for which no fully satisfactory answer has been, or perhaps ever can be, given: namely, what is, or was, a Nazi? Before going into the official answer that was in fact given to this question, it is worth examining the nature of the problem in its historical, moral, political and emotional aspects.

Yet first, behind this problem there lurks another which is in some ways even thornier: what was Nazism? Scores of thousands of pages have been written on this subject over the past forty years by Nazis, anti-Nazis, economists, journalists, politicians, theorists of many nations, psychologists, historians, theologians, and philosophers. Few men can have even browsed in this massive and depressing literature without becoming aware that what they are hearing is a mounting cacophony. And this in turn can be traced back to the fact that Hitler and the other 'theorists' of National Socialism were, in most cases, intellectually incapable of defining their 'view of the world' and in many cases deliberately obfuscated the issues by squirting forth great inky clouds of abstract, semi-abstract and not infrequently quite meaningless jargon.

Thus the very name National Socialist German Workers' Party contains at least two paradoxes, one of which was deliberately exploited. During Hitler's struggle for power in the 'twenties and early 'thirties, there were three main political power blocs which he had to absorb, neutralize or conquer. These were the Nationalists, the Socialists (who posed as internationalists and deplored the chauvinism of 1914-18) together with the trade unions, and the Communists. The Nazis' spokesmen alternately, and sometimes simultaneously, attacked and wooed the Nationalist 'reaction'. They did much the same with the members of the great Social Democrat Party (though they never wooed the S.D.P. as such), posing as the 'true' German Socialist Party, and there can be little doubt that many leading Nazis, including the Strasser brothers and, to a considerable extent, Dr Goebbels himself, believed in the socialist content of the Party. Roehm and Heinrich Himmler, though far from being socialists, were firmly on the side of the 'workers' in what the Marxists call the class struggle, while Hermann Göring was equally firm on the other, the Nationalist, side. Finally Hitler's declared detestation of the Communists was almost as sinuous in its application as the Communist Party line itself in those days. Before Hitler came to power he was prepared to collaborate with his declared enemies in a transport strike of purely political intent: afterwards he signed a pact with Stalin. And among the militant street fighters, the shift of individuals between the two totalitarian parties was always very great. Perhaps the one political quality which Hitler never claimed for himself or his party was any democratic allegiance; and the one hard policy from which he never deviated was anti-semitism.

Indeed the NSDAP though calling itself a party and fighting a long and successful series of local and national elections, was not, in the normal sense, a political party at all. Hitler himself preferred to call it a 'movement', a *Bewegung*, a phrase he had neatly lifted from the Marxists. And like the German Communist Party, it was dedicated in the first instance to the destruction of the 'system', and ultimately to the supplanting of the old ruling class—whether aristocrats, churchmen, democratic politicians, cultural leaders or trade unionists—by its own people. In this again its rôle was similar to that of the Communist parties in Germany and elsewhere when not in power. It was a conspiracy. But here the parallels end. Whatever one may think of the Marxist interpretation of history, at least the Marxist dialectic has a considerable logical coherence, which was far more acceptable to, and accepted by, clever and idealistic men thirty-five years ago than it is today. The Nazi dialectic—the phrase itself is really meaningless—had for all intents and purposes none. What the Nazis stole from the Marxists were their methods and their immediate motive—power at any cost. Thus Hitler's movement had the appeal of a violent crusade, but what that crusade was *for* was never really identified by its leaders: it was thus in some measure impervious to intellectual criticism, since it was *for* every vote-catching concept and so ultimately for none. What it was *against*, however, was made very apparent. Its appeal was essentially negative, and when Rauschnigg spoke of the Revolution of Nihilism he was entirely right. At the centre of Nazism, as at the centre of Hitler's own book, *Mein Kampf*, there was a vacuum, a nothingness. In Goethe's phrase, 'noise and smoke and nothing more'.

If, in the years before March, 1933, Hitler and his Nazis appeared to have almost no constructive policy, they compensated for this by the number of institutions, persons and social groups whom it was their intention to destroy. The Weimar constitution was to go, and with it the men who had created it after the 1918 defeat (men known in Nazi parlance as the 'November criminals') and who had done their best to keep it going since then. The Treaty of Versailles was, somehow, to be scrapped and German power and might restored with the slogan, 'Germany awake!' The political autonomy of the German states who had formed the Empire and had survived into the Weimar Republic was likewise for the trashcan in the interests of centralized authority. All other relicts of independence in the future Nazi State were to be similarly *gleichgeschaltet* or 'geared to equality', a typically vague Nazi semantic coinage (and these included not only the massive trade unions and the smaller but powerful professional and even sporting associations, but also such organizations as the Boy Scouts, the Freemasons and other such societies, while the threat to the Churches, if muted, was audible). Economic matters were treated more gingerly, since there was no wish to antagonize unduly the industrialists whose money was needed and given, but there were promises of a re-organization of the economy in order to 'abolish unemployment'. There were other threats of social re-organization, but the last, as it had been almost the first, was the destruction of 'international Jewry', which was to begin with the exclusion from German life of the German Jews and of those Eastern European Jews who had entered Germany since the Russian pogroms of the 1800s and as the result of Polish anti-semitism since 1918.[1] The Jews were destined, from the very beginning, to be the principal victim of that *furor teutonicus* which provided the explosive power for Hitler's nihilistic revolution.

[1] The number of these 'foreign Jews' was much exaggerated by the Nazi propagandists. Nevertheless, since their very 'foreignness' made them more identifiable and thus spectacular, this propaganda was widely accepted, even by some German Jews. In fact far more Eastern European Jews seem to have emigrated to England and America than to Germany. Reliable statistics, however, are not available.

The means by which these destructive aims were to be achieved were left vague, probably because neither Hitler nor his closest associates knew enough about economics, international politics or social organization, and certainly because he had no wish deliberately to antagonize any major element of the electorate other than the Jews and the Communists. Specifically omitted from his levelling plans was the German Army, the neutrality of which would be essential when the time came to seize power and carry out these 'reforms'. The one really potent innovation that was introduced into the Nazi Party before the seizure of power was, once again, a very woolly concept, the 'leadership principle'.

This was trumpeted forth as an alternative method to the theory of government-by-the-choice-of-the-governed which is in many ways the essential justification of the democratic system. By contrast, the Leader, Adolf Hitler, demanded unquestioning obedience and unswerving loyalty from his followers—first the Party members, later the German nation as a whole. His total authority would be delegated, as through a pyramid, from him to his principal lieutenants and thus on downwards. In theory, a monolithic state would then respond, as a single organism, to the wishes and wisdom of a single, wise, beloved leader. Thus would national unity and national purpose be ensured, freed from the divisive forces of self-interest that plague democracy.

This was of course no new concept. All autocracy is based on the theory that the autocrat is always right and invariably obeyed. Even in normal political parties, what the leader of the party decides is of primary importance. And even at that time Mussolini had, in some degree, tried to put into practice what Hitler was preaching. However, even within the comparatively small Nazi Party before it came to power such monolithic control was almost unobtainable. The Party was constantly threatened or actually confronted by schisms and heresy, with the resultant expulsions and, in 1934, massacres of the faithful. Indeed, a case could be made that Roosevelt's or Baldwin's control of his party in 1936 was as great as Hitler's in the same year. If Hitler succeeded in retaining control of his party, and later of his country, for twelve years, this was due less to the monolithic nature of that party than to his own skill in dividing his followers and playing them off one against the other. The animosity and even hatred that prevailed not only between many of Hitler's principal satraps but also between the organizations they controlled were often bitter, of his making and, it would seem, to his liking. This went on to the very end, when at last Hitler saw fit to anathematize most of his principal colleagues as traitors.

But if a modern dictatorship is scarcely more 'monolithic' than a democratic state, at least it can in great measure disguise its internal tensions until the pressure finally bursts the shell of censorship and silence, and at last the purges begin and the 'traitors' are duly condemned and the tanks rumble through the streets. But certainly any modern industrialized state is far too complex an organization to be run on principles as simple as those which Hitler advocated but failed to implement. This has been the case in the more advanced European societies for the past three hundred years and more, which is presumably the very good reason why the concepts of autocracy and of the divine right of kings long ago gave way to those of aristocracy and democracy. This, however, has not prevented almost every great European power in this century from embracing a 'national' government when a period of crisis, political, military or economic, seemed to call for unity of purpose and an end of partisan squabbling. In 1932 the German crisis was very profound. Hence the appeal of Hitler's leadership principle which, no matter how meaningless it was then and became later, was in reality the only constructive choice he could offer the electorate. His main appeal was to a vast, popular disillusion with the Weimar parties. Political cynicism was both deep and widespread in pre-Hitler Germany.

In the matter of revolutionary theory the Nazis were thus far behind the German Communists, let alone the Russian ones. Lenin's famous apothegm: 'Who whom?' was of directly nihilist ancestry, but by the time the Nazis were again an important force in Germany—by 1929 or 1930—the Russians and their German associates had learned a great deal about the actual exercise of power. Throughout the world the Communists were becoming ever more aware that their principal enemies were those 'left-wing' parties, organizations and groups of individuals which still prized the value of the individual above the value of power for its own sake. The Nazis, unlike the other parties of the extreme left, had almost no such 'philosophical' schisms. Indeed Nazism has made very little appeal, then or now, to anyone with any interest in ideas. This, however, does not mean that it was without any appeal to persons interested in abstractions, in system-making, in ideology. For the unimaginative the mere arrangement of ideas provides a tolerable alternative to their formulation, and some of the German tribes are as lacking in imagination as any groups of Europeans. This can clearly be a virtue in some ways. It is, for instance, desirable that technologists should not confuse their dreams with their technology. This is no doubt also desirable among civil servants and soldiers of all but the highest quality. The vivid imaginative powers of the Southern Latin nations and of the Celts have often inhibited their ability to organize and to act successfully in these three—and other—important fields, fields in which the Germans have frequently excelled. The Germans have of course produced many great poets and musicians and a few great painters, but essentially the qualities that the Germans admire (or at least admired during the period with which we are here dealing) are those which enabled certain great German thinkers to 'systematize' the chaos of the unimaginative mind. The artist is the man who makes the pattern for his imaginative fellowmen: for the unimaginative it is the political theorist, the philosopher, maybe the scientist, perhaps the musician. The great men of modern German culture are Marx, Nietzsche, Einstein, perhaps Schoenberg. Göring is said to have once remarked: 'When I hear the word culture I reach for my gun.' For men of his sort culture means the arts: technology, economics, low-level science and entertainment did not cause him to reach for his gun. Thus again Nazism was a nihilism in that it repudiated so many of the greatest men of that German *Kultur* which it professed to respect. All was paradox: it was a revolt of the weak against the strong, in the name of strength: it was a revolt of the stupid against the clever, in the name of intellectual integrity: it was the revolt of failure against success, in the name of glory. It was one of the great 'levelling' movements which have periodically and temporarily wrecked most of the great nations of Europe.

The Nazis came in from below. But again, the paradox is there. Because they were fighting their rivals, the Communists, for totalitarian power, and because—though stupider than their chosen enemies—they did not have to take orders from any equivalent of Stalin's post-revolutionary Comintern, this revolutionary party, devoted to *Gleichschaltung*, could also pose as a counter-revolutionary party and enlist the support of strong segments of the stupider middle and upper classes. In fact the 'leadership principle' meant that whereas every Nazi supporter in 1932 thought that he was forwarding his own interests, he was, in both the short and the long term, merely supporting Hitler's. And Hitler, as we now know, was interested in nothing save his own power—not even, and finally not at all, in the interests of the German people who voted him in, and fought for him, and died for him, and murdered for him.

If we are, as the Allied powers found themselves forced to do, to decide who or what was a Nazi, we must think in terms of dates. Those who voted Nazi in the many elections of 1932 and early 1933 which buried the Weimar Republic were of at least three sorts:

There were the Old Fighters, the *Alte Kämpfer*, who, at least in theory, dated from the days of Hitler's first attempted seizure of power in 1923, and who derived their name not only from this but also from the fact that many of them had fought both in the First World War and in the *Freikorps* that had taken part in the various frontier, and internal, skirmishes of the immediate post-war years. (They were a minority. The *Stahlhelm*, or Steel Helmet, was the principal ex-soldiers' organization. Its political affiliation lay, in general, with the German Nationalists.) They might be generally described as tough, brutalized and neurotically nationalistic.

Secondly, there were the down-and-outs, victims of the depression from the lower or lower-middle class. Many of these had joined the combatant, street-fighting organization of the NSDAP, the *Sturmabteilungen* or Storm Battalions (henceforth abbreviated to SA), some for ideological reasons, some because they liked a punch-up, some because they were given food and on occasion a little money. Many of these men had fluctuated between the SA and the Communist equivalent, the *Rotfrontkämpfer* (RFK) or Red Front Fighters. They had won the Battle of the Streets for the Nazi Party, and they were its most socialist element. Their leader was a drunken homosexual named Ernst Roehm. Anti-social elements who lacked the wit to understand Marxism were attracted to the SA. From its ranks were to come, in due course, the middle-level bosses of the concentration camps and other repulsive elements of the Nazi régime. But not all of them were criminals.

Thirdly, there were those deluded opportunists of the upper-middle class, and more rarely of the aristocracy, who imagined they could use the Nazi movement for their own purpose, to prevent a swing towards Communism or even Socialism and to crush the apparently powerful trade unions. Others of this group had less selfish motives. They saw the chaos all around them: they had lost what little confidence they may have ever had in the Weimar Republic and German democracy, and, as has since happened in other European countries, they believed that a 'strong man' was needed. The natural political resting place for these people was the German National People's Party of which Alfred Hugenberg, former general manager of Krupp's, and later a great newspaper owner and film magnate, had become the leader in 1929. In October 1931 a mass meeting was held at Harzburg attended not only by German Nationals and the Nazis, but also by the *Stahlhelm*. Dr Schacht, the brilliant banker, economist and former Reichsbank President who in large measure spoke for German heavy industry and big finance, brought Hitler and Hugenberg together and an alliance was forged. By this the Nazi Party was given a bogus air of respectability in the eyes of those administrative and managerial classes which could only view Roehm's street fighters with disgust. Thenceforth many more members of the bourgeoisie joined the Nazis than before.

There was thus very little homogeneity in the Nazi Party that had its first taste of national power in January of 1933. Its nebulous policy was well suited to so disparate a cross-section of the German nation. And if there was little that was coherent either in the make-up or in the views of the Nazi Party, there was even less among the millions of voters who voted for that Party's list of candidates in the numerous elections of 1932. The science of psephology did not then exist, nor were there public opinion polls in those days, but it is generally agreed that the massive increase in Nazi support throughout 1931 and 1932 was at the expense of all the other political parties, from the Communists to the German National People's Party, while the Communists managed to maintain or even increase their voting strength principally at the expense of the Social Democrats.

But many of the votes that the Nazis collected in the elections of 1931 and 1932 were purely negative, as negative as the party's politics. Hitler promised to 'save' Germany, a task that the multiple political parties were proving themselves incapable of doing. All right, why not give him a chance? He'd probably fail, anyhow.

What he asked for, and was given, was a blank cheque. He did not hesitate to fill it in.

As soon as Hitler became Chancellor, and even more so after the March 1933 General Election which—with the exclusion of the Communists—gave him, through the Enabling Act, absolute power, there was a vast influx into the Nazi Party. The atmosphere of those days is admirably described in William Sheridan Allen's *The Nazi Seizure of Power*[2] in which the process of nazification is given in detail with reference to a single, real but pseudonymous German town, which he calls 'Thalburg'. He writes:

> Many people felt the need to protect themselves by joining the NSDAP. In some cases club leaders or artisan masters joined so that they could stay on executive committees. Others wanted job insurance. Still others joined in response to the growth of terror. The great rush to join the NSDAP began in February, immediately after the announcement that Hitler had been named Chancellor. People who had been wavering or who had held back for fear of compromising themselves now submitted applications. In January, 1933, there were fewer than a hundred dues-paying Nazis in Thalburg. By March the Nazi Local Group swelled to almost four hundred. By mid-March there began a veritable flood of membership. This great climbing-on-the-bandwagon became so pronounced that old Nazis referred to the newcomers as the *Maerzgefallene*—the 'March casualties'.
>
> The NSDAP had so many applicants that it was forced to declare that it would accept no new applications after May 1, so that the existing backlog could be cleared up. This, of course, produced a still greater rush in April. Von Altberg remembered seeing bushel baskets full of applications in the Nazi county headquarters on April 20. By May 1 close to 1,200 Thalburgers had joined the Nazi party. Almost 20 per cent of the town's adults had been enrolled.
>
> Not all of these new members joined as a result of commitment to Nazi ideas. One of the Nazi methods of bringing institutions under control was to require their leaders to become members of NSDAP. This was the case with the County Prefect, von Altberg, and also with the TNN's (the local newspaper's) reporter, Erhardt Knorpel. Both were exceedingly sceptical about Nazism and both joined because it was demanded of them. Others joined because they saw membership in the NSDAP as an indispensable prerequisite for personal advancement. This was admittedly the case with two teachers who confidently expected that by joining the Nazi party they would ensure themselves a promotion. Still others joined out of a pure desire to conform, i.e.,

[2] Eyre and Spottiswoode, 1966, pp. 233-35.

to go along with the majority, as illustrated by the following story:

Hugo Spiessman was a curious case. Until the March Reichstag elections he was in an agony of indecision. I remember him frequently asking me for advice: should he or should he not join the party? I always told him to do whatever he wanted, but this didn't seem to help. But the day after the Nazi electoral success the SA gave a victory parade which I witnessed. At the very end of the parade was Hugo Spiessman with a happy smile on his face. As he marched by he waved to me and yelled, 'I've done it!'

Many men were forced to join by the pressure put on them at home. As one man described it, 'there were wives whose constant words were "Think of your family!" There were wives who actually went out and bought a brown shirt and put their men into it.' Still others entered the NSDAP in the belief that what Nazism needed was a leaven of decent people and that by working from within they could steer the revolution into moderate paths.

Thus, at the very least, the level of commitment varied considerably among the new members. But once they had joined the NSDAP these people were trapped. They were now under party discipline and had to aid in the whole process. The organization of the party (in cells and blocks down to the smallest unit) kept them under constant surveillance. Instead of ensuring their future, they became even more insecure, for if they were ever expelled from the NSDAP they would be marked men. Furthermore their consciences were hopelessly compromised, for as members they partook of responsibility in the most immediate sense.

This process was taking place all over Germany. In order to keep their jobs many men felt forced to join the Party, whether they sympathized with its aims or not. As the process of *Gleichschaltung* became accelerated whole professions, such as the school teachers and not much later all government employees of any stature, were forced to join or resign. In many of the professions, such as the law and journalism, membership of the appropriate Nazi Party professional organization was an essential. Thus a friend of mine, a lawyer and at all times a convinced anti-Nazi, maintains that he deliberately joined the Party because only thus was he able to defend anti-Nazis in court. And finally there was the omnipresent fear, particularly among men of the old left-wing parties, of the Nazi terror. It was rumoured at the time that members of the now illegal RFK had received orders from their KPD leaders to infiltrate the SA. It seems unlikely, and this writer has seen no evidence to support that story. But with Communists being murdered, tortured and carted off in their thousands to Göring's new concentration camps, the safest place for a former or present Communist was in the ranks of the Nazis. Many changed sides, as many had done—in both directions—during the last years of Weimar. This may well have served to give Roehm's SA an even more radical hue. And, of course, an ex-Communist would have to be even more zealous than another man in his service to the Nazis.

Thus the Nazis of 1933 were a very different collection of men from those of 1932. The term *Müssnazi*, or 'Nazi by necessity' was coined about this time. It was one which was to be heard, *ad nauseam*, by the Allied authorities and the denazification tribunals after the war. It sometimes seemed as if the millions of German Nazis had all been compelled to join the Party. This was of course nonsense. But still, there were large numbers of *Müssnazis*, and it is not for those who were not there, and did not experience the pressure and the terror, to condemn their lack of heroism in not refusing to join.

A much smaller category of Germans also confuse the issue of what was, and what was not, a Nazi, even at this early date. There were a number of people, some of them extremely prominent, who helped the Nazis into office, supported them with great ability and zeal throughout the lifetime of the régime, and yet never joined the Nazi Party. The most spectacular of these was Baron Franz von Papen, whose rise is discussed in Chapter Nine below, though there were many others too. Again, there were men who, because of their past, could hardly be victimized by the Nazis provided they kept quiet. Pastor Niemoeller, the former U-boat ace, was one who did not keep quiet when his Christian conscience was outraged: it is safe to assume that had he not been a famous war-hero he would have died in Dachau, as so many clergymen of both persuasions did, instead of being given preferential and comparatively kid-glove treatment and kept alive in another, slightly less savage, camp. Ernst von Salomon, on the other hand, did keep quiet. An extreme nationalist in his youth, an accomplice in the murder of Walther Rathenau (a Jewish politician of great brilliance who had served both the Kaiser and Weimar), Salomon had been imprisoned for his crime and was thus, from the Nazi point of view, as much above suspicion as any man can be in a totalitarian state. Though he was not a Nazi and lived with a Jewish mistress, he kept his mouth shut, and he survived and prospered throughout the Third Reich. After the war and his release from the American imprisonment he so bitterly resented, he wrote a brilliant *apologia pro vita sua* which was perhaps the most damning, as it is certainly the wittiest, attack on the whole concept of denazification. It is called *Der Fragebogen* and will be quoted in this book. A bestseller in Germany in the 1950s, it is at times immensely moving, though often cynical beyond belief, and is a remarkable indictment both of himself and of the sort of German 'hero' whose heroism consisted principally in the saving of his own skin.

There was another group of Germans, in 1933 and the years that followed, which is extremely hard to categorize as either Nazis, non-Nazis or anti-Nazis, and that is the German Army and particularly its officers. The picture here is one of immense complexity. Again, paradox is the only description.

The German Army had survived the defeat of 1918 and the subsequent political turmoil for two main reasons: it had retained the respect of the nation, which had enabled it to assume an almost regal authority as the ultimate arbiter of that nation's fate, and, being a very small and entirely professional army, it was kept under the closest political supervision by its commanders, who had decided that it would serve the State but not in any way the parties. Though most of its senior officers cared nothing for democracy or the democratic politicians, they had defended Weimar against its internal enemies and had ordered their soldiers to shoot at Nazis and Communists alike. The Army defended the State in so far as it regarded the State as a useful adjunct to the Army itself. It was not a-political—for the camouflaged General Staff was quite prepared to topple by intrigue or direct demand any government of which it disapproved—but it was above party politics. And any form of party politics was forbidden to its soldiers and, in theory, to its officers.

Such a divorce from the nation's life was almost impossible for most officers, as individuals, and totally so for some, in the heightening political crisis of Weimar's decline. In 1930 three junior officers were arrested for having joined the NSDAP. They were defended by Dr Carl Sack (who died for his complicity in the attempt to kill Hitler on July 20th, 1944) and the colonel of their regiment gave strong testimony against their conviction by a civil court. His name was Ludwig Beck. As General Beck he was leader of the military opposition to Hitler from 1938 on, and was also one of those who died on July 20th, 1944.

On that same fateful date Colonel von Stauffenberg had planted the bomb that failed to kill Hitler. Eleven and a half years earlier this same officer, then a lieutenant, had been reprimanded: he had taken part in a torchlight procession to celebrate Hitler's appointment as Chancellor.

Two more profoundly proved anti-Nazis than Beck and Stauffenberg would be hard to find in the subsequent history of the German Army. Yet had they lived, and had they not done what they later did, both would have been highly suspect to the Allies in 1945.

Some senior German officers, such as General von Hammerstein, were outspoken opponents of the Nazis in the period which is here under consideration—the early days of the Nazi revolution—and were to remain so. Others, such as Reichenau and to a lesser extent Blomberg, were pro-Nazi. The majority of the senior officers, and most of the junior ones, adopted the attitude of their class towards the new régime. While disliking its vulgarity and deploring the coarse brutality of the SA, they believed that they could use this new régime for their own ends, which were, in essence, a stronger Germany with a more powerful army. Meanwhile the Army was the only major organization of the German nation (with the exception, for different reasons and here only partially, of the Churches) strong enough to resist the torrent of *Gleichschaltung*. The Army was not Nazi, but no more was it anti-Nazi, and it did not need to be *Müssnazi*. It stood aloof. It was at worst a passive accomplice to the brutality that was rampant in Germany between January 31st, 1933 and June 30th, 1934.

By the spring of 1934 the tensions within the Nazi Party were close to breaking-point. The 'radicals' looked to Ernst Roehm and the armed strength of his SA to force through a second revolution. The 'reactionaries', who looked to the Vice-Chancellor, Papen, felt that the first revolution had already gone too far and that it was time the terror be ended, or at least legalized. Neither of these groups contemplated the dropping of Hitler, for he had led them both to believe that he sympathized with their views. Hitler seems to have hesitated, but when the heads of the Army and of the Navy spoke out in favour of the reactionaries and against the radicals, he decided. Roehm and his henchmen were murdered, principally by Heinrich Himmler's *Schützstaffeln* or SS (the 'Protection

Squads' who had initially been Hitler's personal bodyguard) and with the tacit approval of the Army. Hitler also took the opportunity of this bloodbath to liquidate a number of 'reactionaries' —including General von Schleicher—whose existence irked him. Papen was lucky to escape with his life. The number killed is unknown, but it was probably some five thousand at least. As a political force, the SA ceased to exist.

The Night of the Long Knives was, on a national level, the equivalent of the murder by gangsters of gangsters in Chicago a few years earlier. Roehm, Ernst, Heines and the other dead SA bosses were neither more nor less repulsive and brutal than their assassins, Göring, Goebbels, Himmler and the rest. What was significant was the fact that the Army, which had sat back and allowed this bloodbath, thus became Hitler's accomplice both during and after the crime. A few weeks later, when the aged President Hindenburg died and Hitler succeeded him as Head of State, the soldiers accepted a personal oath of allegiance to the dictator. The *Gleichschaltung* of the Army had begun. The generals, and not only the generals but also many respectable persons both inside Germany and abroad, began to believe that the gangster-type murders had somehow made the German Government itself a more respectable body. The terror did not cease, the concentration camps were not closed, anti-semitism was increased, but all this was done under a cover of 'legality' and, more or less, out of sight. It seemed that the Nazi state, having conquered Germany, might digest its conquest. And so it did, a gorged python. The process of *Gleichschaltung* continued, but less brutally. For four years and more there was very little opposition to Hitler from any quarter but the extreme Left, and, on honourable occasions, from the clergy. His economic policies seemed to work, as unemployment sank: his country increased in size, with the incorporation of the Saar by the vote of its inhabitants, the unopposed re-occupation of the Rhineland and the incorporation of Austria: Germany's strength grew with its expanding army and navy and air force: the foreigners flocked to the Berlin Olympic Games of 1936 and admired the orderliness of the new Germany: the Third Reich seemed to be becoming, perhaps even to have become, a civilized society.

And so, during the period 1934-1938, the nature of Nazi Party membership changed. To be a German and an anti-Nazi meant, increasingly, to be unpatriotic. *Gleichschaltung* had worked, precisely as the Nazis had intended that it should. The former governing class, college presidents, the leaders of industry, diplomats and even some bishops of both faiths found that they could accept the régime. It was now even more difficult to become a Nazi Party member, but men of substance were acceptable, and accepted. The old governing class became nazified, even if with personal reservations.

As for the mass of the population, the process was still more successful. It is well-known that a plebiscite is a very dubious way to determine the wishes of a people, but it now seems that the Nazi plebiscites were not faked. Vast majorities, amounting to near-unanimity of 95%, 98%, 99% were turned in at these mock-elections. True, they had the fear of the concentration camps behind them—all Germans knew of the existence of those fearsome places, but few knew the details, which ignorance added to the terror—but that is not at all an explanation of their massive *Ja* votes. Hitler was Germany, the Germans were Nazis or at least Nazi sympathizers, and by 1937 the python had digested its first meal. It was, indeed, beginning to feel the pangs of hunger. Hitler looked abroad, at the rabbits awaiting beyond the frontiers. As 1937 became 1938 he had a solid Germany behind him.

The Nazi Party, however, was no more homogeneous than it had ever been. Indeed, since it had become almost synonymous with the German nation it was, in some ways, even less so. The smart young business executives who wore a discreet swastika button on the lapel of their dark suits as they danced with the daughters of country estate owners (who were rather less likely to wear such an emblem) had little in common with the SS man, whose uniform was his badge, and who wore a whip when doing his rounds at Dachau or Sachsenhausen. For no matter how 'respectable' Nazi Germany might appear in 1937 and 1938, it continued to be based on terror, though the terror was better hidden now. The terrorists were mainly drawn from the *Allgemeine* (or General) SS. This was a very different type of organization from the SA, its original parent, just as its cold, cranky, efficient and ambitious leader, Heinrich Himmler, was a very different man from the drunken, ebullient and swaggering Ernst Roehm. Under Himmler, terror had become a Department of State, to be conducted with all the secrecy of a totalitarian civil service. It was no less terrible. The men who served in that branch of the Nazi Government were similar to those who had tortured their enemies in Göring's day as concentration camp bosses, often indeed the same men in new uniforms. One of them, Rudolph Hoess, who was later to be Commandant of Auschwitz and to supervise the massacre of several million Jews, wrote his autobiography while awaiting execution.[3] In this document he describes not only his own bestial indoctrination into depravity but also the nature of his brutalized colleagues. These too were Nazis, during the days of Nazi 'respectability'. When Hoess was a camp guard at Dachau, Theodor Eicke was Inspector of Concentration Camps. Hoess writes of his captives:

What did I find? A small number of dyed-in-the-wool communists and social-democrats, who, if they had been given their freedom, would have stirred up unrest amongst the people and would have stopped at nothing to make their illegal work effective. They quite openly admitted this.

But the great mass of them, although they had indeed been communist or social-democrat officials, who had also struggled and fought for their ideals, and who had in some cases done considerable harm to the nationalist concepts of the NSDAP, appeared at closer glance, and after daily contact, harmless and peaceable men who, having seen their world destroyed, wished only to find some quiet job and to be able to go home to their families. I am certain that during the period 1935 and 1936 three-quarters of the political prisoners in Dachau could have been released without any resultant harm whatsoever to the Third Reich.

There remained, nevertheless, that quarter who were fanatically convinced that their world would rise again. These people had to be kept shut up and it was they who were the 'dangerous enemies of the State'. They were, however, easily recognizable, even though they did not openly express their views but on the contrary tried skilfully to disguise them.

Far more dangerous to the State and the people as a whole were the professional criminals, a-socials with more than twenty or thirty convictions behind them.

It was Eicke's intention that his SS-men, by means of continuous instruction and suitable orders concerning the dangerous criminality of the inmates, should be made basically ill-disposed towards the prisoners. They were to 'treat them rough', and to root out once and for all any sympathy they might feel for them. By such means, he succeeded in engendering in simple-natured men a hatred and antipathy for the

---

[3] *Commandant of Auschwitz*, Weidenfeld and Nicolson, 1959.

prisoners which an outsider will find hard to imagine. This influence spread through all the concentration camps and affected all the SS-men and the SS leaders who served in them, and indeed it continued for many years after Eicke had relinquished his post as Inspector.

All the torture and ill-treatment inflicted upon the prisoners in the concentration camps can be explained by this 'hate indoctrination'.

This basic attitude towards the prisoners was exacerbated by the influence of the senior commandants, such as Loritz and Koch, who did not regard the prisoners as men but as 'Russians' or 'Kanakas'.

The prisoners were of course not unaware of this artificial hatred that had been whipped up against them.

The more fanatical and stubborn amongst them were only reinforced thereby in their attitudes of mind. The men of goodwill, on the other hand, were hurt and repelled.[4]

In the Polish prison where he wrote his memoirs, he was to have doubts about his past. He wrote:

Outwardly cold and even stony, but with most deeply disturbed inner feelings, I attended the enquiries and examined the bodies of those prisoners who had committed suicide, or had been shot while trying to escape and I was well able to recognise whether such cases were genuine or not, or had been accidentally killed at work, or had 'run into the wire', or had been legally executed and now lay in the dissecting-room.

It was the same with the floggings and other punitive measures ordered by Loritz, most of which he supervised himself. These were 'his' punishment fatigues, 'his' executions of sentence.

My stony mask convinced him that there was no need to 'toughen me up', as he loved to do with those SS-men who seemed to him too weak.

And it is here that my guilt actually begins.

It was clear to me that I was not suited to this sort of service, since in my heart I disagreed with Eicke's insistence that life in the concentration camp be organised in this particular way. My sympathies lay too much with the prisoners, for I had myself lived their life for too long and had personal experience of their needs.

I should have gone to Eicke or to the Reichsführer SS[5] then, and explained that I was not suited to concentration camp service, because I felt too much sympathy for the prisoners.

I was unable to find the courage to do this.

I did not want to make a laughing-stock of myself. I did not wish to reveal my weakness. I was too obstinate to admit that I had made a

[4] ibid., pp. 78-79.
[5] Heinrich Himmler: abbreviated RFSS.

mistake when I abandoned my original intention of settling on the land.

I had voluntarily joined the ranks of the active SS and I had become too fond of the black uniform to relinquish it in this way.

My admission that I was too soft for a job assigned to the SS would unquestionably have led to my being cashiered, or at least immediately discharged.

And this I could not face.

For a long time I wrestled with this dilemma, the choice between my inner convictions on the one hand and my oath of loyalty to the SS and my vow of fidelity to the Führer on the other. Should I become a deserter? Even my wife knows nothing about my mental struggle on this issue. I have kept it to myself until this very moment.

As a National Socialist of long standing, I was convinced of the need for a concentration camp.

True opponents of the State had to be securely locked up; and a-socials and professional criminals, who under the law as it then stood could not be imprisoned, but must be deprived of their freedom in order to safeguard the rest of the people from their evil deeds.

I was also convinced that this task could only be carried out by the SS in their capacity as the guardians of the new State.[6]

This happened during the 'good' years of the Nazi régime. Men were being prepared for the python's next meal. The well-dressed young men at *thé-dansants* knew that something unpleasant was happening in support of 'their' society. They would have hardly invited Hoess to join their tables and they did not realize that they had joined his on the day they put the swastika button into the lapel of their jackets. Many of them have not realized it today.

The violence of the concentration camps was an essential ingredient of National Socialism, not only as a means of canalizing anti-social elements into the interest of the Nazi State (they used their Communist prisoners of 'anti-social intent' as deputy guards or *Kapos* in many of the camps) but also because the existence of camps is an essential element of totalitarian power. As Hannah Arendt has very truly stated:[7]

Torture, to be sure, is an essential feature of the whole totalitarian police and judiciary apparatus; it is used every day to make people talk. This type of torture, since it pursues a definite, rational aim, has certain

---

[6] ibid., pp. 80-81.

[7] Hannah Arendt: *The Burden of Our Time* (The Origins of Totalitarianism), George Allen & Unwin Ltd.

limitations: either the prisoner talks within a certain time, or he is killed. To this rationally conducted torture another, irrational, sadistic type was added in the first Nazi concentration camps and in the cellars of the Gestapo. Carried on for the most part by the SA, it pursued no aims and was not systematic, but depended on the initiative of largely abnormal elements. The mortality was so high that only a few concentration-camp inmates of 1933 survived these first years. This type of torture seemed to be not so much a calculated political institution as a concession of the régime to its criminal and abnormal elements, who were thus rewarded for services rendered. Behind the blind bestiality of the SA, there often lay a deep hatred and resentment against all those who were socially, intellectually, or physically better off than themselves, and who now, as if in fulfilment of their wildest dreams, were in their power. This resentment, which never died out entirely in the camps, strikes us as a last remnant of humanly understandable feeling.

The real horror began, however, when the SS took over the administration of the camps. The old spontaneous bestiality gave way to an absolutely cold and systematic destruction of human bodies, calculated to destroy human dignity; death was avoided or postponed indefinitely. The camps were no longer amusement parks for beasts in human form, that is, for men who really belonged in mental institutions and prisons; the reverse became true: they were turned into 'drill grounds', on which perfectly normal men were trained to be full-fledged members of the SS. . . .

If we take totalitarian aspirations seriously and refuse to be misled by the common-sense assertion that they are utopian and unrealizable, it develops that the society of the dying established in the camps is the only form of society in which it is possible to dominate man entirely. Those who aspire to total domination must liquidate all spontaneity, such as the mere existence of individuality will always engender, and track it down in its most private forms, regardless of how unpolitical and harmless these may seem. Pavlov's dog, the human specimen reduced to the most elementary reactions, the bundle of reactions that behave in exactly the same way, is the model 'citizen' of a totalitarian state; and such a citizen can be produced only imperfectly outside of the camps.

The uselessness of the camps, their cynically admitted anti-utility, is only apparent. In reality they are more essential to the preservation of the régime's power than any of its other institutions. Without concentration camps, without the undefined fear they inspire and the very well-defined training they offer in totalitarian domination, which can nowhere else be fully tested with all of its most radical possibilities, a totalitarian state can neither inspire its nuclear troops with fanaticism nor maintain a whole people in complete apathy. The dominating and the dominated would only too quickly sink back into the 'old bourgeois routine'; after early 'excesses', they would succumb to everyday life with its human laws; in short, they would develop in the direction which all observers counselled by common sense were so prone to predict. The tragic fallacy of all these prophecies, originating in a world that was still safe, was to suppose that there was such a thing as one human nature established for all time, to identify this human nature with history, and thus to declare that the idea of total domination was not only inhuman but also unrealistic. Meanwhile we have learned that the power of man is so great that he really can be what he wishes to be.

It is in the very nature of totalitarian régimes to demand unlimited power. Such power can only be secured if literally all men, without a single exception, are reliably dominated in every aspect of their life.

The 'respectable' period of Nazi Germany was a mere façade. If it was a period of consolidation it was also a period of the most intensive preparation, both military and psychological. Just as Hitler could never have conquered Europe with the old Reichswehr, so he could never have hoped to terrorize and crush an occupied Continent with the drunks and thieves, homosexuals and psychopaths of the old SA. The Wehrmacht was a-building, openly and fast. The SS was being forged, largely in secret and in the concentration camps, into the most monstrous instrument of cruelty and tyranny that the world has ever seen. Himmler's SS was not only the nucleus of the Nazi Party in which the concept of honour had been replaced by the concept of loyalty (its motto was: *Meine Ehre heisst Treue*): it was also designated by its leader to be the governing class not only of Germany but of all Europe, and to contain men not merely of German but of any Nordic stock. Indeed towards the end of the war Himmler was privately expressing disgust with the German race and was talking of creating a new SS state, to be called Burgundia, stretching from the Alps to the mouth of the Rhine, whence the SS supermen would rule all Europe and fight a perpetual war against the Asiatics.[8] These dreams lay in the future, but already in the late 'thirties the instrument intended to implement them was being forged. What Hannah Arendt has called 'the nuclear troops', the very kernel of the Nazi movement, were from an early date above, and therefore outside, the German nation. For them nationalism was but a means to an end, that end being absolute power for themselves, as Hitler's

[8] Felix Kersten: *The Kersten Memoirs*, Hutchinson, 1956.

paladins or janissaries, over an absolutely impotent populace stretching from the Atlantic to beyond the Urals.

So that by 1938 the nature of Nazism, and therefore of the Nazis, had once again been profoundly modified. On the one hand there was the German nation, prosperous, growing stronger every day, and in appearance at least almost unanimous in its loyalty to its Füehrer. If some members of the upper classes remained sceptical and viewed the Nazi bosses with distaste, if some members of the lower classes regretted the disappearance of their trade unions and other workers' organizations and resented the regimentation to which they were increasingly subjected, there was no real opposition to Hitler inside Germany. Even had such an opposition existed, its potential leaders were, almost without exception, dead, in the camps or in exile. On the other hand there was the SS, which might be described—paradox again—as an official conspiracy within the Third Reich, biding its time, building up its strength, being psychologically prepared, or as we would now say brainwashed, for its future, monstrous rôle.

Finally there was the Army, which can be more conveniently dealt with in the next chapter. This concerns the Nazis at war. And from the point of view of the Army's most senior generals that war began on November 5th, 1937, when Hitler informed the Commanders-in-Chief of the Army, Navy and Air Force together with his Foreign Minister that he intended to solve Germany's territorial 'problems' by force, not later than by 1943 and, if need be, in the course of the next year.[9] The Army, which had stood aloof, kept its kid gloves clean, and had been merely an accomplice in the domestic crimes of the Nazis, was now ordered to be the instrument of Nazi aggression across the frontiers. The Army was the only important organization in Germany, again apart from the Churches, that had not been *gleichgeschaltet*. It was also the only force in Germany that could then overthrow the Nazi Party, and the few German anti-Nazi and the many German non- or *Müssnazis* had long hoped the generals would do so. Now those generals were faced with alternatives which directly concerned themselves and in which they could no longer be mere accomplices.

---

[9] William Shirer: *The Rise and Fall of the Third Reich*, Secker and Warburg, 1960.

Chapter Four

As said in the previous chapter, the soldiers of the post-1918 Germany had been trained to believe that they were 'above' party politics, but that their generals were the ultimate custodians of conscience who could, and did, intervene in times of crisis to save the country. So long as Field-marshal Hindenburg, their own supreme representative, was Head of State, this was a comparatively simple rôle for the generals to fill: they were Germany's army and Hindenburg incorporated their idea of an *ersatz* Kaiser. It was very different when Hitler succeeded the old gentleman in 1934 and exacted an oath of personal allegiance to himself, something which Hindenburg had never done or indeed ever needed to do.

Furthermore, with the introduction of conscription in the spring of 1935, the 100,000-man Army (it was already considerably larger) received a great and growing flood of new recruits, most of whom were Nazi sympathizers if not Party members. The Reichswehr had been created and organized precisely for the purpose it was now being asked to fulfil. In anticipation of the day when the Versailles Treaty would be flouted, and a huge army rebuilt, the 100,000-man Army had regarded itself as 'an army of N.C.O.s'. This is what it now became. Lieutenants were promoted major and given the command of battalions, privates became sergeants and commanded platoons. And the new privates and the new lieutenants were frequently, indeed usually, followers of Adolf Hitler.

The men of the old Reichswehr still held, of course, all the important positions and indeed were to continue to do so until the end of the Nazi régime. But in 1938 it was not easy for these men to tell their Nazi soldiers that they must be a-political, particularly as they themselves had sworn a personal oath to the leader of the Nazi Party in his capacity as President of Germany.

Furthermore, throughout the first five years of his government Hitler treated his regular soldiers with the greatest consideration and respect. To please them, as they thought and as he said, he murdered his old friend, Ernst Roehm, who had dreamed vaguely of supplanting their regular army with an SA army, and its commanders with his men and with himself. They did not guess that Himmler and his SS were to prove far more formidable rivals. Hitler showered promotions upon the regular officers, gave them the equipment they wanted, and scarcely interfered with their affairs. They, it seemed were to be exempt from *Gleichschaltung*, and if the senior officers spoke with some contempt of the Bohemian corporal and his government-from-the-gutter, they were hardly likely to turn him out—even if their troops were prepared to obey them, which they probably would have done in the early years—in favour of a restoration of Weimar. Their motto might well have been: what is good for the Wehrmacht is good for the Reich. They saw the threat of conquest by an aggressive France, or even an aggressive Poland, gradually receding. Although all General Staffs must pigeonhole plans against all possible contingencies, the thinking of the German General Staff during the first few years of rearmament was still essentially defensive, as is shown by the equipment and fortification which they bought and built, though the emphasis was shifting somewhat to offensive weapons by 1937.[1] (The distinction between defensive and offensive weapons is extremely hard to draw, as endless disarmament conferences have discovered. One might assume that armoured divisions and heavy bombers are offensive, fortifications and anti-aircraft systems defensive. In 1937 the Germans were creating armoured divisions, the British not, but the British were building long-range bomber fleets, which the Germans never did. A year later the Maginot Line was not only defensive, but the whole organization of the French Army made offensive operations almost impossible: the German West Wall, known as the Siegfried Line, was also defensive, but gave the German Army the protection in its western rear that permitted offensive operations in the East.)

The head of the German General Staff, General Beck, was, in early 1938, defence-minded. Neither he nor the other experienced staff officers believed that Germany could, in the foreseeable future, fight and win a major European war. Furthermore, he had great distrust of, and distaste for, the Nazi leaders. And the conclusion

---

[1] Heinz Guderian: *Panzer Leader*, Michael Joseph, 1957; *The Memoirs of Field Marshal Kesselring*, William Kimber, 1953, and other memoirs of military men.

which he drew from Hitler's sabre-rattling was that the Army should act as it had done in Weimar days, refuse to accept senseless orders and even, in extreme circumstances, take charge. The only two soldiers immediately above him, General von Blomberg, the War Minister, and General von Fritsch, the Commander-in-Chief of the Army, though less determined than Beck, were equally doubtful about the viability of Hitler's military plans.

Hitler acted quickly. Blomberg and Fritsch were fired. Hitler himself became War Minister and General von Brauchitsch, a more pliable figure, replaced Fritsch. In an attempt to demonstrate the Army's disapproval of the threatened war over the Sudetenland in the summer of 1938, Beck himself resigned. From then until July 20th, 1944 there was an almost constant conspiracy within the Army, and particularly within the General Staff, to get rid of Hitler and the Nazi government.[2]

This was the first real anti-Nazi movement inside Germany. There were other and smaller anti-Nazi groups during the war, such as the gallant Munich students who called themselves the White Rose, and the Communist espionage organization known as the Red Choir. There were brave individuals, such as Bishop Wurm and Cardinal Galen, who spoke out against the Nazi atrocities. But the 'men of 20 July', as they later came to be called, were the only group who offered Germany an alternative government, without which offer revolution or counter-revolution is little more than a gesture.

How many men were involved it would be hard to say. It is not even satisfactorily established how many were executed—very few survived—and the figure of 7,000 dead does not necessarily mean that that number was directly implicated. But certainly from 1938 on there was a small resistance movement inside Germany.

Its matrix was the Army General Staff and in particular that part of it, the *Abwehr*, which dealt with espionage and counter-espionage. German officers of that period made, in general, very poor conspirators, but the men of the *Abwehr* were more experienced in this field and also had means of communication, both internal and with foreign countries, that were out of reach of the Gestapo and the other agencies of what was now a ubiquitous Nazi apparatus. It was inevitable that if any resistance to Hitler were to be mounted, only the Army could do it, since the Army alone had

[2] See my *Shirt of Nessus*, Cassell, 1956.

the organization, means of communication, and above all the sheer physical strength. Unfortunately, what could have been so easily carried out during the period of the Night of the Long Knives failed, perhaps only by a hair's breadth or the thickness of an oaken table, eight and ten years later. The Army, or rather the authoritative generals, had waited too long, had been too busy with their rearmament and later with their victorious campaigns of 1939-1942, had been too aloof from 'politics'.

If the General Staff was the command centre of the German resistance, it did not have a monopoly. There were trade unionists such as Leber and Leuschner involved, lawyers such as Moltke and Sack, diplomatists such as Hassell and Trott, administrators such as Goerdeler, apparent Nazis such as Schulenburg (deputy police president of Berlin) and Helldorf (chief of police in the capital.) The colour of the uniform and the holding of a Party card meant little. By the time the war broke out almost everyone in Germany with any form of authority or influence outside the Army was, apparently, a Nazi, and many of the conspirators actually had been. This, again, was to cause severe headaches and anger to the denazifiers. If all those who claimed to have been involved in the German resistance had in fact been active anti-Nazis, Hitler's régime would have collapsed long before 1945.

After the annexation of Austria and the Sudetenland, there were some 80,000,000 Germans. Apart from the refugees and the victims within the camps, there were perhaps some 10,000 who were prepared actively to resist the criminal government. This minute percentage is outweighed in some measure by the fact that so many of them held important positions in their society and in the Army. It is not possible to give any sort of figure for the *Müssnazis*, but here again nonentities were not *compelled* to join the Party. Karl Jaspers estimates the number of Germans who were unincriminated at a mere half-million. Excluding children this gives a figure of about 1%, and tallies with the plebiscites.[3] As in all societies, and at almost all times, a very large part of the population is not interested in 'politics'. This was particularly true of Germany in the early years of the Third Reich. The people were sick and tired of the endless squabblings of Weimar's political parties which, apparently, did the people only harm. This fatigue was one of

[3] Karl Jaspers, *The Future of Germany*, University of Chicago Press, Chicago 1967, p. 65.

the principal, if not the principal, reason why almost half the electorate of Germany voted Nazi in the last free election. They would leave it all to *him*. And they did, and for a while it seemed to work. I remember that when, as a very young man, I was in Germany in 1935-1936 and wished to discuss politics with my German contemporaries, I was told that my interest in such dull matters was hopelessly old-fashioned. *Nous avons changé tout cela, Georges Dandin.*

Yet when Hitler tried to launch his aggressive war in 1938 there was remarkably little public approval. When he succeeded in so doing a year later, there was no more. The military parades were a flop, for the crowds refused to cheer. The mass of the German people, of all classes, had no more wish to go to war than had the mass of the British or the French in 1939. But since they had abdicated, or in the case of the more militant had had stolen from them, any right to participate in their government's choices of policy, they had no alternative to acceptance of that government's actions.

Of course patriotism, in time of war, is a very strong emotion indeed. This Hitler and Goebbels knew. The Nazi-Soviet Pact of August 25th 1939 was accepted by the mass of the German people as an example of their Leader's wisdom. In view of what they had heard from their Leader over the years, they could now obviously accept anything. And they accepted the war their Leader had started in the same dull-witted way. 'The Füehrer knows best.'

Then came direct patriotism—Karl and Heinz at the front, Ernst wounded, Werner a war hero—and the incessant propaganda of Goebbels' superlative machine. And, on top of that, the spectacular victories: Poland, ten days; France, six weeks; Britain, isolated; the gates of Moscow, four months. And the parcels home from the victorious soldiers, and the soldiers themselves on leave, with their tall tales and new medals. It was powerful, heady stuff. We must have been wrong to fear the war: the Füehrer knows best: the German way is sure to triumph, and *Deutschtum* is Nazism.

In those unconquered western lands, such as Britain and a still neutral America, these German emotions produced their echo. In the winter of 1939-1940, before the real fighting began on the Western Front, the Royal Air Force had flown over Germany dropping leaflets, not bombs, urging the German people to persuade their government to discontinue the war. The fatuity of this operation is, in retrospect, almost unbelievable, but it is pertinent to this study. The assumption can only have been that the Germans who might read these leaflets were intellectually rather like Englishmen at a by-election. The fact that most English voters are never influenced by leaflets is neither here nor there: the pieces of paper are handed out, for this is part of the civilized way of deciding differences of opinion. There is no evidence that one single German was influenced in any way by a British leaflet. Some may have been convinced that Nazi methods were more effective, and therefore better.

Then, when the 'Phoney War' ceased to be phoney, there was a contrary reaction. Since the Germans did not respond to bundles of leaflets, it meant that all Germans were Nazis. From 1940 until 1945 and later, in the popular press and in popular thinking the words 'Nazi' and 'German' became synonymous.

If, from the point of view of the Army's leaders, the war may be said to have begun on November 5th 1937, from the point of view of the SS it began just one year later, on November 9th 1938. On that day Reinhard Heydrich, the second most powerful man in the SS, received orders from Goebbels to organize a massive and nationwide 'spontaneous' demonstration against the Jews as a reprisal for the murder of a German diplomat by a Jewish refugee in Paris. The result was the so-called 'Crystal Night', when Jewish shop windows were smashed and the shops looted, the synagogues burned and many Jews murdered on the streets or in their homes while tens of thousands were carted off to die in the concentration camps. This was very far from being a spontaneous demonstration. It was an SS operation of a type that was to become sickeningly familiar in the occupied countries in the years to come. Ernst von Salomon has vividly described the atmosphere in Germany in late 1938. He writes:[4]

> That November evening of 1938 Ille and I had stayed rather late at the home of my friend Axel, playing dice. I was at the time very preoccupied with my work; not only was I writing a script and a film treatment simultaneously, but I was also preparing a thick volume of endless material concerning the rôle of the public official in the German postwar, one of the most interesting subjects of our age and one of great importance. (This book has never been published.) I had arranged an interview with Minister of State Dr Meissner for the purpose of discuss-

[4] Ernst von Salomon: *The Answers*, Putnam, 1954, pp. 217-220, pp. 280-283.

ing with him his activities during 1919, and I had already made a draft of the principal points I intended to raise.

Alex lived in the Sächsischer Strasse, in Wilmersdorf, and I some ten minutes' walk away in Charlottenburg. To reach our home by the shortest route Ille and I had to cross the Olivaer Platz, a pretty little square just off the Kurfürstendamm, which contained the shops where we bought our daily groceries. At the corner of the square where the Konstanzer Strasse joins the Kurfürstendamm, was a small wineshop; it was here that we occasionally bought a bottle or two when we had unexpected guests. As Ille and I passed this little shop I suddenly became aware of the crunch of broken glass beneath my feet, and looking about me saw that the plate-glass front of the shop was smashed and that the bottles were quite unprotected—anybody could have stolen them.

'Some drunk must have crashed into it,' I remarked to Ille, who had stopped and was gazing at the damage. She thought we should notify the proprietor, but we did not know whether he lived in the building.

At this moment we heard a loud crash followed at once by the tinkle of falling glass. We turned around. On the other side of the street a group of apparently young men, dressed in riding boots and civilian jackets, were standing outside a café. One of them was even then picking up a stone, which he put into a cloth that he used as a sling and which, with practised skill, he hurled at one of the café's great mirrors. There was an echoing crash and again the tinkle of falling glass.

A taxi was parked at the corner of the Konstanzer Strasse and the Kurfürstendamm. I hurried towards it while Ille, clinging to my arm, ran along beside me.

'What's going on here?' I asked the driver. He was an elderly man who wore a military badge in his hat in place of a cockade. He looked at me and said, in his Berlin accent:

'Go on home and don't ask questions. I ain't taking no more fares tonight. Me, I'm keeping out of trouble.'

He drove off and disappeared around the corner. Ille still clung tightly to my arm as we hurried along the short stretch of the Kurfürstendamm that separated us from the Clausewitz Strasse. I could feel that she was trembling and I said:

'Don't get so upset. After all, what is it? A handful of hooligans smashing other people's windows!'

Ille said nothing. We saw no one in the streets. Only now and then did we hear the distant crash of breaking glass.

We had a little two-room apartment at the back of the courtyard of 5, Clausewitz Strasse. Apart from Herr Cetteler, the porter, the proprietor of a little dairy next to the front door, and a retired Foreign Ministry official who lived on his pension in the front part of the building, all the other tenants were Jewish. I double-locked the front gate, and we hurried across the courtyard to our apartment. Ille, without even taking off her coat, ran through the kitchen, the hall, and our two rooms, as though to make sure that nothing had been touched. She even looked in the bathroom and the broom cupboard. Then she came up to me and asked, with trembling lips:

'What do we do now?'

I said, as surlily as I could:

'Nothing. Go to bed and get some sleep!'

But she shouted at me:

'Your name is on the door outside! If they start forcing their way into people's houses do you think they'll give you time to explain who you are?'

'You're crazy,' I said. 'Cetteler would have to let them in, and Cetteler would explain—he's a decent man.'

'There aren't any decent men!' shouted Ille.

'Don't shout like that,' I told her, and she lowered her voice as she said:

'But we must do something! We can't just . . .'

I said:

'I'll call Axel and tell him what's happening.'

I telephoned Axel and described to him what I had seen. He asked, at once:

'Have you informed the police?'

This was an idea which, I admitted, had not occurred to me. Axel said that in that case he would do it for me and would ring me back.

Meanwhile Ille had called Herr Cetteler. He was already on his way up, wearing his blue boiler suit. He knew what was going on and he said:

'Don't you worry, lady, they've got proper lists all drawn up. Nothing's going to happen to you. I'll be there and I'll see to that.'

'Are they coming, then?' Ille asked. He said:

'They're coming right enough. Maybe not today and maybe not tomorrow, but they're coming.'

Ille cried:

'But then you must warn the other tenants!'

'I shall, I shall. . . . But what can I do? On the other side there lives an old girl, for years now she hasn't been quite herself. Then they took her companion away, because of the Nuremberg Laws, you understand, been with her for years she had too . . . and now the old girl's got nobody to look after her and she's just kind of rotting away. What can I do? You know what Jews are like, but now they've all got so many worries of their own they can't bother about each other. . . .'

He left. At the door he turned back and said:

'Boy, this is all we needed!'
Then he rang the bell next door and I heard him say:
'Its me, Cetteler, you needn't be scared. . . .'
Axel rang. He said, with agitation:
'The police station wouldn't even let me finish. The man who answered the phone said they knew all about it but they couldn't do anything. . . .' Axel added, emphatically: 'And he didn't even sound ashamed!' Then, somewhat ceremoniously, he went on to say that he would willingly have walked round to see us but that he had friends at his place. 'Friends. Do you understand me? Friends.' They planned to stay the night.
'All right,' I said, and I added: 'Now say your little piece.'
Axel was firmly convinced that all telephone wires were tapped, and it was therefore his habit to end all conversations with a political platitude. He thought that in case of trouble this would count in his favour. He now said, calmly enough:
'The Jews are our misfortune!'
Suddenly his voice became hysterical and he screamed:
'An unutterable misfortune! Our misfortune, *ours*! Do you understand me? *Ours*!'
'Yes, yes,' I said. 'I understand you. Now ring off. We'll phone each other tomorrow.' And I rang off. . . .
There I sat, in the back room with the curtains drawn, while outside the glass smashed and tinkled, telling a trembling young woman of things that had been.
The telephone rang shrilly. It was Axel. He told me that synagogues were burning. From his balcony he could see the glow of the fires. I thought that Axel would now produce his political platitude, his insurance. Instead he said:
'Please make a careful note of this. Early tomorrow morning it will be announced on the radio that the German people, infuriated by the criminal action of the Jew Grünspan who shot the Councillor attached to the German Embassy in Paris, rose spontaneously and set fire to the synagogues. I assert here and now in most solemn terms that I have never risen spontaneously, that I have never committed arson. Since the Reichstag fire arson has been a capital offence, to be punished by hanging.'
I said:
'Yes, yes. Good. I'm sitting here quite quietly with Ille, too, discussing this and that. I'll call you in the morning.'
But Axel did not ring off. He said, pronouncing his words with icy clarity:
'It is extremely interesting. For years these people have announced officially that it was not their intention to attack the Jewish religion,

that they were simply fighting against the danger of contamination by the Jewish race. They have even published laws to this effect. Are the synagogues places of worship or are they institutions for racial interbreeding?'

I said:

'Yes, I know all about that. But at least the burning synagogues cast a clear light on our situation.' And I rang off.

I told Ille what Axel had said. I went on:

'Why are Axel and I not standing in front of the synagogues with outstretched arms protesting and accusing at the top of our voices? Because we know that what we might say would have no echo? That's not the reason. It is something far worse. We are in reality already dead. We can no longer live from within ourselves. Everything that is happening about us is not the product of the internal life of those who are doing it; it is the product of a collective. And a man who will not accept and believe in that collective is dead. The collective always acts unconditionally. It also demands our unconditional faith and acceptance. But this collective has not gathered us up into itself, it has atomised us. Atomised fragments cannot constitute a community, but only an explosive mass. Ernst Jünger said once that the saint on a pillar, the stylite, presented socialism in its most accomplished form. That is certainly true: the deliberate act of the individual for the sake of solidarity. I have never recoiled from true solidarity, or from a collective society, but this collective is now destroying itself, it is a false collective. It offers the individual no chance to perform his deed of solidarity.'

I said:

'This collective is a *reductio ad absurdum* and that is the greatest crime that it can commit. I know, of course, what is happening to the Jews. Were I not myself a witness I should still know, for it has been announced often enough what would happen. The burning synagogues simply show that it is happening now. The appalling thing is that nobody can help 'the Jews', because any attempt to do so simply increases their peril. The appalling thing is that we cannot help ourselves, and far more is happening to us than to the Jews. And far more is happening to the collective than is even happening to us.'

I said:

'Last winter I had occasion to come home by streetcar 176. I was standing on the front platform. Besides the driver there were also two SS people there. Then an elderly lady got on. Suddenly the two men began to talk filth. It began with one saying: "terrible stink of garlic here!" and you can imagine how it went on from there. The old lady tried to open the door leading to the interior of the car. It was only then that I realized the men's filth was directed at her. Now I am not accustomed to let old ladies be insulted in my presence, as you know. Maybe it's an old-fashioned atavism, but there you are. What should I do? Set upon the two oafs? That would have been just stupid. Do nothing, as though it were no concern of mine? That would have been cowardice. I was interested by the alternatives, and I tried hard to think of a third solution. Of course! The simplest! I helped the old lady in her attempt to open the door. It would not move. I called the conductor and he walked the length of the swaying car. I shouted through the little hole in the door that he should open it. He shouted back that in winter the door had to be kept closed. I bellowed through the hole that he must open it at once, an old lady was here in need of help. The conductor cried that she would have to get down at the next stop and re-enter the car by way of the back platform. While I was still arguing with the conductor I suddenly saw the old lady's face, only a few inches from my own. She was looking at me with undisguised hatred, a hatred that came from her sensation of complete helplessness, the worst sort of hatred there is. And I understood: of course! This woman wanted, more than anything else in the world, to avoid attracting attention. To be conspicuous might mean anything, martyrdom, death. And I, it was I who was creating this danger. It was I, not the two SS oafs, who just stood there grinning spitefully though in silence. The car stopped, and the old lady hurriedly got off. It was not my stop but I followed her. I wanted to help the old lady, I wanted to try to explain why I had behaved as I had done, I don't really know what I wanted, I was acting "spontaneously". The old lady did not get back on the other platform. She disappeared into the darkness. I walked along the Kurfürstendamm and I thought as intensively as I could—there must be a third solution. And if there is in fact none, which was preferable: to behave like a fool or to act like a coward?

'At the corner of the Clausewitz Strasse there stood a lamppost. Near the lamppost I saw, hanging on a tree, a piece of cardboard as big as a poster. I walked up to it and read: "The seamstress Frieda Junge, who lives at Weiz Strasse 14, commits racial infamy with the Jew Victor Aaron."

'There it was, written on the poster. Not far from the lamppost stood an ordinary policeman. Now then, here was a chance. I decided to be a fool and not a coward. I ripped down the poster. Immediately the policeman came up to me. He asked:

' "Are you authorised to remove the poster?"

I said:

' "No. But it's a piece of filth."

The policeman said:

' "Quite agree. That's why I'm here, to nab the fellow who keeps hanging them up on this tree. There are special columns for posters at the street corners." He went on: "If you've nothing to do with it, go on home. And give me the poster, I'll stick it up again so as I can catch the fellow. If this goes on anybody will think he can just come here and stick posters to this tree."'

I said to Ille:

'But if this is the truth: if the provocation of the Reichstag fire served to destroy Communism but also, and simultaneously, destroyed the actual legitimacy of the party's road to power: if the events of June 30 ended the revolution but simultaneously created the police state instead of the people's society: if tonight the true central point of the party, its racial doctrine, has been reduced to an absurdity and the Jewish problem has really been transformed into a German problem: if at the same time we are all atomised, isolated, incompetent, sterile, without any direct connection with the new discredited collective—and that is perhaps the most monstrous aspect of the whole process; the hope of our age, the real objective of civilization, the constructive element for the future, the collective discredited by its own most fanatical exponents—if this is the truth, then what remains?

'Now since in these circumstances all action is crime, all that remains is to do nothing. It is at any rate the only decent course. And it is also the most difficult thing in the world, a sort of Gandhi-ism without Gandhi. The individual solution has here a solitary constructive force. It is really the most difficult course of all, and it looks so easy, doesn't it? All honour to him who can follow it—as to myself I am not sure whether I can or not.'

With the state-organized, publicly-enacted, atrocity of the Crystal Night, Nazism had thrown away its mask of moral respectability. All the horrors and bestialities, up to and including genocide, were foreshadowed in the shadows cast by the burning synagogues. As Salomon truly remarks, whether or not there had ever been a 'Jewish problem', there was to be henceforth a very real 'German problem'. Denazification was the first attempt to solve it, after its armed forces' defeat by force of Allied arms.

The mask of political respectability was cast aside four months later, on March 15th 1939, when Hitler tore up the six-months-old Munich Treaty and invaded and occupied the rump of the Czech state. Even Neville Chamberlain now realized that war was inevitable.

The last faint thread of intellectual integrity was snapped when Nazi Germany signed a pact with Soviet Russia and the totalitarian dictatorships proceeded to partition Poland between them and wreak their vengeance on its now defenceless people.

Even before the war began the Nazi leaders had committed two of the major crimes, crimes against peace and crimes against humanity, for which the survivors among them were to be tried by the International Military Tribunal at Nuremberg in late 1945. It has become customary to speak of 'war crimes' and 'war criminals', but it is important to remember that the criminal nature, in all respects, of the Nazi régime was fully established before ever the war began.

The nature of the crimes was not increased by the conditions of war, only the scale escalated as the SS perfected the techniques of mass murder and the Nazi government ordered the invasion of more and larger neutral states. Had the Germans not been defeated, the escalation in atrocity would almost certainly have increased.[5] Although almost all Europe's Jews within their grasp had been murdered in the death factories of Poland before these were overrun by the Red Army, the Nazis had continued to enlarge the largest of these, Auschwitz, until the very end. Had the Nazis won the war, there seems little doubt that genocide, on an even greater scale, would have become a permanent element of their policy.

It is not necessary for the purpose of this book to repeat once again the disgusting chronicle of Nazi crimes during the war years. They are fully documented.[6] What is of relevance to a study of denazification is, first of all, who committed them? secondly, who was responsible? and thirdly, who were the accomplices?

The answer to the first question is, primarily, the SS including the SD (*Sicherheitsdienst* or Security Service). It was primarily the SS who ran the camps, both the concentration camps and the extermination camps. The Gestapo (*Geheime Staats Polizei* or Secret State Police) was also guilty of many crimes. These were all to be branded as criminal organizations by the Allies. However, it was not only their members who committed 'war crimes'. Ordinary German policemen committed crimes against, for instance, prisoners of war. Individuals and even units of the Wehrmacht were also guilty of 'war crimes'. Civilians lynched, with government encouragement, British and American fliers shot down over Germany. The civilian employers of slave labourers from the occupied countries frequently treated their 'employees' with a brutality that led to death or permanent maiming from beatings or starvation.

---

[5] See *Kersten* op. cit.
[6] Lord Russell of Liverpool, *The Scourge of the Swastika*; Gerald Reitlinger, *The Final Solution*; and many other works.

This happened both in Germany and in the occupied lands, both from huge industrial combines such as Krupp's or I.G. Farben and at the hands of individual farmers, artisans or mere housewives, and at all intermediate layers of 'employment'.

Furthermore, if the SS were the principal criminals, this cannot be a blanket condemnation of all the members of that organization. Himmler's SS expanded faster than any other organization during the war. By the end it contained, apart from its other units, many divisions of SS troops, the Waffen (or Armed) SS, who were essentially combat troops with little or no connection with concentration camp guards and extermination squads (*Einsatzkommandos*), though there was some passing to and fro between all the branches of the SS. The Waffen SS, intended by Himmler to supplant the Wehrmacht, was an extremely tough, very well equipped and usually highly skilled fighting force. Some of its divisions—there were nearly thirty of them by 1945—were recruited from foreign Nazis, such as the *SS Viking*, the *SS Nordland* and an Albanian division. It would seem, though this has not been fully authenticated, that not all Waffen SS soldiers were genuine volunteers, and that sometimes both Germans and foreigners were drafted into this special Nazi army. But if the Waffen SS was not *ipso facto* a criminal organization, its soldiers were certainly more brutal, more 'war criminal' than the equivalent units of the regular German Army. Thus it was a regimental staff of the 12th SS *Hitlerjugend* Panzergrenadier Division (commanded by a certain 'Panzer' Meyer, of whom more later) which ordered and supervised the shooting of Canadian prisoners of war in Normandy in 1944. It was men of the 2nd *Das Reich* Panzer Division who massacred the inhabitants of Oradour in France at approximately the same time. On the Eastern Front their record was even worse. In the West at least German regular units did not behave in this way, though again their record on the Eastern Front was worse. To risk a broad generalization, the men of the German Army in Western and Southern Europe behaved much as all soldiers do and their attitude towards the civilians was neither better nor worse than that of the Allied troops who occupied Germany in 1945. With this distinction: the Army's men were passive, and on occasion active, accomplices of the General SS in their terrorist operations against the Jews and other civilians in areas where the resistance fighters were active. The soldiers of the Waffen SS were far more brutal, often criminally so. The members of the General SS, including the SD, the Gestapo and other ancillary, essentially non-military, organizations, were entirely incriminated.

The second question, that of responsibility, is almost equally complex. Certainly all the Nazi bosses, down to quite a low level, were fully implicated in their party's, and hence their country's, criminal policies. So too were large sections of the civil service, particularly the police, as well as parts of the Army and of industry. In popular thought these crimes are often limited to the genocide of the Jews, for this is the best documented as it was the most spectacularly 'successful' aspect of Nazi policy. But it seems probable that even more non-Jewish Eastern Europeans (Russians, Poles, inhabitants of the Baltic States and so on) were killed in one way or another, excluding death in military action, than were Jews. Prisoners of war, for instance, were systematically starved or worked to death. The shooting of 'hostages' was not only limited to the East. Such brutalities involved not merely the SS but also elements of the regular armed forces and most of the government departments, including their regular, respectable civil servants, as well as the whole of the Nazi Party's administrative apparatus all the way down. There were, of course, also individuals, brutalized by circumstances or by psychological malformation, who were enabled to realize their fantasies in the fantastic atmosphere of Nazi Germany and its occupied territories.

After the war, when called to book for their crimes, men of all these categories claimed as exoneration that they had merely been obeying orders. Even Eichmann, the prime instrument in the genocide of the Jews, made this claim when kidnapped in the Argentine and taken to Israel for trial. And there is some truth in this, though that truth is usually irrelevant so far as justice is concerned. Eichmann, as his trial and as Alex Weissberg's book have shown,[7] had very considerable latitude, both in Hungary and elsewhere, concerning his own participation in 'the final solution'. Even the acceptance of bribes from his intended victims was not refused, either by himself or by his immediate administrative superiors. The repeated claim by the murderers that any refusal to obey orders would have resulted in their own instant execution is not generally supported by the facts. Having spent more time than I care to recall delving into

---

[7] Alex Weissberg: *Advocate for the Dead*, André Deutsch, 1958.

these disgusting facts, I know of no case of an SS man, let alone a soldier, being shot for refusing to obey a criminal order. Some SS concentration camp guards were former members of Penal Battalions (men convicted of military crime) who were offered this employment as an alternative to a short life-expectancy on the Eastern Front. It may be assumed that any man would have been returned to his very unpleasant unit had he refused to obey the orders of his officers at Auschwitz. So far as I know, none did, and finally, many of the atrocities, such as the shooting of the Canadian prisoners of war, were carried out on purely local initiative.

Of course they 'pleaded superior orders', all the way up, and ultimately and indeed exclusively assigned total responsibility to the dead Adolf Hitler. Not only is such a shuffling of responsibility upwards a national characteristic of the Germans of that and preceding generations—the blame, like the praise, goes to the *Obrigkeit*, and we are just 'little people' who obey orders and do our jobs—but it is also the marvellous, built-in excuse for the servants of all totalitarian tyrannies. Thus a Krushchev can serve a Stalin with absolute, fawning loyalty and then blame all the horrors which he helped implement on the dead tyrant he had served so well during the monster's lifetime. Like Stalin, Hitler could not have carried out his policies without a vast, loyal and highly efficient apparatus of soldiers, scientists, industrial managers, party officials, propagandists (not artists: artists were not needed, scarcely existed in Nazi Germany, and if they failed to emigrate were highly suspect), and above all brutalized butchers.

The answer to the third question—who were the accomplices?—now becomes sadly easy. It was the entire population of the Great German Reich, including Austria, the Sudetenland and the other linguistically German territories incorporated therein, with the exception of those few thousand men and women who were prepared actively to oppose the criminal régime. This does not include these post-war anti-Nazis who boasted of having listened to the British Broadcasting Corporation behind closed shutters, when so to do was an offence. To be an active anti-Nazi in wartime Germany was so dangerous that it cannot be held against any man that he failed to be one. Ernst, Kurt and Werner were fighting and dying for their country: at home, in an almost atomized land, that was what counted. Few could be asked to think more deeply. Yet some did. One who did not fail in his conscience, but failed in his endeavour, was Henning von Tresckow. He said, on the day of his death, July 20th 1944: 'The worth of a man is only assured if he is prepared to sacrifice his life for his convictions.' It is a barbed remark from a brave and dying man. The conviction may, always, be a wrong conviction. Of educated sensitive Germans (but how many men with both qualities inside Germany had survived the 'respectable' years?) only a handful in that large country had the right convictions. A high proportion of those few thousands lost their lives for their convictions after July 20th 1944, when Stauffenberg's bomb failed by a table's breadth to kill the dictator.

The Germany that the Allied armies occupied in 1945 had, as it then appeared, nothing. It had been smashed completely. Nothing more than even a handful of real men, but only yes-men, who had said yes to the Nazis and were, quite obviously, prepared to say yes again just as quickly as they could to anybody else. A new generation was needed, and a generation takes many years to grow.

Chapter Five

There were, then, two basic groups of Nazis with whom the Allies would have to deal in the immediate post-war period, although the categories overlapped. These, for the sake of convenience, can be described as the criminals, usually referred to as 'war criminals', and their accomplices. The war criminals were those who had themselves committed crimes or had ordered that such crimes be committed by others under their command. Since many of these crimes were of a novel nature and committed outside German territory—a fact which posed certain juridical problems—the Control Council, containing the senior representatives of the American, British, Russian and French administrations in their respective zones, in order to regularize what was becoming a somewhat chaotic and legally unsatisfactory situation, on December 20th 1945 passed *Control Council Law No.10: Punishment of Persons Guilty of War Crimes, Crimes against Peace and against Humanity,* which was published in the *Official Gazette* of the Control Council on January 31st 1946. This supplemented the setting up of the International Military Tribunal, created in the previous August, of which more later. Article II of this Order defines the men whom it was intended should face trial, and reads as follows:

1. Each of the following acts is recognized as a crime:

(a) *Crimes against Peace.* Initiation of invasions of other countries and wars of aggression in violation of international laws and treaties, including but not limited to planning, preparation, initiation or waging a war of aggression, or a war of violation of international treaties, agreements or assurances, or participation in a common plan or conspiracy for the accomplishment of any of the foregoing.
(b) *War Crimes.* Atrocities or offences against persons or property constituting violations of the laws or customs of war, including but not limited to murder, ill treatment or deportation to slave labour, or for any

other purpose, of civilian population from occupied territory, murder or ill treatment of prisoners of war or persons on the seas, killing of hostages, plunder of public or private property, wanton destruction of cities, towns or villages, or devastation not justified by military necessity.
(c) *Crimes against Humanity*. Atrocities and offences, including but not limited to murder, extermination, enslavement, deportation, imprisonment, torture, rape, or other inhumane acts committed against any civilian population, or persecutions on political, racial, or religious grounds whether or not in violation of the domestic laws of the country where perpetrated.
(d) Membership in categories of a criminal group or organization declared criminal by the International Military Tribunal.

2. Any person, without regard to nationality or the capacity in which he acted, is deemed to have committed a crime as defined in paragraph 1 of this Article, if he was (a) a principal or (b) was an accessory to the commission of any such crime or ordered or abetted the same or (c) took consenting part therein or (d) was connected with plans or enterprises involving its commission or (e) was a member of any organization or group connected with the commission of any such crime or (f) with reference to paragraph 1(a), if he held a high political, civil or military (including General Staff) position in Germany or in one of its allies, cobelligerents or satellites or held high position in the financial, industrial or economic life of any such country.

3. Any person found guilty of any of the crimes above mentioned may upon conviction be punished as shall be determined by the tribunal to be just. Such punishment may consist of one or more of the following:

(a) Death.
(b) Imprisonment for life or a term of years, with or without hard labour.
(c) Fine, and imprisonment with or without hard labour, in lieu thereof.
(d) Forfeiture of property.
(e) Restitution of property wrongfully acquired.
(f) Deprivation of some or all civil rights.

Any property declared to be forfeited or the restitution of which is ordered by the Tribunal shall be delivered to the Control Council for Germany, which shall decide on its disposal.

4. (a) The official position of any person, whether as Head of State or as responsible official in a Government Department, does not free him

from responsibility for a crime or entitle him to mitigation of punishment.

(b) The fact that any person acted pursuant to the order of his Government or of a superior does not free him from responsibility for a crime, but may be considered in mitigation.

5. In any trial or persecution for a crime herein referred to, the accused shall not be entitled to the benefits of any statute of limitation in respect of the period from 30 January 1933 to 1 July 1945, nor shall immunity, pardon or amnesty granted under the Nazi régime be admitted as a bar to trial or punishment.[1]

This is all very explicit. It codifies, in some measure, though it does not clarify, the comparatively new concept of 'Crimes against Peace' and 'Crimes against Humanity'. This admirable concept, however, has never, to this writer's knowledge, been used in a court of law save only against the nationals or the foreign supporters of the Axis powers in the Second World War. Though the phrases are frequently bandied about in the United Nations and elsewhere for propaganda purposes, no Russian national has been tried for the invasion of neutral Poland or Finland nor for the Katyn massacre; no American for the atomic bombing of Hiroshima and Nagasaki; no Briton for the destruction of Dresden. Indeed so far as Second World War crimes went, this new concept was employed by the Russians, Americans and Britons, sitting as judges, in order to bring to justice German, Japanese, and to a lesser extent Italian and other pro-Axis criminals. And since then it has not been used legally at all to fix criminal guilt on the men responsible, say, for French atrocities in Algiers, for the Franco-British invasion of Egypt in 1956, for Russian intervention in Hungary at the same time, for the deaths of millions in the Soviet concentration camps and the near genocide of certain Soviet minority groups, for American aggression against Cuba and in Vietnam. In the twenty-two years that have passed since Control Council Order No. 10 was issued, there have been many crimes against both peace and humanity in almost all parts of the globe. The fact that none has been legally punished would seem to bear out the contention of certain Germans that these were no 'legal' measures but mere

[1] Beate Ruhm von Oppen: *Documents on Germany under Occupation 1945-1954*, O.U.P., 1955, pp. 97-99.

'legalistic' methods of revenge against the Nazis and particularly the Nazi leaders. This is, however, not the whole truth. The men tried and sentenced were criminals, often of the foulest sort. If anyone is ever to be tried for a crime of any sort, these criminals richly deserved the trial and punishment they received, punishments that were often absurdly light. By an accident of history, the circumstances that enabled such trials to be held have so far only existed in the immediate post-war period, particularly in Germany and Japan. It may be assumed that in the event of legal apparatus of any sort surviving another holocaust, their precedent would be invoked, but again presumably only by the victors, if any, against the vanquished, if they too should survive. The fact remains that it would not have been possible, either psychologically or politically, simply to ignore the monstrous crimes committed in the name of the Third Reich.

The decision to punish these men, and some women, was taken quite early in the war.

In October 1943, the Foreign Secretaries of Britain, Russia and the United States met in Moscow to try to consolidate Allied wartime and post-war policy. On the 12th of that month Winston Churchill cabled as follows:

Prime Minister to President Roosevelt and Premier Stalin

Would you very kindly consider whether something like the following might not be issued over our three signatures:

Great Britain, the United States, and the Soviet Union (in whatever order is thought convenient, we being quite ready to be last) have received from many quarters evidence of the atrocities, massacres, and cold-blooded mass-executions which are being perpetrated by the Hitlerite forces in the many countries they have overrun and from which they are now being steadily expelled. The brutalities of the Nazi domination are no new thing, and all peoples or territories in their grip have suffered from the worst forms of government by terror. What is new is that many of these territories are now being redeemed by the advancing armies of the liberating Powers, and that in their desperation the recoiling Hitlerites and Huns are redoubling their ruthless cruelties.

Accordingly the aforesaid three Allied Powers, speaking in the interest of the thirty-two United Nations, hereby solemnly declare, and give full warning of their declaration, as follows:

At the time of the granting of any armistice to any Government which may be set up in Germany those German officers and men and members of the Nazi Party who have been responsible for or have taken a consenting part in the above atrocities, massacres, and executions will be sent back to the countries in which their abominable deeds were done, in order that they may be judged and punished according to the laws of these liberated countries and the free Governments which will be erected therein. Lists will be compiled in all possible detail from all these countries, having regard especially to the invaded parts of Russia, to Poland and Czechoslovakia, to Yugoslavia, Greece, including Crete and other islands, to Norway, Denmark, the Netherlands, Belgium, Luxemburg, France and Italy. Thus Germans who took part in the wholesale shootings of Italian officers or in the execution of French, Dutch, Belgian, or Norwegian hostages, or of Cretan peasants, or who have shared in the slaughters inflicted on the people of Poland or in the territories of the Soviet Republic, which are now being swept clear of the enemy, will know that they will be brought back, regardless of expense, to the scene of their crimes and judged on the spot by the peoples whom they have outraged. Let those who have hitherto not imbrued their hands with innocent blood beware lest they join the ranks of the guilty, for most assuredly the three Allied Powers will pursue them to the uttermost ends of the earth, and will deliver them to their accusers in order that justice may be done.

The above declaration is without prejudice to the case of the major criminals, whose offences have no particular geographical localization.

ROOSEVELT
STALIN
CHURCHILL

If this, or something like this (and I am not particular about the wording), were put over our three signatures, it would, I believe, make some of these villains shy of being mixed up in butcheries now that they know they are going to be beaten. We know, for instance, that our threats of reprisals about Poland have brought about a mitigation of the severities being inflicted on the people there. There is no doubt that the use of the terror-weapon by the enemy imposes an additional burden on our armies. Lots of Germans may develop moral scruples if they know they are going to be brought back and judged in the country, and perhaps the very place, where their cruel deeds were done. I strongly commend to you the principle of the localisation of judgment as likely to exert a deterrent effect on enemy terrorism. The British Cabinet endorses this principle and policy.[2]

And he adds: 'This was accepted and endorsed with a few verbal changes.'

In the following month Churchill met with Stalin and Roosevelt

[2] Winston S. Churchill: *Closing the Ring*, Cassell and Co. Ltd., London W.C.1.

in Teheran. In a private conversation between Stalin and Churchill Stalin advocated something not unlike pastoralization for the whole of Germany. Stalin at that time seems even to have advocated the elimination of German watchmakers who might make parts for shells and the furniture-makers who might produce toy rifles. And a little later, Churchill writes:

Stalin asked again what was to happen to Germany.

I replied that I was not against the toilers in Germany, but only against the leaders and against dangerous combinations. He said that there were many toilers in the German divisions who fought under orders. When he asked German prisoners who came from labouring classes (such is the record, but he probably meant 'Communist Party') why they fought for Hitler, they replied that they were carrying out orders. He shot such prisoners.[3]

This, from the very beginning, sums up the basic difference in attitude towards the Germans held by the Russians and by the Western powers. In 1943 the British, like the Russians, had no love for the Germans whatsoever, but the British and the Americans still wished to 'legalize' their disgust in the post-war world. The Russian leaders of that period did not give a fig for legality. How could they, in view of the way they had, for a quarter of a century, been running their own country?

However Churchill's views prevailed and the Moscow Declaration of October 30th 1943 provided the basis for official Allied policy as regards this matter of war criminals. It is so cited in the preamble to Control Council Law No. 10. A year later, indeed, Stalin had apparently decided to accept fully the Western attitude. He and Churchill met, in October 1944 in Moscow, and afterwards Churchill sent a cable to Roosevelt. 'U.J.' is 'Uncle Joe', the curious sobriquet that the Russian dictator enjoyed in the West at that time, even at the very highest level.)

On major war criminals U.J. took an unexpectedly ultrarespectable line. There must be no executions without trial; otherwise the world would say we were afraid to try them. I pointed out the difficulties in international law, but he replied if there were not trials there must be no death sentences, but only lifelong confinements.[4]

[3] Winston S. Churchill: op. cit.
[4] Winston S. Churchill; *Triumph and Tragedy*, Cassell & Co. Ltd., London W.C.1.

The next, and last wartime, meeting of the 'Big Three' was at Yalta in February of 1945, when the final collapse of Nazi Germany obviously lay only a matter of weeks ahead. Here the respective Occupation Zones were finally established, but no further decisions appear to have been taken about the treatment of Nazis and war criminals.

At the Potsdam Conference of July 1945, the matter was taken up again. According to Churchill, Stalin's attitude had changed. He now called all the refugees from the zones his armies had occupied 'war criminals', some eight and a half million Germans of all classes: for many years all anti-Communists everywhere had been, in Communist parlance, 'Fascists'. Now it seemed that all non-Communist Germans, whether in the Russian zone or the zones occupied by the American, French and British armies were to be 'war criminals'. Later, of course, all west Germans were to be labelled 'revanchistes'. Stalin prided himself, in public, on being a master of philology.

Even before the Potsdam Conference, and indeed just before the end of the war in Europe in April of 1945 the United States Joint Chiefs of Staff had issued a directive (JCS 1067) to the Commander-in-Chief of the United States Forces of Occupation in Germany concerning his duties then and for the future. Paragraph 6 is relevant. It reads:

6. *Denazification*

(a) A proclamation dissolving the Nazi Party, its formations, affiliated associations and supervised organizations, and all Nazi public institutions which were set up as instruments of Party domination, and prohibiting their revival in any form, should be promulgated by the Control Council. You will assure the prompt effectuation of that policy in your zone and will make every effort to prevent the reconstitution of any such organization in underground, disguised, or secret form. Responsibility for continuing desirable non-political social services of dissolved Party organizations may be transferred by the Control Council to appropriate central agencies and by you to appropriate local agencies.
(b) The laws purporting to establish the political structure of National Socialism and the basis of the Hitler régime and all laws, decrees and regulations which establish discrimination on grounds of race, nationality, creed or political opinions should be abrogated by the Control Council. You will render them inoperative in your zone.
(c) All members of the Nazi Party who have been more than nominal

participants in its activities, all active supporters of Nazism or militarism and all other persons hostile to Allied purposes will be removed and excluded from public office and from positions of importance in quasi-public and private enterprises such as (1) civic, economic and labour organizations, (2) corporations and other organizations in which the German Government or subdivisions have a major financial interest, (3) industry, commerce, agriculture and finance, (4) education, and (5) the press, publishing houses and other agencies disseminating news and propaganda. Persons are to be treated as more than nominal participants in Party activities and as active supporters of Nazism or militarism when they have (1) held office or otherwise been active at any level from local to national in the party and its subordinate organizations or in organizations which further militaristic doctrines, (2) authorized or participated affirmatively in any Nazi crimes, racial persecutions or discriminations, (3) been avowed believers in Nazism or racial and militaristic creeds, or (4) voluntarily given substantial moral or material support or political assistance of any kind to the Nazi Party or Nazi officials and leaders. No such persons shall be retained in any of the categories of employment listed above because of administrative necessity, convenience or expediency.

(d) Property, real and personal, owned or controlled by the Nazi Party, its formations, affiliated organizations and supervised organizations and by all persons subject to arrest under the provisions of paragraph 8, and found within your zone, will be taken under your control pending a decision by the Control Council or higher authority as to its eventual disposition.

(e) All archives, monuments and museums of Nazi inception, or which are devoted to the perpetuation of German militarism, will be taken under your control and their properties held pending decision as to their disposition by the Control Council.

(f) You will make special efforts to preserve from destruction and take under your control records, plans, books, documents, papers, files and scientific, industrial and other information and data belonging to or controlled by the following:

(1) The central German Government and its subdivisions, German military organizations, organizations engaged in military research and such other governmental agencies as may be deemed advisable.

(2) The Nazi Party, its formations, affiliated associations and supervised organizations.

(3) All police organizations, including security and political police.

(4) Important economic organizations and industrial establishments, including those controlled by the Nazi Party or its personnel.

(5) Institutes and special bureaux devoting themselves to racial, political, militaristic or similar research and propaganda.[5]

At the Potsdam Conference, in July 1945, this U.S. military directive was given three-power approval. On August 2nd, the Control Council's *Official Gazette* (Supplement 1, p. 13 *et seq.*) published, among many other matters, the following outline for the future programme of denazification:

A. *Political Principles*

1. In accordance with the Agreement on Control Machinery in Germany, supreme authority in Germany is exercised, on instructions from their respective Governments, by the Commanders-in-Chief of the armed forces of the United States of America, the United Kingdom, the Union of Soviet Socialist Republics, and the French Republic, each in his own zone of occupation, and also jointly, in matters affecting Germany as a whole, in their capacity as members of the Control Council.
2. So far as is practicable, there shall be uniformity of treatment of the German population throughout Germany.
3. The purposes of the occupation of Germany by which the Control Council shall be guided are:

(i) The complete disarmament and demilitarization of Germany and the elimination or control of all German industry that could be used for military production. To these ends:

(a) All German land, naval and air forces, the SS, SA, SD and Gestapo, with all their organizations, staffs and institutions, including the General Staff, the Officers' Corps, Reserve Corps, military schools, war veterans' organizations and all other military and quasi-military organizations, together with all clubs and associations which serve to keep alive the military tradition in Germany, shall be completely and finally abolished in such a manner as permanently to prevent the revival or re-organization of German militarism and Nazism.
(b) All arms, ammunition and implements of war and all specialized facilities for their production shall be held at the disposal of the Allies or destroyed. The maintenance and production of all aircraft and all arms, ammunition and implements of war shall be prevented.

(ii) To convince the German people that they have suffered a total military defeat and that they cannot escape responsibility for what they have brought upon themselves, since their own ruthless warfare

[5] Ruhm von Oppen, op. cit., pp. 16-18.

and the fanatical Nazi resistance have destroyed German economy and made chaos and suffering inevitable.

(iii) To destroy the National Socialist Party and its affiliated and supervised organizations, to dissolve all Nazi institutions, to ensure that they are not revised in any form, and to prevent all Nazi and militarist activity or propaganda.

(iv) To prepare for the eventual reconstruction of German political life on a democratic basis and for eventual peaceful cooperation in international life by Germany.

4. All Nazi laws which provided the basis of the Hitler régime or established discrimination on grounds of race, creed, or political opinion shall be abolished. No such discriminations, whether legal, administrative or otherwise, shall be tolerated.

5. War criminals and those who have participated in planning or carrying out Nazi enterprises involving or resulting in atrocities or war crimes shall be arrested and brought to judgment. Nazi leaders, influential Nazi supporters and high officials of Nazi organizations and institutions and any other persons dangerous to the occupation or its objectives shall be arrested and interned.

6. All members of the Nazi Party who have been more than nominal participants in its activities and (all other persons hostile to Allied purposes shall) be removed from public and semi-public office, and from positions of responsibility in important private undertakings. Such persons shall be replaced by persons who, by their political and moral qualities, are deemed capable of assisting in developing genuine democratic institutions in Germany.

7. German education shall be so controlled as completely to eliminate Nazi and militarist doctrines and to make possible the successful development of democratic ideas.

8. The judicial system will be reorganized in accordance with the principles of democracy, of justice under law, and of equal rights for all citizens without distinction of race, nationality or religion.

9. The administration of affairs in Germany should be directed towards the decentralization of the political structure and the development of local responsibility. To this end:

(i) Local self-government shall be restored throughout Germany on democratic principles and in particular through elective councils as rapidly as is consistent with military security and the purposes of military occupation.

(ii) All democratic political parties with rights of assembly and of public discussion shall be allowed and encouraged throughout Germany.

(iii) Representative and elective principles shall be introduced into regional, provincial and state (*Land*) administration as rapidly as may be justified by the successful application of these principles in local self-government.

(iv) For the time being no central German government shall be established. Notwithstanding this, however, certain essential German administrative departments, headed by State Secretaries, shall be established, particularly in the fields of finance, transport, communications, foreign trade and industry. Such departments will act under the direction of the Control Council.

10. Subject to the necessity for maintaining military security, freedom of speech, press and religion shall be permitted, and religious institutions shall be respected. Subject likewise to the maintenance of military security, the formation of free trade unions shall be permitted.[6]

Two months later a first attempt was made to reconstitute the internal German legal system which, like almost everything else, had been ruined by the Third Reich and reduced to rubble with its collapse. This was a particularly sensitive part of the German organism upon which to apply artificial revivification. As stated earlier, to all intents and purposes all the active judges and almost all the attorneys and other members of the legal profession had, for years, been at least nominal Nazis. Furthermore, the institution of the People's Courts had given Nazi justice a merely semi-professional quality. These were indeed legal quicksands on which to build. In an attempt to do so, Control Council Proclamation No. 3, dated October 20th 1945 and published nine days later, reads:

By the elimination of the Hitler tyranny by the Allied Powers the terrorist system of Nazi Courts has been liquidated. It is necessary to establish a new democratic judicial system based on the achievements of democracy, civilization and justice. The Control Council therefore proclaims the following fundamental principles of judicial reform which shall be applied throughout Germany

I. EQUALITY BEFORE THE LAW

All persons are equal before the law. No person, whatever his race, nationality or religion, shall be deprived of his legal rights.

---

[6] Ruhm von Oppen, op. cit., pp. 42-44.

II. GUARANTEES OF THE RIGHTS OF THE ACCUSED

(1) No person shall be deprived of life, liberty or property without due process of law.

(2) Criminal responsibility shall be determined only for offences provided by law.

(3) Determination by any court of any crime 'by analogy' or by so-called 'sound popular instinct' as heretofore provided in the German Criminal Code, is prohibited.

(4) In any criminal prosecution the accused shall have the rights recognized by democratic law, namely the right to a speedy and public trial and to be informed of the nature and cause of the accusation, the right to be confronted with witnesses against him and to have process for obtaining the witnesses in his favour and the right to have the assistance of counsel for his defence. Excessive or inhuman punishments or any not provided by law will not be inflicted.

(5) Sentences on persons convicted under the Hitler régime on political, racial or religious grounds must be quashed.

III. LIQUIDATION OF EXTRAORDINARY HITLER COURTS

The People's Court, Courts of the NSDAP and Special Courts are abolished and their re-establishment prohibited.

IV. INDEPENDENCE OF THE JUDICIARY

(1) Judges will be independent from executive control when exercising their functions and owe obedience only to the law.

(2) Access to judicial functions will be open to all who accept democratic principles without account of their race, social origin or religion. The promotion of judges will be based solely on merit and legal qualifications.

V. CONCLUDING CLAUSE

Justice will be administered in Germany in accordance with the principles of this proclamation by a system of Ordinary German Courts.

Done at Berlin, 20 October 1945.[7]

And this was followed ten days later by Control Council Law No. 4, which was not published until November 30th, and of which Article III reads:

[7] Ruhm von Oppen, op. cit., p. 81-82.

Jurisdiction of German Courts shall extend to all cases both civil and criminal with the following exceptions:

(a) Criminal offences committed against the Allied Occupation Forces
(b) Criminal offences committed by Nazis or any other persons against citizens of Allied nations and their property, as well as attempts directed towards the re-establishment of the Nazi régime and the activity of the Nazi organizations.
(c) Criminal offences involving military personnel of Allied Forces or citizens of Allied nations.
(d) Other selected civil and criminal cases withdrawn from the jurisdiction of German Courts, as directed by the Allied Military Command.
(e) When the offence committed is not of such a nature as to compromise the security of the Allied Forces, the Military Command may leave it to the jurisdiction of German Courts.[8]

Thus was the basis laid for four distinct but interlocking operations.

The first was the trial, by Allied military courts, of the major Nazi criminals and most compromised military leaders. The most spectacular of these, of course, was the great Nuremberg Trial of Göring, Hess, Keitel and other policy-makers of the defunct Third Reich.

The second was the trial by military courts of other major criminals in the various Zones of Occupation and in the former occupied countries. These were conducted by the nationals of the occupying or sovereign powers in question, though witnesses were called from outside those areas in order to testify concerning crimes committed elsewhere. Perhaps the last such trial, neither more nor less 'legally' justified than the others, was that of Eichmann in Israel in 1964. In all these trials, including the Eichmann trial, the defendant was entitled to, and almost invariably had, where Western justice was concerned, at least one German defence attorney. If one accepts the basis of the justice administered by the American and British Courts, the procedure was fair and the sentences in general mild. Many men who might, by any moral standard at all, have been shot out of hand for their past crimes were given comparatively mild prison sentences, and most of these were later remitted. As will be seen, some of these war criminals, after release from Allied

[8] Ruhm von Oppen, op. cit., p. 84.

gaols, were later re-tried by the newly reconstructed German courts and given much stiffer sentences. The British and Americans leaned over backwards to avoid the nagging fear that what they were exercising in their courts in Germany was not justice but revenge. In view of the type of criminals with whom they were dealing, and also in view of the climate of opinion of the time, this is presumably an admirable example of self-restraint. There was, after all, no force on earth apart from educated public opinion in their own countries to prevent the American and British military from massacring all suspected Nazis in their respective Zones, and even at home few tears would have been shed for SS men and such.

Thirdly, and this has happened, it was intended that the trial of war criminals should eventually become the duty of the new German courts.

Finally, there was the problem of denazification. This became, inevitably, a German problem, but powerfully stimulated by the occupying powers. Once the past had been cleared away by the trials of the criminals—or in Russian territory more frequently by their liquidation—the next problem was the elimination from public life or re-education of their accomplices, and the creation of new administrations in accordance with the approved model of the occupying force. Up to this point even the Russians and the Americans could work in agreement. But since the models were so alien, and soon to be involved in a 'cold war' the one with the other, their solutions were to be very different.

This whole scheme for Germany was outlined and rapidly implemented in the first year after the end of the war. From the Western point of view, at least, there seemed to be very little time. At Potsdam President Truman had told Churchill that the American armed forces would only remain in Europe for two years. The Russians were in no such hurry to go home. They would in any event be in Europe forever, nor could they anticipate that within those two years their own misinterpretations of American policy would have caused the Americans to reverse it, and to remain. Gradually the military demarcation line became the Cold War frontier, a Soviet-type state or satellite was created to the east of it, an American-type to the west. And inevitably the attitude of the two great powers to their Germans changed. There will be a little more to say about the Russians' and East German Government's attitude towards the Nazis, but not a great deal. In general the Russians were prepared to accept Nazis who publicly or even privately renounced their previous views, and indeed to maintain them in office if useful enough. They knew how similar the RFK and the SA had been in days not long past and that one form of totalitarianism is not unlike another. The Americans, and to a lesser extent the British, did not understand this, for they remembered and regretted Weimar. What they knew was that Germany had once been a democracy, and they wished to see the Germans turn their country into a new democracy once again. The French were sceptical, but without real power. The Germans did their best to oblige all their masters. What else could they do?

The atmosphere in Germany during the early months of the occupation was very strange indeed. The armies of the Western Allied powers entered Germany, theoretically at least, as the avenging forces of light which had defeated the powers of darkness. However, those armies were composed of several million men, few of whom aspired to the rôle into which they were cast. The most glaring example of this rôle was the non-fraternization regulation, which laid down that Allied officers and soldiers were to keep relations with Germans to a minimum and conduct them in the coldest and most formal manner possible. This stemmed from United States directive (JCS 1067) of April, 1945, already quoted:

> Germany will not be occupied for the purpose of liberation but as a defeated enemy nation. Your aim is not oppression but to occupy Germany for the purpose of realizing certain important Allied objectives. In the conduct of your occupation and administration you should be just but firm and aloof. You will strongly discourage fraternization with the German officials and population.[9]

Non-fraternization was a failure. It was neither possible nor really desirable to prevent private soldiers from handing out sweets and chewing gum to German children, nor from getting hold of liquor, and above all girls.

Saul K. Padover, a historian and psychologist who was a member of the psychological warfare branch of the U.S. Office of Strategic Services, entered Germany with the leading troops of the United States Twelfth Army Group. He wrote a book about his experiences there, based on his diary, and he published this at once. Highly emotional, with the standard left-wing views of intellectuals in

---

[9] Ruhm von Oppen, op. cit., p. 16.

those days, violently pro-Russian and anti-German, it reflects very accurately the atmosphere of those first chaotic months. On non-fraternization he has this to say:

The non-fraternization rule had been a mockery from the beginning. It was, as I pointed out in a confidential memorandum to S.H.A.E.F. at Christmas time, an ill-advised, though well-meaning order and one based upon faulty intelligence. Our soldiers treated the order not to fraternize with Germans much the way their fathers treated the Eighteenth Amendment, only more so. This was notably true where women were concerned. Non-fraternization was wrecked on sex, and the order to have no contact with Germans made the soldiers more careful but not less hungry for German women. War is compounded of one-tenth discomfort and nine-tenths boredom, and it is the latter that over-stimulates sex in soldiers who have little else to think about. To a man bored and fed up with the company of other men, almost anything in skirts is a stimulant and a relief, and German women were not just skirts. They were undeniably attractive in a wholesome, physical, sexy way, and, unlike most non-professional French women, they were neither shy nor unwilling. They were what the boys called 'easy', perhaps the easiest white women in the world; and in their approaches to men their subtlety was not greater than that of the soldiers. G.I. and Fräulein were magnet and steel.

This created a psychologically, and perhaps also a politically, complicated situation. We were particularly interested in the German reaction. How did they feel about an order which by implication placed them in a position of untouchables during the day and which was being violated in bed at night? Was this merely one more proof of the well-known 'Anglo-Saxon hypocrisy'? And did it undermine the respect of the vanquished for the conqueror who showed so little dignity and decency where his passions were concerned? We asked a number of thoughtful Germans, leaders in their communities for their opinions.

At Kornelimuenster we talked to Mayor Huepgens and his deputy, Wagemann. They told us that the people were unhappy at the ban on fraternization, particularly since it came suddenly and without any public announcement or explanation. One day the soldiers and officers were friendly and polite, and the next day they were cold and reserved. 'People are upset and worried. They think it is fear of spying that makes the Americans so reserved. They don't understand what we understand, namely, that this is war and that friendship is impossible.' Huepgens, an elderly anti-Nazi school teacher, remarked that when the Americans entered town, his wife said to the first doughboy she saw, 'You bring us peace and freedom.' And the soldier replied, 'I hope so.' Wagemann observed dryly that despite the order against fraternization, there was secret sexual contact between soldiers and women in town. Most of them, he added, were 'bad women', and among them was one aged sixty-seven, a harridan who wore pants and was *'verrueckt* (crazy)' but who had nevertheless sexual success with the soldiers.

At Bardenberg, Father Wirtz, the Catholic priest, condemned non-fraternization as a reflection on the whole German people. 'If the United States fears spiritual infection,' he said, 'I can understand. But this is not the way to do it, because it is a condemnation of everybody, the guilty and the innocent alike. It treats all Germans as inferiors. As a German, this hurts me. Your Military Governor refused to shake hands with the priest. We think that this is frightful and no way to build up new relations between the two nations. Your radio, moreover, said that you are fighting only against the Nazis. Why, then, do you treat us all the same?' As we left his parish study, he remarked that the American ban on fraternization was bound to be violated just as surely as was the Nazi ban on listening to the foreign radio. Other Germans to whom we spoke expressed fundamentally the same views.[10]

At the grass roots level Allied occupation policy first fell down over the non-fraternization rule which foundered on the indestructible reefs of human nature, a nature that may often be vile but which contains many qualities that are quite the reverse. It was, the soldiers felt, all very well for senior officers in Washington, London, Paris or at S.H.A.E.F. to lay down a rule forbidding fraternization—weird word: as one G.I., punished for breaking this regulation, remarked: 'I never wanted to treat her like she was my brother'—but the soldiers in the ruined German cities, most of whom were about to be demobilized and knew so could not care less whether the pretty blonde had been a Nazi youth leader or not.

And then there was the emotion of pity. Starvation tightened its grip on Germany. A quarter of Germany's arable land had been lost to the Russians and the Poles, and despite Churchill's pleas to Stalin during the Potsdam Conference, the Russian dictator would not consider the export of foodstuffs to feed the eight and a half millions of Germans who had fled or were being driven from those areas into the Western zones. In the British zone the basic ration sank to 1,048 calories, just enough to keep an idle man alive, and it remained at this figure until August, 1946. In the French zone,

---

[10] Saul K. Padover: *Psychologist in Germany*, Phoenix House, 1946, pp. 211-212.

on February 1st, 1946, it was in theory slightly higher at 1,075, while in the U.S. and Russian zones it remained at about 1,500. There were very few fat Germans in 1946 and 1947.[11] In fact the soldiers found themselves surrounded by a starving population consisting largely of children, women and the old. It was too much to expect all of them not to give some of their rations away.

The circumstances in which these starving people lived were atrocious. Brett-Smith has described Berlin as it then was:

> After a time those who had to live among the ruins became inured or deadened to them; this was very noticeable, especially among the children, many of whom themselves were little veterans without an arm, an eye, or a leg, at the age of seven or ten or twelve. They took their disablement with amazing calm, but they grew up fast. They had to, to survive. Noticeable too was the almost unbelievable way in which people managed to live in some of these ruins. A new race of troglodytes was born, one or other of whom periodically would bob up from nowhere at one's feet among rank weeds and rubble, to explain, on being questioned, that his 'cellar' was really quite stylish compared to some. Shrubs, dirty but determined, and weeds, grass and wispy flowers, forced their way up through stones and masonry and among rusty iron and steel. The greenery of the ruins was forlorn, but it throve mysteriously and lavishly. Ruins take on a vague but formidable personality of their own. If there is one thing about them above others, it is their agelessness. Six months before a part of the unremarkable living scene, that much later they might have been ruins for half a century. At night they achieve a sort of beauty sometimes, for their grimness is softened, but their foreboding awe better defined. They seem to lean towards you, and the starlight and the winds play tricks among their gaps and crannies. Whether they have any lasting effect upon the men and women who daily pass among them, is hard to say. It is tempting to exaggerate their significance. But in Berlin, where more than anywhere they have, so to speak, frozen into permanence, it is possible that in some measure they have entered into everyone's subconscious feelings—subconscious because in Berlin of all places the inhabitants seem utterly to ignore them.[12]

The Germans were puzzled and disappointed by the non-fraternization law. At first many of them seem genuinely to have

---

[11] Richard Brett-Smith: *Berlin '45: the Grey City*, Macmillan, 1966, p. 111.
[12] Richard Brett-Smith, op. cit., p. 126.

believed that the British and above all the Americans came as 'liberators', to save them from the Russians. They were then bewildered by the failure of the soldiers to obey that law. But it may be suggested that the disobedience did more to bring the Germans back into the Western fold than any acts of the Control Council during its first year or so of existence.

If the non-commissioned ranks thus flouted Allied policy from the start, the officers were scarcely more obedient. They, quite naturally, tended to look for comfortable billets in large houses, nor did they invariably, as they were supposed to do, evict the German owners. Contact became inevitable and from these contacts with members of their own class, maybe with shared interests, emotions as strong as friendship arose.

But perhaps more important than this was the partial failure to implement Allied policy concerning the purification of the German administration at medium and low level. Although Nazi mayors, chiefs of police and so on were in general dismissed, and even arrested, immediately, this did not apply at first to anything like the same extent with the more a-political jobs, at least not while the combat soldiers retained responsibility. Writing about this period of direct military rule at all levels, Brett-Smith says:

> Our Military Government was an unqualified success, on the whole. The chief reason for this, I think, was that we had not in any way been trained for it, nor told how to catch out the gas works manager or check the harbour-master's returns. We knew nothing whatever about Military Government as practised by those who came after us. We relied, therefore, upon the rule of thumb and common sense, and left Germans who knew their business to get on with it.[13]

It was much the same in the U.S. zone in the beginning, but the Americans had a larger staff devoted to military government, G-5, which moved in very rapidly behind the combat troops to take over. They were not invariably successful. There were repeated scandals about Nazis being retained in office: these often got into the American press and caused understandable bitterness and anger among the large Jewish population and others in the United States. Indeed the first large German city to be captured in the West, Aachen, was the scene of the first of these scandals, as early as

[13] op. cit., pp. 7-8.

January of 1945. Padover, who was there at the time, describes the situation in great detail.

Aachen had been captured on October 21st, after a long and ferocious battle which had reduced most of the city to rubble and destroyed all its utilities. The German Army had then looted it, before withdrawing, taking with them a large part of the population and leaving mines and booby traps behind. Since for the next four months Aachen remained within a few miles of the front, this semi-deserted ruin was not an easy place to administer. A military governor was appointed, and Padover discovered that among his staff there was only one American who spoke German. (This was not at all uncommon. There were very few American officers who spoke any German at all. This did not make local administration any easier.)

What happened in Aachen was this. A lieutenant-colonel had been appointed Military Governor and had been ordered to find a mayor for the city. The Bishop of Aachen, a Roman Catholic, had a perfectly clean record, and though urged to leave by the Wehrmacht had preferred to remain within his diocese. It was to him that the American Military Governor went, in search of a suitable mayor, and the bishop suggested a man well known to himself, a lawyer by the name of Franz Oppenhoff.

Oppenhoff was in 1944 a man of forty, who had never been a Nazi Party member. Indeed he had been brave enough to defend half-Jewish firms and Roman Catholic priests in the pre-war courts. That was how he had come to the notice of the Bishop, who had appointed him diocesan lawyer. During the war Oppenhoff had avoided military service because he had taken an administrative job in Aachen's largest war-plant, the Veltrup, and was thus exempt. If not a Nazi, he had shown no signs of anti-Nazi activity other than those legal cases long ago. His political views, however, were extremely right-wing and anti-democratic. He hated and feared Communism, disliked all forms of Socialism and trade unionism, and according to Padover would have felt thoroughly at home in Dollfuss's semi-fascist Austria or in the Italy of Mussolini, whom he admired.

As *Oberbürgermeister* or Chief Mayor he now appointed a number of deputy Mayors to handle, as is usual in Germany, various aspects of city administration. These were all personal friends of his, most of them drawn from the administration of

Veltrup or other armament works. None was a Nazi, but none had been an anti-Nazi either. They seem to have shared Oppenhoff's political views.

They proceeded to appoint the city administration. They did not hesitate to give jobs to Nazi Party members, though Oppenhoff maintained that these were all *Müssnazis*. They gave no administrative jobs to Social Democrats or trade union leaders, though some of these had survived in what, in pre-Hitler days, had been a predominantly Social Democrat society. This caused considerable bitterness among the working population of Aachen, or what was left of it. It seemed to them that a small right-wing clique, having no particular objection to Nazism and prepared to employ Nazis, had taken over their city, backed by the Bishop and by the Americans. Certainly where the Aacheners were concerned Oppenhoff and his pals had far more direct power in Aachen so far as patronage—and hence in the distribution of heat, food and light—than had the American Military Governor. And the Military Governor apparently did not mind.

The C.I.C., or Counter Intelligence Corps, a branch of the U.S. Army that contained many German refugees and could therefore get the feel of the place far better than the non-German-speaking members of the Governor's staff, pointed out the dangers inherent in the Oppenhoff administration, all the more since this was the first German city to be occupied and a dangerous precedent might be being set. However, the Governor was not obliged to listen to the C.I.C. He preferred to consult the Bishop, who continued to support Oppenhoff. Still, rumours reached Twelfth Army Group that all was not well in Aachen, and though this was not strictly his job, Padover and some others were sent there and he was told to write a report of what he found. He quotes from this report of his, which began:

In the last three months a new élite has emerged in Aachen, an élite made up of technicians, lawyers, engineers, businessmen, manufacturers, and churchmen. This élite is shrewd, strong-willed, and aggressive. It occupies every important job in the administration. Its leader is Oberbuergermeister Oppenhoff. Almost all the Buergermeisters and key functionaries were chosen by him and most of them think his way. Behind Oppenhoff is the Bishop of Aachen, a powerful figure with a subtlety of his own and a programme of the Church. Nearly all of these men have known each other for a long time. Three of the

Buergermeisters live together in one house, two in another house. Oppenhoff had been, among other things, the lawyer for the Bishop and the diocese. His collaborators are Faust and Op de Hipt, both of them executives in the Veltrup (armaments) works. Buergermeisters Hirtz and Schefer are old school-mates. All of these men managed to stay out of the Nazi Party; most of them were directly connected with the city's leading war industries, those of Veltrup and Talbot.

Their strong point, especially in dealing with Americans, is that they are 'anti-Nazi' or 'non-Nazi'. Their proof is that they never joined the Party. How and why did they escape Party membership? Oppenhoff says his circle did not depend on the Party because they were in the *freie Berufe* (free professions) or were closely connected with the Church and thus 'could not join'. Schefer, now Chief of Police, was protected from Party membership by working as an assessor for the Wehrmacht High Command in Berlin. Buergermeister Mies was manager of a big war industry whose contribution to the Nazi war effort was important enough to earn him the *Kriegsverdienstkreuz* (War Service Cross) in 1943. Buergermeister Hirtz was not eligible for Nazi Party membership because he says he had a Jewish mother (he admitted he would have joined otherwise). Buergermeister Breuer could not join because he was a Papal Legate.

These leading officials kept out of the Wehrmacht because they volunteered their services to the war industry. Some of them, notably Oberbuergermeister Oppenhoff and his chief assistants Faust and Op de Hipt, sought 'refuge' in Aachen's leading war plant, the Veltrup works. Veltrup was under the jurisdiction of the German High Command's *Wehrkreiskommando*, and since the Wehrmacht was primarily interested in war production, Veltrup was not ordered to force his group of experts to join the Party.

A striking fact about this new Aachen élite is its comparative youth. Their ages run from thirty-three to fifty. They all represent the upper-middle class; their earnings in the last ten years under Hitler have been high, ranging from seven thousand to two hundred thousand marks yearly, with the average about thirty thousand marks. None of them ever suffered under the Nazi régime—or ever, by word or deed, opposed it. The record shows that they prospered under Hitler.

These men around Oberbuergermeister Oppenhoff are not democratic-minded. They profess a marked distaste for the Weimar Republic, an abhorrence of party government, a dread of labour, and a fearful suspicion of liberal movements. In varying degrees and tones, one or the other repeats the slogans and clichés of the Nazis and the 'eternal Germans'—that Germany was 'dishonoured' by the Versailles Treaty, that the latter was too harsh, that France is the permanent hereditary enemy, that Germany was betrayed when the Fourteen Points were not kept, that the 'poor' Reich is a 'land without space' and must expand. They attribute the outbreak of the war to these 'evils' and charge the working-class with being the main support of Hitler . . .

That this situation was allowed to develop may be explained on the ground that M.G. seems to have no sharply-defined policy, and that M.G. officers tend to approach their problems from a personal viewpoint. Unless they are given unequivocal guidance based on a clear policy of what we want to achieve politically in occupied Germany, M.G. will continue to flounder in a mass of contradictions, and M.G. officers will improvise policies according to their temperament, convictions, and personal prejudices.

An M.G. team is judged on its efficiency and 'performance record'. Thus when an M.G. group enters a city, its first consideration is functional, not political. No political intelligence officer accompanied the M.G. team into Aachen. In fact, no officer, outside the medical officer (Hungarian-born), could speak German; none had any firsthand German experience.

An M.G. team, therefore, will employ almost anybody it believes capable of putting a town on a functioning basis. Thus Nazi sympathizers, Party members, or German nationalists, are appointed by M.G. officers, as the only available specialists. These specialists, who look extremely presentable and have professional backgrounds similar to those of M.G. officers, then place their like-minded friends in secondary positions. As a consequence, M.G.'s initial indifference to the politics of the situation leads in the end to a political mess. Then come the complicated attempts by C.I.C. to weed out the undesirables, and M.G. officers find themselves in the unpleasant position of having either to defend Nazis or of starting all over again.[14]

The scandal was a most disagreeable one for the American authorities and at the highest level all attempts were made to ensure that it was not repeated. Aachen was 'cleaned up' and, a little later, Oppenhoff was murdered, though by whom is not clear. But of course it *was* repeated and finally at a very high level.

General George S. Patton was one of the greatest tank generals of all time—according to Captain Sir Basil Liddell Hart, not only superior to any American or British tank general of the Second World War, but also on a par with the greatest Germans, Rommel and Guderian—and perhaps the greatest American army commander since Sherman. The brilliance of his campaign in Sicily was only surpassed by that of his Third Army in France and

---

[14] Padover, op. cit., pp. 179-181, 202-203.

Germany. His great victories then would have been even more spectacular had he not been held back, perhaps for inter-Allied political reasons, by his Supreme Commander in Europe and by his Commander-in-Chief in Washington.

He was a most curious man, with his adolescent passion for personal display, padded shoulders like an All-American footballer and a brace of pearl-handled pistols as if he were a latter-day Jesse James. His attitude towards the army he commanded was in some ways extraordinarily old-fashioned. It resembled that of some eighteenth-century general such as the Maréchal de Saxe or Prince Eugene. For him, Third Army was 'my' army, and he treated it as such. In matters of discipline, the wearing of ties and so on, he treated 'his' men far more roughly than did the other American army commanders in Europe. He was quite capable of losing his temper, and he once slapped a soldier in a Sicilian hospital who, he believed, was malingering and being impertinent. This may have cost him command of the United States Twelfth Army Group in the French campaign. If so, it was a fortunate slap, for he was undoubtedly far better at commanding fighting troops than at dealing with the more 'political' responsibilities that bedevil the lives of senior officers above army level. Most of his staff loathed him, and whether his soldiers loved him or not would be hard to say. The newspapers called him 'Old Blood and Guts': the soldiers knew that it was their blood and their guts; but what counts for soldiers is that their army commander wins great victories, and at such speed that the cost in lives is comparatively slight. He was a great American general and, in 1945, a great American hero.

His political views were those of the extreme American Right. He loathed Communism and, therefore, President Roosevelt's long flirtation with 'Uncle Joe' and the whole American liberal establishment. He had seen the Red Army limping into Berlin and it has been said that in 1945 he wished to push straight through to the Urals: the Americans would have to fight the Russians eventually, so why not do so now, while he had his superb army ready and the Russians' was on its last legs? He could, he believed, have been in Siberia in three weeks. From a military point of view he may have been right. Politically it was utter nonsense, and of course anathema in Washington.

He despised the Nazis whom he had, as he would have put it, 'licked'. According to his nephew he habitually referred to them as 'slimy scum', 'filthy murderers' and, strange epithet, 'purple-pissing Nazis'. He had compelled leading Germans to visit the concentration camps and had rubbed their noses in the filth. On the other hand his general political views were probably closer to those of Herr Oppenhoff than to those of Mr Padover. His appointment to take over the military government of Bavaria was unfortunate in view of the policies that Washington was determined to enforce through the obliging and uncritical General Eisenhower. Nor was this the sort of job for which Patton, for whom the 'progressives' were already gunning, had the slightest ability. The job bored him. In a private letter, dated August, 1945, he wrote:

> To keep busy, fortunately I also have to occupy myself with the denazification of Bavaria, and the recruiting of the industries of the German people so that they can be more self-supporting.[15]

By this time denazification had really begun, and the many *Fragebogen* had been sent out. American military authority in Germany was shifting from a combat to a clerical capacity, a shift that was not likely to appeal to General Patton who, after being relieved of his command, referred to his troops of the post-war Third Army as 'a group of soldiers, mostly recruits, who rejoiced in that historic name'.

He took his job seriously. He believed he must make Germany prosperous and productive once again if it were not to become another Communist state. This belief was contrary to many of the powerful currents in Washington where the Morgenthau Plan was not entirely dead and Roosevelt's belief in the importance, if not perhaps the potential permanence, of the U.S.-Soviet alliance was accepted dogma. In trying to carry out his duties, Patton found himself increasingly hampered by the mounting programme of denazification. As his nephew remarks, he was ordered to remove men 'with Nazi affiliations' from 'the running of waterworks, power stations, medical laboratories, subway systems, even hospitals'. (There are no subway systems in Bavaria, but perhaps Mr Ayer is referring to the Berlin U-Bahn.) Patton reacted with characteristic bravura and tactlessness. He is reported to have said that *he* decided who had been a Nazi in Bavaria. (This may be

---

[15] Fred Ayer: *Before the Colours Fade*, Cassell, 1965. Mr Ayer is a nephew of General Patton. I am principally indebted to him for this account of 'the Patton incident'.

untrue: Ayer does not quote the remark. Whether true or not, it was an unfortunate echo of a remark, perhaps equally apocryphal, attributed to Göring: that *he* decided who was a Jew.) Patton was in fact treating Bavaria as he had treated *his* Third Army, and finally said: 'If there was an election I could be President of Bavaria', which was probably true but scarcely tactful. When he was quoted as saying: 'Nazis and anti-Nazis. Why, it's only the ins and outs, just like Republicans and Democrats at home', and again: 'It's just as if the Democrats in power at home threw out every Republican who held any kind of civic job or vice versa. Nothing would run', he was talking about his job of rehabilitating South Germany and completely ignoring his secondary—and, from the point of view of Washington, more important—job of getting rid of the Nazis. The *New York Times* made a great splash of all this, and one of America's greatest war heroes was fired. A few weeks later he was dead, in a car crash. For a time there were rumours in Germany that he had been murdered by his political enemies: these are certainly untrue. He had gone from power because he no longer fitted into the age of the *Fragebogen*, which had already opened. The war was over: reconstruction had begun.

Chapter Six

In the earliest days of the Occupation there was much muddle. This was not merely due to apparent contradiction of Allied administrative policy such as led to the 'Patton incident' nor even to the partial inefficiency, and at times blatant corruption, of the men in the armies of occupation. There was also a basic flaw in Allied thinking about what Salomon has called 'the German problem'. This was exemplified by the concept of collective guilt.

James Stern, who had known Germany well before the war, found himself in Bad Nauheim in May of 1945, only a week or so after the German act of unconditional surrender. Bad Nauheim is a pleasant little spa, not far from Frankfurt-am-Main. Apart from the *Kurhaus*, which had been precision bombed under the mistaken belief that it housed a senior German headquarters, the little place was almost undamaged, its stolid, bourgeois inhabitants still well-dressed and comparatively well-fed. The day after his arrival, James Stern went for a walk, past the ruins of the *Kurhaus*. He has written:

While this building, now a shell half-hidden by scaffolding, may have acted as a magnet to newly arrived Americans, the natives of Nauheim were not interested. They were drawn elsewhere. We found them in small groups, standing in front of trees, before the town's proclamation board and the empty windows of closed shops. They stood there, silent, motionless for several minutes; then, shaking their heads, they walked slowly away. What they saw on these trees, boards and shop-windows, what faced them in some prominent spot in every street in every village and town, was a large notice from which glared a heading in immense black letters:

WHO IS GUILTY?

Under the heading were a number of enlarged, rather blurred photographs: hundreds of naked human skeletons were piled high on the open wagon of a goods train; what looked like a mountain of garbage was a mountain of ash and charred human bones; men in striped prison clothes hung from gallows, while children and babies lay on their backs on the ground, dead from starvation. Under each photograph a caption informed the observer where the picture had been taken.

Standing behind these groups of spectators, I never heard anyone utter a word. A woman would occasionally put a hand or a handkerchief to her mouth as though to stifle the moan or cry of horror; an elderly man with his mouth open would stare as though hypnotized for a few minutes; then one by one they would walk slowly away.

I tried to put myself in the place of these people to imagine what they were thinking. I followed them in my mind as they wandered slowly through the sunlit park, past the man whose spiked stick, in this murderous world, prodded at pieces of paper under benches and dropped them carefully, tidily, into the wire basket; I watched them pass a line of wounded ex-soldiers of the Wehrmacht whose hands sprang to their peaked caps as they encountered American officers, who were not permitted to return the salute; I followed them through the *Sprudelhof* where wealthy invalids had once hoped to cure their ills in sulphur baths; I saw them shuffle by, unseeing, a photographer's window-display of ski scenes and close-ups of laughing German children and babies; and I came out with them into the streets of Victorian hotels and was close behind them as they slowly mounted the staircase to the stuffy, cluttered room where I imagined them to live. There, sitting invisible in their presence, I watched the trembling hand go out to the radio for relief, and I listened to the voice of accusation resounding through the room:

WHO IS GUILTY?

Who is guilty of the atrocities committed against humanity in your midst . . .?

As the voice continued, minute after monotonous minute, describing in dreadful detail the endless list of crimes, I sat watching the dumb, expressionless face. And when the voice ended and started all over again with its 'WHO IS GUILTY?' I watched the hand go out to the knob, saw the knob turned, and in the hollow silence that followed I tried to put myself in the place of this anonymous native of Nauheim; but no mental effort I ever made could have been more vain.

The native reaction seemed no different, one's efforts to penetrate the silent masks no less futile, when this notice was taken down and another put up in its stead. Asking no question, this placard stated a fact. Over clearer, more detailed photographs ran the bold black headline:

THIS TOWN IS GUILTY!
YOU ARE GUILTY!

Back in the hotel, during a discussion of German guilt and allied propaganda, an officer interrupted. 'I think,' he said, 'that the manner in which we use the word "allied" is a little loose. There are no guilt placards, such as we see here, in the Russian zone. And do you know what the Berlin radio is telling its listeners, what people in this zone who can tune in to Berlin are hearing? They hear details about the destruction of the city and what is being done to clear it up; about the water, gas, electricity and food situation and what is being done to increase rations; about housing, clothing, and other bare necessities of life. After this they are treated to a round-the-clock program of music, including the works of the Jewish composers, Mendelssohn and Offenbach—which have not been heard in this country for twelve years. The Germans, you know, are great music lovers . . .'

This information did not, needless to say, end the discussion. But it set some of us thinking about the larger issues of propaganda and collective guilt.[1]

This concept of collective guilt is queer. Guilt is a theological, a legal and only at second-hand a political word. Theologically 'collective guilt' must be a meaningless term, since there is no such thing as a 'collective soul'. Legally it makes more sense: accomplices are also found guilty in courts of law, and, as I have shown, a good case can be made for the contention that almost all the Germans were accomplices, active or passive, in the crimes of the Nazis. (But the children? The anti-Nazis dead or in the camps? The incorrigibly and hopelessly stupid who form a sizeable portion of any community, and quite simply do not understand anything beyond their own utterly narrow and personal view of the world?) In a political sense 'collective guilt' seemed obvious in the immediate post-war period to the Allied nations who had had to batter their way to the very heart of Germany and who had then been nauseated by what they found there, at Auschwitz, Belsen, Buchenwald, Ravensbrück and the other camps. It was hard then not to loathe and despise the whole German race. And from this it follows that all Germans should be punished, maybe even exterminated. Indeed, a few weeks after James Stern took his walk through Bad Nauheim I heard precisely this idea expressed by a highly educated young woman in New York City. She was herself a German, a Jewish refugee. When I tried to explain that her favoured choice would only 'justify' Hitler's atrocious treatment of her own people she

---

[1] James Stern, *The Hidden Damage*, Harcourt, Brace, 1947, pp. 79-81.

became extremely angry. Politics are, of course, usually more a matter of emotion than of reason, and seldom has there been so intense a politico-emotional climate as that which prevailed concerning Germany and the Germans in 1945.

Historically the idea of collective guilt, again from the Western point of view, is explicable. The British used it, repeatedly and for years, in their colonial wars. When pestered by armed bands on the Northwest Frontier of India or in Arabia, say, the penultimate deterrent (the ultimate was annexation) was first to warn the inhabitants and then to destroy by aerial bombardment the villages which the armed enemy was believed to regard as his home. The French had behaved similarly: furthermore their dislike and fear of the *Boche* was still endemic and in many ways reinforced by the Occupation. (Yet in some respects the generally good behaviour of the German Army in France from 1940-1944 had increased French respect for their Teutonic neighbours, while there was also a sort of sneaking solidarity of the defeated nations against the triumphant 'Anglo-Saxons'. Besides, the Germans had often beaten the French, as the French had often defeated the Germans. The parts in the play were accepted by the actors.) As for the Americans, if my earlier analysis is acceptable and they tend to judge all wars in terms of their own Civil War, the Germans were not merely enemies but 'traitors'. A defeated enemy is treated with a measure of respect, while a captured traitor deserves, and gets, none. As early as 1943, when Colonel General von Arnim had surrendered in Tunisia, General Eisenhower had refused to accept his sword or, indeed, to receive him at all, let alone to treat him with the civilities customary in the old Europe on such occasions. A tiny, but significant, straw. Nobody suggested then nor has since that Arnim was a Nazi, let alone a war criminal. But for Eisenhower, even in 1943, he was already 'collectively guilty', whatever that phrase may mean.

Meanwhile for the Germans of 1945 and the years immediately to follow, the concept was bewildering to the individual civilian or soldier who had committed no crime, but had merely carried out his 'normal' life despite the abnormalities both of the Nazi government and of wartime conditions. He might feel ashamed of his government and of his country when confronted by the evidence of what that government had done, but any attempt to force the stolid citizens of Bad Nauheim to accept personal guilt for the horrors of Buchenwald was asking both too much and too little. It was clearly right to force the facts upon them, and clearly wrong to imagine that they would, both individually and in the mass, accept the almost meaningless guilt of the 'collective'. Some did, but one essence of totalitarianism, as was pointed out in a quotation from Salomon earlier in this book, is that totalitarianism atomizes society and destroys the 'collective'. There was, in Germany in 1945, no form of collective society left to accept the guilt for what had happened, and without acceptance guilt becomes meaningless or, worse, mere masochism.

Secondly there was one gross internal contradiction in Allied policy, as seen through many German eyes. While it was generally accepted that the real criminals among themselves be tried and punished for specific crimes, it did not make sense that men should be tried and punished merely for having been Nazis if it were also and simultaneously the belief of the conquerors that all Germans, whether Nazis or not, were collectively guilty. The idea of supplanting a Nazi harbour-master with a non- or even anti-Nazi successor made no sense whatever if the collective guilt of the whole German nation embraced them both equally.

There can be little doubt that this philosophical bewilderment further confused a nation already numbed by the terrors of total defeat, stunned by the horrible revelations concerning its own immediate past, and now almost totally engaged as individuals in a desperate struggle for food, warmth, survival. In intellectual circles a sterile debate about collective guilt, its validity or otherwise, rumbled on for years. Its echoes can still be heard from time to time. The great majority of the Germans simply shrugged their shoulders at last, and often opted out of their incomprehensible society. '*Ohne mich!*' (without me) was later to become a commonplace attitude, comparable to the 'I couldn't care less' of fed-up wartime and post-war Britons, sick of governmental and newspaper exhortations. For such people denazification was just another meaningless gimmick on the part of the occupying powers. This became, and has remained, the general attitude of the public to what was initially a well-intended and sensible policy decision: to get the Nazis out of public life forever. At the time of writing a former Nazi Party member is Chancellor of the German Federal Republic, and despite the constant reminder of this fact from the Communist propaganda apparatus few people who are not of that persuasion think any worse of Herr Kiesinger for this.

In the summer of 1945, however, it was very different. Each zone adopted its own attitude towards the problems of denazification.

In the Russian zone denazification played a subordinate rôle to the destruction of capitalism, though the dismantling of the Nazi apparatus, in the civil service, industry and social life generally, was frequently invoked as the reason for the construction of a Communist apparatus in its place. The Russians explicitly and repeatedly stated that they were not interested in whether a man had or had not been a Nazi, but only in whether he had been an 'active' Nazi—a distinction which is extremely hard to draw—and in whether, as a Nazi Party member or not, he had been guilty of crimes and had helped forward the criminal policies of the defunct Nazi administration, governmental or local, or of the industry that supported it. This elastic formula gave the Russian authorities and the German Communists complete freedom to punish or to employ any man they chose. Of course many Nazis were dismissed. The official figure given is something over half a million.[2] Nazis who had served the Americans in the areas originally seized by the United States and later handed over to the Red Army were, of course, doubly suspect and the object of a special operation. Official figures of those imprisoned, sentenced to forced labour, deported to Russia or executed are not available, and would be almost worthless if they were.

'Denazification' in the Russian zone was largely completed by the end of 1945, in the first weeks of occupation and the last of that year. Thus in Thuringia on November 15th 1945, there were from official statistics still 142 departmental heads, 374 officials and 2,030 public employees who had been Nazi Party members. Of these 120, 268 and 1,475 respectively had been dismissed by January 15th 1946, or approximately two-thirds, with emphasis inevitably on the more senior among them. No *Fragebogen* were issued. The operation was carried out in a more or less haphazard fashion, and by an order of the Soviet Military Administration, No. 201, dated August 16th 1947, denazification was to end within three months. In fact it was officially pronounced that the programme had been completed on February 26th 1948. Finally, on January

[2] Stefan Doernberg: *Die Geburt eines Neuen Deutschland 1945-1949*, Ruetten and Loening, Berlin, 1959.

14th 1950, the Soviet Control Commission ordered the provisional government of the German Democratic Republic to dissolve the forced labour camps in which, it may be assumed, many Nazis unacceptable to the new régime had been incarcerated. Since their creation the two German governments have carried on a lengthy slanging match, each accusing the other of employing former Nazis in high places and producing lists of these men and even short biographies to prove their point. Both are undoubtedly correct, though the East Germans are more mendacious: almost any man they dislike is branded as an ex-Nazi, which accusations, whether true or false, are then repeated by Communist parrots in the West. In fact it would seem a fair estimate that approximately the same number of former Nazis, proportionate to the population, are employed in both the Germanies.

The French shared one problem with the Russians. The British were in Europe, but the Channel separated them from the Continent. It was assumed by everyone in 1945 that the Americans would soon withdraw behind the Atlantic. The French, like the Russians, would have to live cheek by jowl with the Germans forever. Just as the Russians had been invaded twice, and defeated once, in the past forty years, the French had been invaded three times and conquered twice in the past seventy-five. Therefore while denazification might, for the Americans and to a lesser extent the British, be in some ways an almost abstract exercise in justice, for the French, as for the Russians, it appeared in 1945 a political problem which, if correctly solved, should prevent German aggression for a very long time and with luck forever.

The Russian solution politically was to incorporate as much of Germany as they controlled—and they would have liked to control it all—in their Communist Empire. And for this they used the totalitarian methods that they favoured and that the Germans knew so well under differently coloured shirts. The French had had no such ideological *imperium* to offer foreigners for a hundred and fifty years. In certain French circles in 1945 the break-up of the German State into smaller units was considered desirable, as it had been desired by many Frenchmen in 1919. However, this was clearly impossible without the approval of the three great powers (France was not even invited to participate in the Potsdam Conference, though had a peace conference taken place the French would have been present) and for various reasons none of the Big Three wanted to see Germany broken up: the Russians hoped soon, perhaps as soon as the Americans had gone, to gobble up the lot; the British and Americans had no wish to see Central Europe 'Balkanized' into a series of titbits to be swallowed by the Russians piece-meal, as had just happened to the old Balkan countries themselves. Furthermore even if neither of these major political changes were to follow upon the creation of multiple Germanies, only force in the long run could prevent German nationalism from coalescing once again. And even if a new Confederation of the Rhine were firmly linked to Paris, the nature of modern war would no longer permit such a state to act as a useful buffer against future aggression by a future German state. Partition, like pastoralization, was therefore a non-starter. A devoluted federal state was the best the French could hope for, and this was what they got, but from the French point of view it was still not enough.

The French therefore had to rely on their own resources in order to produce, first in their own zone and later by contagion in all Germany, a neighbour across the Rhine whom they need not fear and with whom they could live in peace. To do this was to rule out French terrorism or even naked power politics, such as the French occupation of the Ruhr in 1923, as a weapon. In 1945 the French were military pensionaries of the British and, even more, of the Americans. It was assumed that the 'Anglo-Saxons' would soon vacate the scene from a directly military point of view. And the French had at least learned enough from the period 1918-1940 to know that their own bitterly divided country was not capable of enforcing its will on Germany for long, single-handed.

Perhaps the strongest 'weapon' at the disposal of the French in the immediate post-1945 period was their assuredness that French culture, French education and French respect for man's individuality were superior to anything in those fields in the world. Certainly many 'good' Germans, particularly in Western Germany, agreed. As will be seen, the French therefore laid, from the very beginning, far greater emphasis on the educational, as opposed to the punitive, aspects of denazification than did the other three Allied administrations. And in dealing with Nazis they preferred to handle these men as individuals, to categorize less, to treat each Nazi as a man rather than as a jumble of facts, derived from a *Fragebogen*, that could be fed into a computer-type bureaucratic machine which would then pronounce a verdict on the 'facts' rather than on the man. This led to some divergence from the American and British attitudes. It was possible for some Germans to obtain public employment in the French zone who had been refused employment or dismissed from it, for political reasons, in those of the other Western Allies. The French were therefore accused, on occasion, of being 'soft on Nazis', and not least by their own Communist press. It is, however, interesting to note that two men, so employed by the French and branded as unemployable in the other zones, were Konrad Adenauer and Carlo Schmid.

The French had another problem in addition to their political and military weakness vis-à-vis their allies, and this was the internal divisions within France herself, many of them so chronic as to be apparently incurable and much exacerbated by the events of the past few years.

Throughout most of the 1930s France had been living in a state that might nowadays be described as 'cold civil war'.[3] The extreme Right is supposed to have said: *Plutôt Hitler que Blum*, while the extreme Left could well have replied: *Plutôt Staline que les deux cent familles*. With the Spanish Civil War, 1936-1939, France became even more polarized, left and right. Then came defeat and another polarization between Pétainistes and collaborators on the one hand and Gaullistes and Resistance fighters on the other. International events made this dichotomy confusing. During the period of the Nazi-Soviet Pact the Communists were ordered to collaborate. After June 21st 1941, they were ordered to turn about. Not all did. Ex-Communists such as Déat and Doriot remained the extremist wing of Pétainism. Others fought bravely in the Resistance and, being well organized, dominated it in large parts of France. Then came the Liberation and the settling of old scores. Just as was to happen in Eastern Germany, the Communists took this opportunity to brand as collaborators many of their enemies to whom this term was hardly applicable. For a brief period lynch law prevailed in France. Many public officials who had 'collaborated' to the extent that they had continued to run the local waterworks or administer the street cleaning system in their home towns throughout the Occupation were murdered, basically because they were anti-Communist. Legality returned soon enough, with de Gaulle, and *comités d'épuration* or 'purification committees' were set up to try known collaborators. But the brief period of terror

[2] See Alistair Horne, *To Lose a Battle; France 1940*, Macmillan, 1969.

had made many of the French, and particularly many of the French officers who now had to administer their zone, highly sceptical concerning man's ability to distinguish between political virtue and political vice. Although most of those officers had no reason to love the Nazis, and many had very good cause to hate them, they saw the problem less in black and white than did the Americans. Scepticism comes easily to the French.[4]

Furthermore the basic split in France was, if anything, accentuated among the army officers who led their troops into Germany and then had initially to administer their zone of the defeated enemy's land. Many French officers were aristocrats, often of extreme right-wing views: indeed, for such men service in the Army or the Navy had, for generations now, offered the chance of serving France, their *pays réel*, and not, as they thought, the contemptible *pays légal* which was the First, Second, Third and embryonic Fourth Republics. Many of these men had begun by supporting the Pétain government, which appealed to their own views on French affairs and which was, after all, for several years the only French government either in France or abroad. Some remained loyal to the Marshal almost to the end and, in their hearts, beyond it. This did not mean that they were fascists, let alone Nazis, though of course the Communists so named them. In fact they were no less bewildered by the kaleidoscopic nature of recent European history than were the French Communists themselves. Patriotism was a uniting force, but in the complexity of post-war politics patriotism was once again not enough.

The units that had fought for de Gaulle's idea of France in Africa, Italy and the Western Campaign were at least equally patriotic and almost certainly both more enlightened and of greater moral courage. Inevitably they viewed the men who had served Vichy, a government that castigated de Gaulle's followers as traitors, with doubt. Soldiers who had fought at Bir Hakeim and elsewhere four and less years before felt in some ways closer to the Communists who had fought in the *maquis* than to those other French soldiers who had obeyed Vichy at Dakar, in Syria and on the Algerian beaches. Finally, the Communists and the fellow-travellers had established a very strong propaganda apparatus in Paris, both in the press and in the Constituent Assembly. General

---

[4] Much of the factual material which follows is derived from F. Roy Willis, *The French in Germany 1945-1949*, Stanford University Press, 1962.

Koenig's Army of the Rhine and the Danube, which was entrusted with the military government of the French zone, was thus not only divided in some ways from its British and American allies, but was subjected to constant, often vicious, sniping from the rear. As Willis writes:

> The vexed problem of collaboration had caused much trouble in France since the Liberation. For many of the Resistance groups, only active participation in the Resistance could be called patriotic. Active and even passive support of the Vichy government was accounted treasonable. However, during 1944-45, the French government had attempted to bring some order into the situation by creating purge committees (*comités d'épuration*) which reviewed the cases of all accused of collaboration with the Germans, whether directly or through the Vichy régime. The parties of the Left were convinced by the summer of 1945 that this process had been far from effective. . . .
>
> The Army was especially susceptible to these charges. The spirit of loyalty to established authority which had been an ingrained feature of the French military spirit had led the majority of the French army to accept the orders of Pétain, until these were countermanded by Darlan after the North Africa invasion. The patriotism of these men was acknowledged by General de Gaulle, but not by the majority of the political groups, as was seen in the parliamentary opposition to the confirmation, in December 1945, of the grant of the *légion d'honneur* to men who had resisted the American invasion of North Africa in 1942. Critics pointed out that others, more gravely compromised, had later fought with the Resistance or with the First Army, and in this way had made less evident their first acceptance of the Vichy régime, while still others had been able to resume their positions in the army through the complicity of friends. Finally the work of the purge committees had been slow and ineffective. The blame for this was laid to the Minister of War, André Diethelm, who . . . was dropped from the cabinet in November 1945. In April of the following year, Diethelm was still the Communists' whipping boy. On April 3 1946, Paul Tabert declared that there was still need for changing all the arbitrary decisions taken by the former minister (Diethelm) who 'was held back by no control, bound by no rulings, and not even stopped by the voice of conscience, either in matters concerning collaboration, promotion or decorations, or in judicial proceedings and disciplinary action'. (*France, Assemblée constituante, Annexe Nr. 959*) . . .
>
> The same charge of 'Vichyism' was also levelled at the Military Government. The method of recruitment in 1944-45 had made it possible for many who were compromised by their past associations with the

Vichy government to find employment in the zone. As the storm over the insufficient purge in the army grew, repercussions were also felt in the Military Government. In January 1946, Pierre Cot complained that denazification could hardly be successful in the French zone. 'Among those who represent us, there are men in whom we cannot have confidence, because we are not sure that in their very hearts they have not been and have not remained fascists.' (*France, Assemblée constituante*, Debates, 16.1.46). In March, 1946, Alfred Biscarlet, a Communist member of the Committee of Enquiry, testified that 'the zone of occupation has been and is still the refuge for thousands of Vichyites who went there either to be forgotten or to carry on with their work of treason'. (Ibid. March 29 1946) Salomon Grumbach, reporting for the Committee of Enquiry in April, 1946, recommended the discontinuation in their posts of all who had served the Vichy government for any continuous period. Thirteen in particular were named, including some of the highest officials in the zone. (Ibid. Annexes 959, 9 April, 1946.)

The army of the Fourth Republic was to enjoy few triumphs, much chagrin, and was to end in a mess of defeated treason against the Head of State of the Fifth. It should, by the rules of international politics, have been the least effective instrument of all the Allied armies in enforcing political decisions on the Germans. It was as sloppy as its soldiers looked, and they looked very sloppy indeed in 1945 and 1946. The level of discipline was low compared to the American, and even more so to the British, armies. Many of the officers were, or had been, not at all anti-Nazi. Perhaps the atmosphere in their officers' messes was essentially a reactionary one, and certainly the French paid more attention to the views of the Roman Catholic priesthood in Germany than did even the Americans, which fact much annoyed French atheists. But, twenty-five years later, theirs is the only country which can be said to have achieved its basic, and comparatively modest, aims in Europe. The Russians, who held all the military trumps in 1945 except the ace, have failed to advance beyond the line that the British and Americans gave them in Germany. The British, who enjoyed universal respect in May, 1945, have become the almost unwanted ally even of the Germans: they are of sadly small interest to the people of post-war Europe today. The Americans, because of their immense power, are still attractive to the Germans, their most loyal ally during the Adenauer-Dulles period, but the attraction is weakening. Meanwhile the French, from an extremely slender base in 1945, have become the most powerful political force in Europe and therefore, after America and Russia, the third in the world. This is due, primarily, to the French capture of German loyalty to a European ideal. By so doing the French have laid the ghost of trans-Rhine hostility, with luck forever. And all this began in 1945, when the French were prepared to accept the fact that all sorts of horrible things had happened for which the criminals should be punished, but were also aware that their own nationals had not always behaved impeccably in the crucible of war, had understood the humiliation of defeat, both as the conquerors and, more important, as the conquered, and had learned in their own country that punishment for past crimes, important and desirable as it may be both to the criminal and to his judges, can deal only with the past, while education can only concern the future.

The French were not loved by the Germans in their zone. They were hardly even respected. But they were surprisingly successful. True, they had in some respects more malleable human material than did the other occupying powers. Most of their zone had at one time formed part of the Roman Empire and it is astonishing, indeed almost inexplicable, what a difference that influence, exerted so long ago, has made in Germany and elsewhere in Europe. Of course there were a great many Nazis in the Rhineland, Baden and Wurttemburg, some, such as Joseph Goebbels, very prominent indeed. But in general these were the least 'nazified' areas of Germany. And to this vague heritage of Latinization must be added—though it may be little more than a corollary of this—that these areas were on the whole devoutly Catholic. So, too, was Bavaria, but here there was no residue of remote Latin civilization, and though there were anti-Nazis in Bavaria these were drawn principally from the intelligentsia and the aristocracy. Munich was the Nazi Party's capital, *die Hauptstadt der Bewegung*, and Bavaria was almost solidly Nazi. The French zone, on the other hand, produced an exceptionally high proportion of anti-Nazis, of 20th July men. The atmosphere which had encouraged these brave men was more susceptible to the influence of French culture and Western libertarian ideas. Furthermore, large parts of the French zone had been thoroughly 'Frenchified' in the not so distant past. This was particularly so in the former kingdoms of Baden and

Wurttemburg,[5] where French had remained the language of polite society until a surprisingly recent date—in some old-fashioned families up to the First World War—while even the Nazis had never succeeded in stamping out altogether a profoundly deep-seated respect for French manners and French culture. Thus in their efforts to dominate the French Zone culturally—as the Russians were determined to dominate theirs politically and the Americans, eventually, to rule theirs economically—the French had foundations which were not negligible upon which to build. This in many ways compensated for the slenderness of the builders' resources and also for the other disadvantages under which the French soldiers and administrators were forced to operate.

The French accepted three of the four stipulations for denazification laid down at the Potsdam Conference.[6] Only paragraph C of the three-power Declaration was interpreted more loosely by the French than by their allies. This was the paragraph which stated: 'All members of the Nazi Party who have been more than nominal participants in its activities (shall be) . . . removed from public and semi-public office, and from positions of responsibility in important private undertakings.' This seemed too simple to the French, and on May 28th 1946, the German State Secretariat of South Wurttemburg, which formed part of the French zone, passed an *Ordinance for Political Cleansing*, with of course the full approval of the French Military Government.

In the preamble to this document, which was really a rationalization of what was already normal practice in South Wurttemburg and throughout most of the French zone, it was stated that 'whereas political cleansing demands energetic action against National Socialism and militarism . . . at the same time a thorough and just consideration of each individual case is also needed. [Denazification] must secure the well-being of all the people.' And it goes on to pronounce that membership of the Nazi Party would not be *prima facie* evidence of guilt nor non-membership proof of innocence.

In order to bring at least the three Western occupation administrations into line in this matter of denazification on October 12th 1946 the Allied Control Council issued its Directive No. 38, published

---

[5] See, among other books, Sybille Bedford's novel, *A Legacy*, Secker and Warburg, 1956.
[6] See Chapter Five, pages 105-106, paras. 3-5.

in the *Official Gazette* on October 31st of that year.⁷ This laid down that the entire German nation was to be divided into five categories and five only. This document was the essential text for denazification in the West, which may be said to have reached high tide at about this time, and therefore the relevant passage must be quoted in full:

PART II

ARTICLE I

Groups of Persons Responsible

In order to make a just determination of responsibility and to provide for imposition (except in the case of 5 below) of sanctions the following groupings of persons shall be made:
1. Major offenders;
2. Offenders (activists, militarists, and profiteers);
3. Lesser offenders (probationers);
4. Followers;
5. Persons exonerated. (Those included in the above categories who can prove themselves not guilty before a tribunal.)

ARTICLE 2

Major Offenders

Major Offenders are:
1. Anyone who, out of political motives, committed crimes against victims or opponents of national socialism;
2. Anyone who, in Germany or in the occupied areas, treated foreign civilians or prisoners of war contrary to International Law;
3. Anyone who is responsible for outrages, pillaging, deportations, or other acts of brutality, even if committed in fighting against resistance movements;
4. Anyone who was active in a leading position in the NSDAP, one of its formations or affiliated organizations, or in any other national socialistic or militaristic organization;
5. Anyone who, in the government of the Reich, the Laender, or in the administration of formerly occupied areas, held a leading position which could have been held only by a leading national socialist or a leading supporter of the national socialistic tyranny;
6. Anyone who gave major political, economic, propagandist or other support to the national socialistic tyranny, or who, by reason of his

⁷ See Ruhm von Oppen, op. cit., p. 168.

relations with the national socialistic tyranny, received very substantial profits for himself or others;

7. Anyone who was actively engaged for the national socialistic tyranny in the Gestapo, the SD, the SS, or the Geheime, Feld- or Grenz-Polizei;

8. Anyone who, in any form whatever, participated in killings, tortures, or other cruelties in a concentration camp, a labour camp, or a medical institution or asylum;

9. Anyone who, for personal profit or advantage, actively collaborated with the Gestapo, SD, SS or similar organizations by denouncing or otherwise aiding in the persecution of opponents of the national socialistic tyranny;

10. Any member of the High Command of the German Armed Forces so specified.

ARTICLE 3

Offenders

(A) *Activists*

I. An activist is:

1. Anyone who, by way of his position or activity, substantially advanced the national socialistic tyranny;

2. Anyone who exploited his position, his influence or his connections to impose force and utter threats, to act with brutality and to carry out oppressions or otherwise unjust measures;

3. Anyone who manifested himself as an avowed adherent of the national socialistic tyranny, more particularly of its racial creeds.

II. Activists are in particular the following persons, insofar as they are not major offenders:

1. Anyone who substantially contributed to the establishment, consolidation or maintenance of the national socialistic tyranny, by word or deed, especially publicly through speeches or writings or through voluntary donations out of his own or another's property or through using his personal reputation or his position of power in political, economic or cultural life;

2. Anyone who, through national socialistic teachings or education, poisoned the spirit and soul of the youth;

3. Anyone who, in order to strengthen the national socialistic tyranny, undermined family and marital life disregarding recognized moral principles;

4. Anyone who in the service of national socialism unlawfully interfered in the administration of justice or abused politically his office as judge or public prosecutor;

5. Anyone who in the service of national socialism agitated with incitement or violence against churches, religious communities or ideological associations;

6. Anyone who in the service of national socialism ridiculed, damaged or destroyed values of art or science;

7. Anyone who took a leading or active part in destroying trade unions, suppressing labour, and misappropriating trade union property;

8. Anyone who, as a provocateur, agent or informer, caused or attempted to cause, institution of a proceeding to the detriment of others because of their race, religion or political opposition to national socialism or because of violation of national socialist rules;

9. Anyone who exploited his position or power under the national socialistic tyranny to commit offences, in particular, extortions, embezzlements and frauds;

10. Anyone who by word or deed took an attitude of hatred towards opponents of the NSDAP in Germany or abroad, towards prisoners of war, the population of formerly occupied territories, foreign civilian workers, prisoners or like persons;

11. Anyone who favoured transfer to service at the front because of opposition to national socialism.

III. An activist shall also be anyone who, after 8 May 1945, has endangered or is likely to endanger the peace of the German people or of the world, through advocating national socialism or militarism or inventing or disseminating malicious rumours.

(B) *Militarists*

I. A Militarist is:

1. Anyone who has sought to bring the life of the German people into line with a policy of militaristic force;

2. Anyone who advocated or is responsible for the domination of foreign peoples, their exploitation or displacement, or

3. Anyone who, for these purposes, promoted armament.

II. Militarists are in particular the following persons, insofar as they are not major offenders:

1. Anyone who, by word or deed, established or disseminated militaristic doctrines or programmes or was active in any organization (except the Wehrmacht) serving the advancement of militaristic ideas;

2. Anyone who before 1935 organized or participated in the organization of the systematic training of youth for war;

3. Anyone who, exercising the power of command, is responsible for the wanton devastation, after the invasion of Germany, of cities and country places;

4. Anyone without regard to his rank who as a member of the Armed Forces (Wehrmacht), the Reich Labor Service (Reichsarbeitsdienst), the Organization Todt (OT), or Transport Group Speer, abused his official authority to obtain personal advantages or brutality to mistreat subordinates;

5. Anyone whose past training and activities in the General Staff Corps or otherwise has in the opinion of Zone Commanders contributed towards the promotion of militarism and who the Zone Commanders consider likely to endanger Allied purposes.

(C) *Profiteers*

I. A profiteer is:
Anyone who, by use of his political position or connections, gained personal or economic advantages for himself or others from the national socialistic tyranny, the rearmament, or the war.

II. Profiteers are in particular the following persons, insofar as they are not major offenders:

1. Anyone who, solely on account of his membership in the NSDAP, obtained an office or a position or was preferentially promoted therein;

2. Anyone who received substantial donations from the NSDAP or its formations or affiliated organizations;

3. Anyone who obtained or strove for advantages for himself or others at the expense of those who were persecuted on political, religious or racial grounds, directly or indirectly, especially in connection with appropriations, forced sales, or similar transactions;

4. Anyone who made disproportionately high profits in armament or war transactions;

5. Anyone who unjustly enriched himself in connection with the administration of formerly occupied territories.

ARTICLE 4

Lesser Offenders (Probationers)

I. A lesser offender is:

1. Anyone including former members of the Armed Forces who otherwise belongs to the groups of offenders but because of special circumstances seems worthy of a milder judgement and can be expected according to his character to fulfil his duties as a citizen of

a peaceful democratic state after he has proved himself in a period of probation;

2. Anyone who otherwise belongs to the group of followers but because of his conduct and in view of his character will first have to prove himself.

II. A lesser offender is more particularly:

1. Anyone who, born after the first day of January 1919, does not belong to the group of major offenders, but seems to be an offender, without however having manifested despicable or brutal conduct and who can be expected in view of his character to prove himself;

2. Anyone, not a major offender, who seems to be an offender but withdrew from national socialism and its methods, unqualifiedly and manifestly, at an early time.

ARTICLE 5

Followers

I. A follower is:
Anyone who was not more than a nominal participant in, or a supporter of, the national socialistic tyranny.

II. Subject to this standard, a follower is more particularly:

1. Anyone who as a member of the NSDAP or of one of its formations, except the HJ and BDM, did no more than pay membership fees, participate in meetings where attendance was obligatory, or carry out unimportant or purely routine duties such as were directed for all members.

2. Anyone, not a major offender, an offender, or a lesser offender, who was a candidate for membership in the NSDAP but had not yet been finally accepted as a member;

3. Anyone being a former member of the Armed Forces who, in the opinion of the Zone Commander, is liable by his qualification to endanger Allied purposes.

ARTICLE 6

Exonerated Persons

An exonerated person is:
Anyone who, in spite of his formal membership or candidacy or any other outward indication, not only showed a passive attitude but also actively resisted the national socialistic tyranny to the extent of his powers and thereby suffered disadvantages.

All very neat and explicit, indeed too much so for the French. Their policy of devolution meant that each *Land* in the French zone exercised considerable latitude in its interpretation of the denazification laws. The Rhineland-Pfalz government promptly decided that five categories were not enough, that seven would be better, and even so that membership of the Nazi Party did not automatically involve categorization in any of those seven. While in *Land* Baden it was arranged that the courts must distinguish between *Will* and *Müssnazis*. Professional men, such as lawyers and even architects, had comparatively little difficulty in proving that they had been *Müssnazis*. One result of this was that, as early as October 1945, the *New York Times* could name twenty-seven Germans dismissed as Nazis in the U.S. zone who had found official employment with the French. The French admitted this. And in Wurttemburg at least the Germans placed in Category Four—the 'Followers'—were allowed to retain administrative jobs, which certainly diminished the confusion in the lower ranks of the administration within the French zone.

Despite this apparent leniency, denazification in the French zone was at least as efficient as in the British and American. As will be seen, the whole operation began to fall apart in 1947. The previous year was the year in which influence upon the future was still possible through administrative and judicial processes, and it is therefore important to note that by the end of 1946 248,845 cases had been examined in the French zone. In 97,517 of these action had been taken, usually dismissal or some other form of punishment. With the French emphasis on education, particular attention had been paid to the teachers, some 50% of whom had been dismissed as politically unsuitable. The greatest success was in South Wurttemburg, where Carlo Schmid was President of the Secretariat and where it was reckoned that approximately 75% of the Nazis were speedily and efficiently dealt with, the emphasis being on public officials, lawyers and teachers. In the Palatinate, on the other hand, the figure was as low as 30%, which is roughly comparable to the overall figures for the British and U.S. zones.

Chapter Seven

The British attitude towards denazification was closer to that of the Americans than was the French, but here again there were subtle distinctions. Each of the Allied powers based its policy in some measure upon its feelings for the Germans, for 'the German problem', as a whole. And in the democracies this led inevitably to a measure of self-contradiction as various voices were raised and different theories predominated for shorter or longer periods of time.

Throughout the war there was surprisingly little hatred of the Germans in Britain. Dachshunds were not stoned nor shops with German-named owners looted or boycotted, as had happened in the First World War. Even when Britain was being bombed more intensively than any country had been up to then (1940-41) the people's attitude was extraordinarily fair-minded. The German or Nazi airmen (the two terms had already become interchangeable in popular parlance) were regarded less as the murderers of innocent civilians than as brave men doing a dangerous and difficult job.[1] For several years almost the only direct confrontation between German and British soldiers was in the North African Western Desert, where there was to all intents and purposes no civilian population to suffer at the hands of the SS and the SD. The men of the Eighth Army respected their enemies of Rommel's Afrika Korps and indeed felt the same sort of kinship towards them that the men in the British trenches had felt for those in German ones in Flanders during the 1914-1918 war. The African campaigns were probably fought as 'cleanly' from a moral point of view as any modern war can be. The war at sea was in some ways dirtier, yet even the publicity given to the acts of individual U-boat commanders who machine-gunned seamen in open boats evoked small response among the British public at large, while the fantastic fight of the *Bismarck*

[1] See my *The Blitz*, Wingate, London, 1957.

against overwhelming odds won general respect. In fact the atrocity propaganda of the First World War boomeranged during the Second. When the popular press tried to whip up hatred of the enemy, the people, and above all the soldiers, merely shrugged their shoulders. It was hard to persuade them even that the concentration and extermination camps were anything more than a British government propaganda stunt exploited by the yellow press. Indeed by early 1942 this respect and even liking for the German enemy was causing serious concern to the military authorities and a 'hate' campaign was initiated throughout the armed forces. It was a failure. Only when the British Army saw the Nazis at work in Europe, and above all when the concentration camps were liberated, did a sizeable proportion of its soldiers realize the nature of the defeated enemy. Yet even this hardly extended to a hatred of the Germans as such. The British soldier not only respected the German soldier but also felt far more comfortable in Germany than he had in France or Italy. It may sound fatuous, but beer-drinkers have something in common that separates them from wine-drinkers, and this goes deeper than the mere beverage. The ordinary British soldier felt, and has continued to feel, almost 'at home' in Germany. This is also in some measure true of their officers as well. The semantic confusion of Nazi and German did not make the task of the British Army any easier when it was ordered to be a force for moral and political reform. This is not a rôle for which any army is well cast, and by 1945 the other ranks of the British Army, when interested in morals or politics at all, were more concerned with altering British than German society. The 1945 Election was the result.

Among the middle and governing classes in Britain there were many differing attitudes. By 1945 the handful of Fascists and pro-Nazis who had seemed a potential menace before the war had been totally and finally discredited and have remained an entirely negligible force. The Conservatives, even the extreme right wing of that party, were anti-Nazi and to some extent anti-German for patriotic reasons, quite apart from the fact that xenophobia must be endemic among imperialists save perhaps where client states are concerned. The only foreign society that the British aristocracy had ever really admired was that of their equivalents in France, and even this was by 1945 an antiquated love-affair. The 'intellectuals' of that time, whom Manes Sperber has described accurately as the cadet branch of the British aristocracy—often impoverished and frequently ignored—had had their own anti-imperialist love affair with permissive Weimar Germany in the 1920s and a hate affair with British society throughout the following decade, with enlistment in the Communist Party as an act of ultimate defiance. This had even led some of the more prominent writers and artists who were outspoken anti-Nazis to prefer neutral America in the early years of the war. The attitude of those left-wing British intellectuals who, while wringing their hands over Europe, retreated into the contemplation of their navels in the United States, is to some extent comparable to that of Ernst von Salomon as expressed by himself earlier in this book. But unlike him, they continued to exercise a considerable influence in British intellectual circles.

Among more serious and better-informed people the attitude towards 'the German problem' was far more complex and, in many ways, more interesting. Some adopted a purely 'racist' attitude: the Germans were a rotten, violent people, always had been and always would be, and deserved no mercy of any sort. Among the more notable adherents of this view was Lord Vansittart whose wartime book, *Black Record*,[2] puts him into almost the same class of polemicists as Dr Goebbels and Julius Streicher of *Stürmer* notoriety. He compares the whole German nation, or race, to a bird called a shrike which apparently murders its natural enemies in a peculiarly horrible fashion. Lord Vansittart had been permanent head of the British Foreign Office: he had been promoted, and put out of power, by Neville Chamberlain because of his violent rejection of that Prime Minister's longing for peace at any price. During one of the most spectacular post-war trials, that of the members of the German Foreign Ministry, he was to make a statement under oath which verged on, if it did not actually cross, the line of perjury, when he denied the existence of any high-level diplomatists' opposition to Hitler during the period of the Third Reich.

Another very senior, and throughout the war far more influential, anti-German was Professor Lindemann, later Lord Cherwell, who was Churchill's scientific adviser. He was subtler than Vansittart. So too was Sir Lewis Namier, accepted by historiographers as one of the most distinguished and brilliant, though not among the most enjoyable, historians of this century. But it is perhaps not

[2] Hamish Hamilton, 1941.

irrelevant that both Namier and Lindemann were German-born naturalized Englishmen, while Vansittart had spent a considerable part of his unhappy childhood in that unhappy land.

Many English Jews, often themselves of German origin, felt emotions which are only too comprehensible in view of what had happened and was happening to other Jews, co-religionists and often to members of their own immediate families. The written word cannot hope, in a book such as this, to evoke the intensity of emotion, from impenetrable silent grief to violently expressed hatred, which the crimes of the Nazis evoked among the Jews of the world, including those who were British. Zionism was one honourable answer. Yet some among them saw another, that the evil was not necessarily national, nor its eradication equally national. The late Sir Victor Gollancz, himself a Jew and a left-wing publisher (he had run the predominantly Communist *Left Book Club* in the 1930s), was sufficiently wise and magnanimous to believe in clemency. In 1945 this convinced and tried-and-true anti-Nazi, who had been on the Gestapo's list for immediate arrest to be followed by torture and execution, organized the *Save Europe Now* movement, the prime motive of which was to prevent the starvation of Germans in Germany: not slave-labourers, not the miserable handful of Jews who had escaped the Nazi murder apparatus, but Germans. In the confusion of the period it would be hard to imagine a more notable action on the part of a man with a record such as that of Gollancz. And there were many other British Jews who reacted as he did. Perhaps more than any other group of people in the Western World they proved, at least to our Western selves, the superiority of our vision of the world over that of our totalitarian enemies.

As in the United States, Germany, Russia, France and indeed in all the world, most of the people cared little or nothing about these problems; happy that the killing had ceased, they wished to resume more sensible lives and forget the past and the foreigners. 'Let the dead bury the dead.' It was against this sort of background that the British tried to denazify Germany.

The British army that entered Germany was commanded by Field-Marshal Sir Bernard (now Lord) Montgomery, an Ulsterman with eccentric views and manners. He was to be head of British Military Government for the first year after the end of the war in Europe. Supreme Headquarters Allied Expeditionary Force

(SHAEF) was disbanded on July 14th 1945, that is to say immediately before the Potsdam Conference, and there was thenceforth no unified command structure for the armies of the Western democracies in Germany. In theory the Control Council was the supreme authority. On it sat Marshal Zhukov for the Soviet Union, General Eisenhower for the United States (until November 1945), Field-Marshal Montgomery for Great Britain and General Koenig for France. However, the Control Council was a committee the command powers of which were dependent on unanimity. As relations between the Russians and their wartime allies steadily and rapidly deteriorated the Control Council grew increasingly impotent: this had less effect, though, in the field of denazification than in most other matters concerning the Germans.

There was, however, no uniform policy even in this field, as has already been shown in the case of the Russians and the French. The British did try to keep in step, more or less, with the Americans. But it is important to realize that after July 14th Montgomery no longer received orders from Eisenhower. He was thenceforth responsible only to his government in London, which was to be a Labour Party government within a matter of days. In his autobiography[3] he regrets the precipitate abolition of SHAEF, but, once again, this scarcely affected the denazification programme.

As already remarked, non-fraternization was far from successful in the British zone, particularly once the fighting was over. On June 12th 1945 Montgomery rescinded the regulation so far as British soldiers speaking to, or playing with, German children was concerned. As he remarks, they were doing so anyway. Three months later he raised the whole matter of non-fraternization in the Control Council and it was agreed that this policy be scrapped in all the zones. However, British soldiers were still not billeted with German families—when billets were required the German inhabitants were turned out, to fend for themselves—and British soldiers were not allowed to marry German girls.

Field-Marshal Montgomery did not share the extreme germanophobia of Lord Vansittart and others, nor did he believe that the Germans were born with more than their fair share of original sin. He was certainly an anti-Nazi, but like many soldiers he was not averse to a certain authoritarianism in government—as his post-war respect for Mao Tse-tung and the South African government has

[3] *The Memoirs of Field-Marshal Montgomery*, Collins, London, 1958.

shown—while he had little respect for the extreme left wing of the Labour Party in Britain. On the other hand, to judge by his memoirs, he did not envisage the British playing a permanent and dominant rôle in German public life. His old and admired adversary, Field-Marshal Rommel, when discussing Germany's post-war future with General Koestring[4] shortly before the attempted rebellion of July 20th 1944, had produced a rather surprising suggestion. Since the Germans had proved themselves politically incapable, for a generation and more, of running their own country properly, why not become a British colony? After all, the British had run Hanover very well for many years: why not all Germany? This idea was totally impractical, of course, for many reasons, not least the climate of opinion in Britain itself where imperialism was almost a dead letter and, in many circles, a dirty word. Thus Montgomery could not hope to turn the Germans, even those of 'his' zone, into second-class Britons. Nor did he aspire so to do. As he has written:

'It would be useless to try to make the Germans like unto ourselves, as some people wanted to do; our aim should be rather to turn them into good and right-thinking Germans.'

In 1945 it would have been hard to define a 'good and right-thinking German', but the Field-Marshal was not much given to metaphysical lucubrations of this sort. As a highly practical soldier, he saw his task in Germany as falling into four phases: the first two were demilitarization and arrest of the criminals, and the avoidance of famine and pestilence during the winter of 1945-1946. These were achieved, and in February of 1946 he turned his attention to what he called phases three and four:

THE PROBLEM IN GERMANY: FEBRUARY 1946

As I was to leave Germany in a few months, I turned my attention to the two matters which in my opinion were the root of the whole matter—the problem of the German people, and the evolution of government in the British Zone in order to cope with that problem.

In my opinion one of our most important objects in Germany was to change the heart, and the way of life, of the German people. For the past thirteen years the Germans had had nationalistic and dictatorial ideas forced into their minds; the authority of the family had been minimised, the influence of the Church reduced, and the power of

---

[4] This story was told to the author by Herr Herwarth, later German Federal Ambassador in London. In those days he was on the staff of General Koestring. He was present when this curious conversation took place.

the State had increased. This period had been one of full employment and a high standard of living for the German people. Now there was nothing but misery. There was a danger that the people would soon begin to look back with longing on the old régime; my information was that a large percentage, probably 60 per cent, were out-and-out Nazis. Opinion in the zone was hardening against the British and a subversive organization had recently been uncovered. The fact was that we had some twenty million Germans in the British Zone who, due to the shortage of food, were going to experience a hard time. Without doubt conflicts with these people lay ahead; in some way they must be influenced for good so that they would not cause trouble in the future. How was this to be done?

It seemed to me that we could divide this mass of human material into three categories for the purpose I wanted to achieve.

First, there were the children. These should not be difficult to handle, though of course there was always the danger of a bad home influence if the older members of the family were Nazis. Then came the young men, and young women too, between the ages of say 18 to 25. Here was a much more difficult problem and this age group was probably the crux of the problem; they had been brought up in an atmosphere of National Socialism—having been taught it at school, in the Hitler Youth, and many of them in the SS also. And lastly there were the older people; amongst these were many who could probably be got on our side.

I decided that the best way to begin influencing all these groups was through economics; this was probably the foundation of the overall solution. We must give the German people hope for the future; they must be made to realize that they could reach a worthwhile future only by their own work. That meant fixing the level of industry so that there would be a decent standard of living with the minimum of unemployment. If this were not done the Germans would merely look to the past and be ready to follow any evil leader who might arise.

With this foundation, and having got the Germans down to work, we must then tackle the political problem. On the practical side, this meant the decentralization of the Government and the Civil Service. I also reckoned that we should encourage contacts with the outside world so that the Germans could study a new ideology to replace that of the Nazis. On the psychological side, we must tell the Germans when the process of denazification would be completed.

And then there was the educational problem. For children still at school we must ensure a good supply of books, reliable and trustworthy teachers, and decent buildings. The troops were living in many of the school buildings; they must hand them back to the Germans at once. Of the age group 18 to 25, a small minority were being educated in universities. But the vast majority of this group were untouched by such advantages; for them the important things were good cinemas, the Press, books, and so on, all controlled and run by the Germans themselves. I thought selected members of this age group might well be sent to England to learn a new way of life, and one which they had never known; they had been children when Hitler came to power and National Socialism was the creed in which they had been brought up.

THE EVOLUTION OF GOVERNMENT IN THE BRITISH ZONE

I had already ordered that on the 15th April 1946, Corps Commanders were finally to hand over their responsibilities for civil administration. Phase Three of my instructions issued in December 1945 would then be complete. It was now necessary to issue instructions to initiate the execution of Phase Four, and on the 25th March 1946 I circulated a memorandum which was intended to do so. In the memorandum I pointed out that the 'Battle of the Winter' had been won. No epidemics had broken out and the general health of the German people had been maintained. But the outlook for the future was now worse than ever before. The food situation overshadowed everything else, and other factors would soon aggravate the situation. The future level of German economy would cause distress and unemployment; the influx of refugees was just beginning; all stocks of consumer goods had now been used up. The next battle was going to be more serious than the 'Battle of the Winter' just concluded. It could not be tackled by Military Government because of the drastic cuts in establishment and the speed of demobilization. It must be tackled by the Germans themselves, but with our aid, especially by the import of food. Moreover, we must give them clear orders on such questions as denazification. In order to make my scheme possible we should have to build up German administrations, staffed by vigorous men who must be supported by us. The most important of these administrations was the Zonal Advisory Council which I had had formed. All domestic matters should be put to it for advice, it should be encouraged to discuss as many matters as possible, and its advice accepted whenever we could do so. These principles also applied to the other functional bodies which were being gradually set up in the zone. All these administrations should eventually be given executive power. What it really amounted to was that the Germans must now be entrusted with the responsibility for their own problems. We would have to help them, but also continue to supervise and control their activities indirectly.

MY MEMORANDUM FOR THE BRITISH GOVERNMENT

I was to leave Germany on the 2nd May 1946, being due to take up my new duties at the War Office in June. After prolonged thought I decided it was my duty to prepare a memorandum for the British Government on the situation in Germany as I believed it to be.

My time in Germany since the war ended had convinced me that a united Germany was at present not possible. I doubted if it would ever be possible without fighting. But the Western Allies had half of Germany, and they would have to continue to strive for a united Germany.

Our object must now be to bring the Western Germans into the community of Western nations, and to make their territory so attractive and prosperous that the Eastern Germans would regard it enviously when comparing it with their own miserable lot. But if we were to do this, we would have to grasp the nettle firmly with both hands. Courageous decisions would be necessary—and without delay.

I devoted my last day in Germany to writing the memorandum. I took it to England with me on the 2nd May and handed it personally to the Prime Minister. This is what it said:

1. I leave Germany tomorrow. I have set out below a concise statement of the situation as I believe it to be. I am not happy about it. I consider the general overall picture is sombre, if not black.

For the present the food crisis overshadows all else, but it is not by any means the only serious factor in the situation.

2. We have a sick economy.

Coal is short; only the basic industries can be developed; the others lie idle, and there are few consumer goods being produced, and nothing in the shops for people to buy.

We have reached agreement on the future level of the German economy; there will soon begin the removal and destruction of a large part of German industry; this will cause distress to the German people and may produce unemployment on a large scale in the British Zone.

The present level of production is such that our exports do not pay for our imports.

3. A sick economy means that we cannot have a sound currency. There is little to buy with marks and the people are tending to use a system of barter to get food. Marks are gradually becoming of no value to people. Under such a system industry cannot be got going, since there is no incentive; this is the beginning of inflation, i.e. the phase when money begins to lose its value.

4. In my Memorandum entitled 'The Problem in Germany: February 1946', I dealt with the subject of how we should handle the great mass of human material we have in Germany. I said we must work on a definite and concrete plan designed to bring about a change of heart in the German people.

I stated that the foundation of the plan must be the economic line of attack.

I said that the Germans must know what is to be the future of their country; they must be given a reasonable standard of living; they must be given some hope for a worthwhile future.

I gave it as my opinion that if we did not do this we would fail in Germany.

We have not done it and I would say that at the moment there is a definite danger that we may fail. By that I mean there is a danger that if things do not improve the Germans in the British Zone will begin to look East. When that happens we shall have failed, and there will exist a definite menace to the British Empire. In this connection, much communist propaganda is coming westwards over the iron curtain.

5. If we are to progress at all we must have:

>a sound economy,
>a balanced budget,
>central financial control.

We must produce consumer goods.

The essential financing of the cost of reparations must be borne by Germany as a whole; at present it falls heavily on the British Zone, which has most of the industries.

I still consider that the real answer to the problem is contained in my memorandum of 1st February 1946. But adequate economic conditions must be established before we can make any progress with the plan set out in that memorandum; at present these conditions do not exist.

6. While we are in this sorry economic condition, good progress is being made with the formation of political parties and trade unions. But we want to be clear that herein lies a possible danger.

There is no doubt that in a contented Germany, a strong Social Democratic party would be a great asset and one making for peace and security in Western Europe.

But, if the Germans become discontented and we get organized hostility of the people against the occupying Power, then they have machinery in the political and trade union spheres which could be used to implement their nefarious purposes. This aspect of the problem needs to be carefully watched during the next few years; close touch must be kept with propaganda coming from the Russian Zone.

BASIC FUNDAMENTALS IN THE SOLUTION TO THE PROBLEM

7. We must decide what is to constitute "Germany". The eastern frontier of Germany was agreed at Potsdam. The western frontier is not yet agreed; it is wrapped up in the whole problem of the future of the Saar, the Ruhr and the Rhineland.

We must tell the German people what Germany is to consist of.

8. The people living inside that Germany must be given a reasonable standard of living, and hope for a worthwhile future. A reasonable standard of living can be set up in Germany on the basis of the level of industry which has been agreed, but only under certain conditions. These conditions were emphasised in our acceptance of the level of industry agreement. The principal one is that Germany should be treated as one economic whole. This is not happening at present, firstly on account of French opposition and, secondly, because of the attitude of the Russians. I do not feel confident that the Russians ever intend to treat Germany as an economic whole as we understand that phrase. I am certain that they will not do it unless we join with the other Allies in exerting strong pressure upon them.

9. The whole country is in such a mess that the only way to put it right is to get the Germans "in on it" themselves. This is being done by Zonal Advisory Councils; but this is not enough.

It means Central Administrations; we do not have these; we must have them. We must secure French agreement on their establishment. We must then take great care to ensure that they are set up under genuine Quadripartite control, and that neither their constitution nor their functions shall be such as to make them susceptible to the influence of one Power more than of others.

10. We must decide whether we are going to feed the Germans, or let them starve. Basically, we must not let them starve; if we do, then everything else we do is of no avail.

It does not look at present as if we can increase the ration beyond the present of 1042 calories; this means we are going to let them starve gradually.

In spite of the difficulties of the world food situation, we must get back to a reasonable ration standard in the British Zone as quickly as possible. The discrepancies which exist between the standard of feeding in our zone and that in other zones must be removed by agreement on a common standard.

CONCLUSION

11. I regard the four points outlined in paras. 7 to 10 as the four pillars on which we must build the new Germany out of the ruins of the old. The master pillar is the fourth, or food pillar; if that breaks, the other pillars fall down.

12. So far, the four pillars do not exist. Therefore we cannot progress.

13. We must start to build the four pillars. And above all, we must tell the German people what is going to happen to them and their country. If we do not do those things, we shall drift towards possible

failure. That "drift" will take the form of an increasingly hostile population, which will eventually begin to look East.

Such a Germany would be a menace to the security of the British Empire.

14. On the other hand, a contented Germany with a sound political framework, could be a great asset to the security of the Empire and the peace of the world.'[5]

Not everybody in British public life was prepared to adopt so matter of fact an attitude towards German problems as was Field-Marshal Montgomery. Many of the lawyers in particular had grave doubts about the legality of denazification (as opposed to the trial of alleged criminals for specific crimes). Indeed the Hague Convention of 1907 appeared to make the whole procedure illegal. That magisterial document lays down that, after a war, 'the authority of the legitimate power having in fact passed into the hands of the occupant, the latter shall take all measures in his power to restore, and ensure, as far as possible, public order and safety, while respecting, unless absolutely prevented, the laws in force in the country'.[6]

In 1907, of course, the crimes of Nazi Germany lay in an almost unimaginable future and forty years later there were few in Britain who would have put the legalism of the Hague Convention over the need to purge Germany (and Japan) of an incriminated governing class. But was such a purge in fact possible? The sociologists also had their doubts. For many of them Max Weber was the most hallowed authority, and he had written: 'Even in case of revolution by force or of occupation by an enemy, the bureaucratic machinery will normally continue to function just as it has for the previous legal government.'[7]

Again, in 1945-1947 it was clearly more desirable to the policy-makers of the Occupying Powers to get rid of Nazi administrators than to follow Max Weber's beliefs, but then the immediate problem arose, in all the zones, of establishing an alternative administration. There were simply not enough 'good' Germans immediately available to run an extremely complex society reduced, by its previous rulers and by defeat, to a state of chaos. The crude nature of direct

[5] Field-Marshal Montgomery, op. cit., pp. 490-416.

[6] Art. 43, Conv. IV of 1907, respecting the laws and customs of war on land, in James Brown Scott (ed.), *The Hague Conventions and Declaration of 1899 to 1907* (New York: Oxford University Press, 1915), p. 123.

[7] Max Weber, 'Essentials of Bureaucratic Organization: An Ideal-Type Construction,' in R. Merton, *Reader in Bureaucracy* (Glencoe: Free Press, 1951), p. 25.

military government could obviously be little better than a stop-gap, all the more so since the British and American armies of occupation were being rapidly demobilized and sent home.

It was not just the German administration that was to be denazified. It was also intended that German industry, and particularly the heavy industry which had supported Hitler and—until the bombers came—had profited greatly from German militarism, be broken up and placed in the hands of more responsible and respectable men than had run it under and for the Nazis. The huge German industrial cartels built up in the 1920s had a great deal to answer for.[8] The vast industrial empires of Krupp, Flick, Thyssen or I. G. Farben were almost government departments and had become little other than just that during the Nazi period. The British, since their zone included the Ruhr complex, had more than their fair share of these people with whom to deal. On the other hand they were in some ways politically less inhibited in dismantling capitalist empires than were the Americans, since they took their orders from a socialist government. In some ways only, though. In Britain the 'socialist' economists and politicians were busy constructing huge nationalized industries, such as the British Coal Board and British Railways, while other Britons in Germany were ordered to devolute great German industrial combines. A measure of confusion ensued, and Krupp[9] and Volkswagen are still with us.

And finally to bedevil the British reformers in Germany even further, there was the Russian problem. The American atomic umbrella did not appear to offer unlimited protection while Henry Wallace was running for President on the one hand and the American right-wing isolationists were emerging from retirement on the other. Few countries have ever been strong and skilful enough to fight two major wars at once without losing both. The British had had really no choice in 1941, while America was still neutral, but to ally themselves with the Russians against Nazi Germany. However, even before the Germans surrendered it had become apparent that Soviet Communism was the great new danger to Western Europe and to Britain, while the attitude of America remained for

---

[8] See *The Weimar Republic* by Godfrey Scheele, Faber and Faber, London, 1946.
[9] For the attempt, and failure, to break up Krupp's see *The House of Krupp* by Peter Batty, Secker and Warburg, London, 1966. It is only fair to say that this failure was perhaps more of American than British origin.

some years uncertain. In these conditions the British, who are not powerful enough to fight two wars at once, were once again forced to accept an almost unacceptable ally. They needed the Germans, and the produce of the German factories and, quite soon, German soldiers too. Good and right-thinking Germans would have been acceptable, but since these were in short supply, particularly in the higher echelons of industrial and military organization, a great gap was created in the denazification process through which large numbers of bad and wrong-thinking Germans were enabled to escape the full responsibility for their past misdeeds.

Chapter Eight

In 1950 General Lucius D. Clay was United States High Commissioner for Germany. By then the Federal Republic was in existence and denazification dead and about to be buried. General Clay took this opportunity to sum up what had been attempted in the U.S. zone in respect of this policy and also what had been achieved. In his letter of transmittal, dated 31 December 1950, covering his office's *Quarterly Report on Germany* for the final quarter of that year, and addressed to Secretary of State Dean Acheson and Economic Cooperation Administrator William C. Foster, he makes these comments:

As one of its last actions before Christmas recess, the Federal Lower House considered legislation to establish uniform principles governing the termination of denazification. Although shortcomings on the Allied and German sides could not be denied, and were indeed inevitable in a process unparalleled in history and involving millions of people, the policy appears to have achieved its primary purpose. Serious offenders have been punished and Nazi activists have been largely excluded from public life during the formative period of German democracy. The awareness of the German people to the evils of the Nazi régime has been awakened and there exists virtually no inclination in West Germany to-day to re-establish a totalitarian government whether Nazi or Communist.

His paper which follows, entitled *The Present State of Denazification* is both so clear and so concise a résumé of endeavours in this field that it would be supererogatory to attempt a paraphrase rather than a full quotation. Here it is:

From the outset the four Allied Powers responsible for the occupation and peaceful development of defeated Germany were determined that Germany should be purged of Nazism. To this end it was agreed that former Nazi party members and collaborators 'who were more than nominal participants in its activities' should be excluded from public and other influential posts and made subject to sanctions under law. To achieve these purposes the Allied Control Council issued two basic enactments: Directive No. 24 of January 12, 1946, concerning 'Removal from Office and from Positions of Responsibility of Nazis and of Persons Hostile to Allied Purposes', and Directive No. 38 of October 12, 1946, concerning 'The Arrest and Punishment of War Criminals, Nazis and Militarists and the Internment, Control and Surveillance of Potentially Dangerous Germans'. These directives were without legal effect until implemented by zonal laws or other enactments.

Responsibility for the implementation of the agreements and directives on denazification was assumed by the military and later by the Allied civilian authorities in their respective zones of Germany. In the U.S., British and French Zones procedures differed somewhat but in general kept closely to the spirit of the agreed directives. In the Soviet Zone the course of denazification was strongly influenced by the drive to communize the population. Many former Nazis, even though seriously incriminated, were acquitted of the charges against them and restored to influence on condition that they engage in active support of the Communist régime. However, the Soviets have never ceased to assert their continued determination to root Nazism out of the German system.

The objective of denazification was not the attainment of a final goal within a specified time, when it could be said: 'The job is done; Germany is now denazified.' It was rather to safeguard the new German democracy from Nazi influence and to make it possible for anti-Nazi, non-Nazi and outspoken democratic individuals to enter public life and replace the Nazi elements which had dominated all life in Germany from 1933 to 1945.

To accomplish this objective the Occupying Powers abolished the Nazi Party and its formations and affiliated organizations, outlawed them and removed the individuals who had been responsible for their operation from positions of influence in both public and private life. It was then possible for non-Nazi Germans to come into the many fields of communal, economic and political activities to rebuild German life on democratic lines. The initial steps in this program had been attained substantially by the summer of 1946.

Once former Nazis had been removed from public life and to a certain extent from private enterprises, a paradoxical situation arose. In a sense the party had been reconstituted by creating a large group of 'ex-Nazis', which in the U.S. Zone alone would have numbered over 3,500,000 persons. They would have been tagged and labelled and largely excluded from civic life and professional activity. This large group, together with their families, relatives and friends, would have become a body of 'second-class citizens' within the state and a constant source of discontent and unrest.

In order to avoid this danger, insofar as it could be done without raising the specter of revived Nazism, and recognizing that not all ex-members of the party and and its affiliates were equally guilty of the crimes of Nazism, it was decided in the U.S. Zone to proceed with the next phase of the program. Military Government had undertaken the task of stating who had been Nazis within the framework of Directive 24; it was to be the responsibility of the German authorities to decide to what extent each person had been an active Nazi and to what sanctions he should be subject under law, or whether he should be exonerated. To this end the German 'Law for Liberation from National Socialism and Militarism', drafted under the auspices of Military Government, was promulgated in March 1946 by the several states of the U.S. Zone. Though direct responsibility was transferred to the Germans under the terms of the law, Military Government actively supervised its enforcement until August 1948. All political parties then in existence supported this law.

The general principles of this law were stated to be as follows:

'(1) To liberate our people from National Socialism and Militarism, and to secure a lasting base for German democratic national life in peace with the world, all those who have actively supported the National Socialist tyranny, or are guilty of having violated the principles of justice and humanity, or of having selfishly exploited the conditions thus created, shall be excluded from influence in public, economic and cultural life and shall be bound to make reparations. (2) Everyone who is responsible shall be called to account. At the same time he shall be afforded opportunity to vindicate himself.'

Every adult in the U.S. Zone was required to register and submit certain details about his or her past activities. On the basis of information thus submitted and available from other sources, each registrant was placed in one of the following categories:

I. Major Offender; II. Offender; III. Lesser Offender; IV. Follower; and V. Exonerated.

Classification was based on the position and rank of the person in the party hierarchy, individual incrimination as indicated in documents or in direct accusations, and upon results of investigations conducted by court officials. Nearly thirteen and a half million persons registered in the U.S. Zone, and of these nearly four million were found to be 'chargeable', that is, subject to classification in categories I through IV.

Trial tribunals (Spruchkammern) were set up in all urban and rural districts. Appellate tribunals were established for the review of decisions. Public prosecutors and assistants were assigned to each tribunal. Spruchkammen personnel were required to be persons who knew their locality and were known to be active opponents of National Socialism. It was the task of the tribunal to evaluate the evidence presented by the public prosecutor, and the defense offered by the defendant and his attorney, to find for or against the defendant and to assess the sanctions prescribed by the law for each of the five established categories. Some penalties were made mandatory under the law, others were optional with the tribunals.

Shortly after the law went into operation it became apparent that there would be such an immense number of persons chargeable (that is, found subject to the law by the prosecutor) that the German Courts would not be able to try all of the cases within a reasonable time. The law, by making chargeable all members of the Nazi party as well as its formations, affected over 27 per cent of the adult population of the U.S. Zone (3,669,239 persons). It was realized that among them were large numbers of persons who had not been active in furthering Nazi ideology. Consequently in August 1946, the Military Governor announced the Youth Amnesty which provided that all persons born after January 1st, 1919, would not be tried by a denazification tribunal unless they were incriminated and chargeable as major offenders or offenders. This amnesty was followed in December by another amnesty, known as the Christmas Amnesty, which provided that persons in low income groups, who had earned less than 3,600 RM per year in 1943-45, and who had less than 20,000 RM property on January 1st, 1945, and persons who were more than 50 percent physically disabled would not be tried unless they came within the categories of major offenders or offenders. By June 1, 1948, 2,373,115 persons had come within the terms of those amnesties. By that time, 865,808 trials had been completed, leaving a total of only 31,707 still to face formal trial. Since that date the trials have continued but new registrations, largely refugees and returning POWs, have made it impossible to complete the program. By September 30, 1950, a total of 13,416,000 persons had been registered; 958,071 trials had been held; and 2,777,444 amnestied, either by the prosecutor or after trial. There remained 1,740 cases to be disposed of.

The Law for Liberation also provided that criminal offenses by National Socialists or Militarists might be prosecuted outside its provisions. This applied particularly to war crimes and to offenses arising out of National Socialist tyranny. Thus, several hundred war criminals, many of whom were active leading Nazis, were dealt with and punished by Allied and German tribunals independently of the Law for Liberation. Likewise, other top Nazis were tried by the International Military Tribunal in 1946 and by the United States Tribunals which imposed death sentences and long terms of imprisonment on those found guilty of major crimes.

Under the various directives issued by the several state governments, the apprehension and prosecution of persons who had been individually involved in the acts of tyranny and terror which were part and parcel of the Nazi régime have been, and continue to be, undertaken with vigor. The extent to which the German communities have denounced their own members for participating in these acts is one indication of the measure of denazification attained by the German people.

The Law for Liberation operates extensively, and dealt with a problem that was without precedent in history. It was both drafted and implemented by persons who had no precedents and no experience on which to draw since nothing of this character had ever been attempted before. The task was done amid a ferment of emotions and during a period of instability and universal hardship and unrest.

The statistical table on the next page gives figures on the operation of the denazification program in the U.S. Zone from the promulgation of the Law for Liberation in 1946 to September 30, 1950. Not much change has taken place since that date, so that the figures with negligible modification can be accepted as correct as of December 31, 1950.

This was, perhaps, the most extensive legal procedure the world had ever witnessed. In the U.S. Zone alone more than 13 million persons had been involved, of whom over three and two-thirds million were found chargeable, and of these some 800,000 persons were made subject to penalty for their party affiliations or actions. All this was, of course, apart from the punishment of war criminals many of whom were high-ranking Nazis.

In fact, of the top Nazis who fell into Allied hands, all have been either tried or interned. Of the 24 most important and prominent Nazi Cabinet Ministers and Nazi leaders appointed to the highest party rank, that of 'Reichsleiter', six were executed, six are still serving sentences up to life, and eight have died or committed suicide. The fate of one is obscure and three are at liberty. Of the 42 persons who held the next highest rank, that of 'Gauleiter' or regional party chief, eight were executed, ten committed suicide or have died; one was shot by his own comrades; eleven are still jailed or interned; while the fate of four is unknown. The eight today known to be at liberty have either completed their confinement or are fugitives.

DENAZIFICATION PROCEEDINGS
in the
U.S. Zone

Total registrants	13,416,101
Not chargeable cases	9,746,862
Chargeable cases	3,669,239

Monthly average of new registrations during period
1 October 1949 to 30 September 1950 ... ... 13,800*
Cases amnestied by Public Prosecutors' categorization 2,456,731
Otherwise quashed by Public Prosecutors 252,875
Classifications by Trial Tribunals:
  Major Offenders 1,698
  Offenders 22,598
  Lesser Offenders 106,995
  Followers 487,996
  Exonerated 18,571
  Amnestied 320,713
Cases to be completed by Trial Tribunals 1,062
Cases to be completed by Appellate Tribunals 678
Inmates of internment camps 73
Persons permanently ineligible to hold public office ... 23,616
Persons restricted in employment 125,510
Subject to confiscation of property 27,587
Persons fined 572,993
Sentenced to Special Labor but not imprisoned ... 30,781

* Returning POWs and returnees from the East.

It cannot be denied that some guilty persons have escaped detection and punishment. It was impossible in dealing with a régime so long existent and so widespread in its ramifications as National Socialism to bring to the bar of justice all who were guilty of participation or collaboration in the misdeeds of the Nazi régime. But a serious effort was made to ascertain guilt and to punish the guilty, while assuring that every individual charged would receive a fair trial in accordance with law.

By the end of 1950 the process of denazification within the Federal Republic was nearing its formal end. The German authorities had by then enacted measures modifying the provisions of the law to exclude from its application nominal Nazis, while leaving the law in operation with respect to active and criminal elements of the party. The various state parliaments had under consideration draft laws for terminating denazification procedures within the respective states. On December 15 the Lower House approved a resolution requesting that the Federal Government recommend to the states the adoption of uniform legislation governing the liquidation of the denazification program. This recommendation did not contemplate the annulment of all denazification decisions but suggested dates to be incorporated into state laws which would assure simultaneous action in the termination of proceedings. Specific criteria were set up to guide the actions of the states. In general, these involved a broad relaxation of restrictions, particularly as applied to categories III, IV, and V. The recommendation emphasizes, however, that prosecutions for any crime committed by Nazis are to be continued.

These recommendations, if carried into effect, would bring about the termination of virtually all denazification operations by April 1, 1951. It was proposed that the Federal Government and the states work out a plan to abandon Nazi classifications III, IV and V by January 1, 1951; to lift all reemployment restrictions, with the exception of those involving categories I and II, by March 31 and to lower all property barriers and restore election rights to all classifications by April 1. Thus it would appear that formal denazification will come to an end early in 1951.

Final evaluation of the denazification program is a task for the historian. It is even too soon to determine whether its implementation by the German authorities since it was turned over to them can be called a success or must be adjudged a failure.

In the operation of the law certain shortcomings have, it is true, become evident. It is generally conceded today, for instance, that it would have been wiser to have applied the penal aspects of the program more promptly and effectively to the real activists, while treating the great mass of lesser Nazis more leniently. As a matter of fact, it was soon recognized that the scope of the trials was too broad. The natural desire of the Germans was to raise the stigma from the innocent and the nominal ex-Nazis as soon as possible. This necessarily delayed the trials of the more serious offenders while, at the same time, the courts became bogged down in a mass of inconsequential cases. Realizing this, efforts were made to speed up the processing of the lesser cases. The amnesties extended in 1946 helped. A 'schnell' (fast) process, adopted in 1948 to dispose of the many cases of persons classified as followers, allowed the prosecutor to determine on the basis of written evidence whether or not the defendant actually was a follower, and if so to assess a fine and notify the accused without a public trial. If the accused was not satisfied he could appeal the decision. This allowed many of the minor cases to be disposed of rapidly, with the aim of devoting more attention to the involved and difficult cases of the major offenders. Despite these measures, the trial of many major Nazis was so long delayed that they benefited from the inevitable change of feeling among the people. It is literally true that by the time many of the more serious cases came up for trial the Germans were too tired of the whole business to care very much whether or not they received their due.

Another point on which critics often dwell is the alleged tendency of the denazification tribunals to exonerate 'big Nazis' while imposing severe penalties or disqualifications on some minor offenders. There were no doubt some instances of such discrimination. Yet this criticism represents only part of the truth.

The 'big Nazi' referred to was sometimes a man of influence, possibly a devoted Nazi, who made large contributions to the party and urged his employees to join. But he may have been a benevolent employer, and one who never persecuted anyone. So when he came before his peers and neighbours who sat on the courts, these people had no grievance against him. They did not judge him by his ideological beliefs but on his day-to-day activities which, from their point of view, were all in his favor. On the other hand the 'little Nazi', who may have been a cobbler, a postman, or a petty foreman, and who received severe sanctions and is often cited by the critics, may have been a fanatical Nazi. He may have denounced his neighbors to the Gestapo, belonged to the 'hoodlums' of the community, caused the arrest of his neighbors, their internment in concentration camps, or damage to their property. When such a 'little Nazi' came before the tribunal composed of his neighbors he was assessed a heavier penalty. It was too much to expect these farmers, artisans and work-a-day people to reason that had it not been for the benevolent 'big Nazi' with his big contributions to the party, hoodlums and Gestapo could not have prospered.

Criticism of the law today, however, is based on knowledge after the event. And in any case, this disadvantage of the law, if such it was, must be set off against the benefits derived from its having forced the local people, all over the Zone, to review actively what had taken place during the Nazi period.

Critics of the denazification program also point to the presence of former Nazis in important positions and in the public service generally. It is true that there are many former Nazis in public positions. Many are school teachers, mail carriers, policemen. Some few occupy higher positions, even in the state and Federal governments. Many business men holding important posts were once members of the Nazi party. Millions of former Nazis are re-employed, most of them in their former vocations. But these are, with few exceptions, persons who were found by the denazification tribunals to have been only nominal party members not personally implicated in the criminal activities of the party, or persons whose minor involvement in such activities has been expiated by legal process.

When exonerated Nazis with an active past seemed to have fared too well in getting cleared, and have been reinstated in responsible jobs, action has been taken. A case in point was that of the teachers reinstated in Wuerttemburg-Baden (U.S. Zone), who had held high positions during the Nazi régime. When the situation was disclosed earlier this year, U.S. officials urged the Minister of Education to re-examine it and to institute dismissals wherever the facts warranted. In the course of

November, the U.S. High Commissioner emphasized the American position by declaring to the Ministers President of the U.S. Zone that enthusiastic propagandists of Nazi doctrines should not be permitted to teach the young generation of a democratic Germany. Although all the former Nazi functionaries who were re-appointed as teachers had been pardoned by the Minister President of Wuerttemburg-Baden, the High Commissioner continued to press for their ouster during the last quarter of the year. It remains, moreover, the prerogative of the Allied High Commission to intervene in cases of appointment to high office of persons dangerous to Allied objectives in Germany.

It was, in fact, one of the primary intentions of the Denazification Law to make possible the reassimilation of the great mass of nominal and minor Nazis into German society at the earliest possible moment. It would have been unthinkable and indefensible to try to keep almost 8 million former members of the Nazi party proper—together with their dependants probably close to 30 million people—outside the community or outcasts from it. With very few exceptions the former Nazis who now occupy posts of any significance have been 'denazified'. In other words, they have been made eligible through legal procedure to hold their present offices. That it would be better if certain individuals were to remain out of public life cannot be denied. Many Germans would rather not see them in the positions they now occupy. Sections of the democratic German press have spoken out unequivocally against certain appointments to public office. However, once such persons have been duly appointed, and in the absence of legal grounds for their removal, there is generally nothing that can or should be done except to rely upon the democratic system which has been constructed in Germany to deal with the problem. No democracy is perfect; a new one may perhaps be allowed more than its normal share of mistakes. To interfere with it from the outside will in many cases do more harm than good. In all cases, intervention must be carefully weighed, being offset against the obvious danger of undermining the system in the confidence of the people it serves.

There have been widely publicized instances of the return of former Nazis to office. But the converse is likewise true, as is illustrated by the case of a former official of a Federal Ministry. The Nazi past of this official had been given wide publicity and was exposed in detail in a pamphlet circulated by the German Trade Union Federation dealing with the return of ex-Nazis to office. The official resigned his post in order to seek an injunction against the circulation of this pamphlet, but his request was denied by the court. In this case German opinion forced a former Nazi out of office, an action far more salutary than the expulsion of such persons at the insistence of the occupation authorities. In the final analysis, Nazism will stay out of German life only if the

German people reject it and continue to ban it even when the occupying powers are gone.

Allied policy at this stage is to repose trust in the German Federal Republic. The Federal Government has already assumed increased powers and will shortly be assigned further prerogatives. Germany is to be admitted eventually into full and equal partnership with the nations of the democratic community. It must be expected that those leaders who will be charged with these new responsibilities and powers will employ them for constructive and peaceful ends. They will also be entrusted with the responsibility of ensuring that the evil elements of the Nazi era do not re-emerge and exercise these powers to the detriment of Germany and of Europe.

The whole issue of denazification as it stands now on the eve of Germany's resumption of the status of a free nation may be simply stated. The occupying powers performed the major surgical operation to remove the evil of the Nazi régime from the German body. The patient must now bring into play his own recuperative powers.

The Office of the U.S. High Commissioner is, however, carrying out a broad program which in reality is an extension of the denazification policy in a positive field. This is the program of helping the Germans build a lasting democracy. In this connection, the difficulties encountered by former German denazification officials in their quest for employment should be noted. It is a situation which undoubtedly requires correction by a responsible and enlightened public opinion.

The success or failure of this effort rests, in the final analysis, on the Germans themselves. The regeneration of a people must come from within. There are in Germany today men and women of real stature, ability and courage who are devoting their energies to this task. There are such people in and outside the Government, in all walks of life. There is a free and democratic press. There are broadening contacts with the free world outside. There exists a deepening conviction among Germans everywhere that the interests of Germany will be best served not by the resurgence of a narrow and chauvinistic nationalism but by the close association of Germany with a free and integrated European community.

Before attempting to evaluate this report of General Clay's in a larger setting than the purely United States zonal one in which it is inevitably cast, it is perhaps convenient to resume the whole process of denazification from the Allied, and particularly the Western Allied, point of view.

The first phase lasted for approximately one year, from the entry of Allied troops into Germany in late 1944 until the end of the year 1945. Although some attempt, particularly at the Potsdam Conference, was made to co-ordinate the policies of the Four Powers, this was really a period of *ad hoc* measures taken by the individual military commanders, often on their own initiative. During this year fugitive Nazi officials, both military and civilian, were arrested and Nazis still in office were deposed, though not invariably, but in the British and American zones (particularly after General Patton's departure) more than in the French zone.

The discrepancy between the French and the Anglo-American attitudes had many causes, some of which have been discussed in an earlier chapter. One that has not been mentioned but was of some importance is a basically different concept both of the function of the law and its best method of enforcement. The difference between French, and indeed most continental, legal practice, and that of the English and the Americans which is derived from British practice, is too complex and technical a subject for discussion here. However, one result was that at no time did the French have any arrangement for the 'automatic arrest' of Nazis, as did their Western allies. French prosecutions were almost invariably based on denunciations, usually by other Germans. And in such cases, whether trials of war criminals or denazification hearings, the defence likewise relied far more heavily, in the French zone, on personal testimony as to past actions than on documentation concerning past membership of condemned Nazi organizations. This in turn meant that considerable 'string-pulling' went on, members of the Roman Catholic clergy being particularly valuable to the accused as defence witnesses. The French, and later the German courts in their zone, often handed out sentences far more savage than did their American and British equivalents. On the other hand they were often far more lenient. If luck were on his side, and particularly if he had a prelate up his sleeve, almost any prominent supporter of the Nazi Party was well advised to establish his residence in the French zone. Many, such as Papen, did. As for the small fry, the French hardly bothered with them except on the basis of denunciations.

By late 1945 there was some anxiety at the highest Allied levels concerning the divergence of methods and policies between the zones. Although the Russians were pursuing their own quite different ends ever more openly, and were clearly not prepared to implement any directives from the Four Power Control Council which did not suit their book, efforts were still being made on all sides to paper over the cracks.

The attempt to bring reason into an increasingly unreasonable situation led to *Control Council Law No. 10*, 24 December 1945, of which the most significant passage has already been quoted on pages 69, 70 and 71. From now on the process of denazification became increasingly a German problem under Allied zonal supervision, and as such it began rapidly to break down. The idea of screening the entire German adult population was impractical and the notion that this could be done fairly by semi-legal German courts even more so. Neither the time nor the personnel was available. Huge *Fragebogen*, or Questionnaires, were prepared. That of the Americans was the most voluminous (see Appendix 1) and the most widely distributed. Indeed it would seem from the statistics—which are here even less reliable than usual—that more copies of the American *Fragebogen* were distributed than there were Germans, adult, infantile or senile, in the U.S. zone, and that only some 25% of the interminable documents were ever processed at all.

For as early as July, 1946, the 'amnesties' began. First the young, that is to say people born since 1 January 1919, were exempted in the American zone, a month later in the British zone, and in the following year in the French. Then at Christmas 1946, exemptions were extended in the U.S. zone to almost all save those classified as Class One or Class Two suspects, which eliminated, with a stroke of the pen, 75% of the population. The British followed suit. Soldiers returning from prisoner-of-war camps were also more than likely to be exempted.

1946 had been the high-water-mark of denazification, as it had been that of the trials of war criminals. By the end of the year it was breaking down. This was due in part to the vast scale on which the operation had been originally envisaged, in part, and as a result of this, to a most unsatisfactory procedural expedient. As General Clay remarked, it was becoming generally believed in Germany throughout 1946 that the 'little Nazis' were being tried and punished while the 'big Nazis' were left alone. There is some truth in this view, but it is not explicable on a paranoiac basis. The first great Nuremberg Trial and many of the other major trials (I. G. Farben, the Foreign Ministry Officials, 'the Doctors', and so on) had shown how extremely difficult, complex, expensive and prolonged these legal ceremonies were. Many years later, when Western Germany had once again become a sovereign state and the Germans were administering their own laws in their own courts, the trial of some of the criminals who had run Auschwitz extermination camp lasted for over a year. The horrible past behaviour of the accused was known to all. Yet a proportion of these men, a proportion which must be seen as absurd to any man who is not a lawyer, got off extremely lightly. Nor was this a case of the Germans defending their own people. If it was in any way 'defensive' it was the German lawyers defending the concept of legality—the laws of evidence and so on—which had been despised by the Nazis and reimposed, in theory and practice, by the Allied powers. The Eichmann Trial was similarly protracted, and nobody has ever accused that Israeli court of being 'soft' on Nazis.

The Allied courts, often multi-national, who tried the major Nazi criminals were hampered not only by the extreme complexity of the cases, the vast numbers of multi-lingual witnesses and so on, but also by the fact that the lawyers were attempting to administer laws, in conditions of sometimes conflicting emphasis on aspects of testimony, that had few precedents and little authority from any other source, while the suggestion, increasingly voiced, that this was the victors passing judgment upon the vanquished hardly eased the task of the judges. Furthermore, the vast scale of Nazi crime far exceeded the number and time of the lawyers, German or foreign, qualified to handle the trials, which perhaps should have been held immediately after the war. Inevitably many of the alleged criminals—and most of them were real ones—were given a judicial reprieve. And, also inevitably perhaps, the semi-legal *Spruchkammern* handled the denazification of the small fry. Such a court can hand out a fine of a few thousand marks or a few months of rubble-clearing, but it would clearly have been against Allied policy for two civilians and an attorney to condemn men to death. Therefore the denazification courts dealt in general with the 'little Nazis' while the big ones sat in jail and, eventually, profited by the change in political atmosphere, often to escape altogether. That is what was going on in Germany in 1946, and it caused some bitterness.

It has, I hope, been shown how extremely complex it was to establish who, or even what, precisely was a Nazi. The courts—I must stress again that I am here referring to the denazification courts and not to those trying criminals for specific crimes—were in essence a confrontation between anti-Nazis (originally of the Allied armed forces, quite soon replaced by German nationals) who sat in judgment, and Nazi Germans who were subject to this judgment. General Clay has said that the success of the operation must be left to the historians to estimate, and time separates the historian equally from the judges and those upon whom they passed their verdicts. Who were the Americans of 1946 who passed judgment on the Germans for political wrong-thinking and passive collaboration in one of history's greatest crimes?

I must here be subjective. I was a staff officer in the United States Army before and during the campaign in France in 1944. For squeamish reasons, I had no wish to enter Germany as a conqueror, a rôle for which I felt myself to be ill-suited and ill-equipped. Many other Americans then felt as I did, no matter how great their detestation of Nazism, like my own, may have been. Unlike most of my contemporaries I was able to have myself transferred to London, and later to Washington, where I spent a year and more studying the history and personalities of the German General Staff. I hope that the papers I then wrote and edited may have contributed, at least marginally, to the decision of the policy-makers in the two principal Western capitals that the German General Staff be not treated as a criminal organization comparable to the SS or the Gestapo. During this time, 1945 and 1946, I had frequent occasion to visit Germany, saw many German prisoners of war, and was in daily contact with other Americans and many Britons who were concerned with German affairs at all levels.

The Duke of Wellington once remarked that it is as impossible to describe a battle as a ball: too much is happening, in too many different places and at the same time. This is certainly true of immediate post-war Germany. But from the perhaps confused fog of memory, here are three items from those confusing days.

A fairly senior Public Relations Officer attached to a very senior U.S. headquarters informed me in mid-1946 that he had 'liberated' $180,000 worth of 'Nazi' property. With this loot he proposed to buy himself a TV station in the U.S. Yet in all other respects he was an honest, decent man.

In Brittany in 1944 a G.I. was arrested for rape, court-martialled and duly sentenced. It was generally agreed among the officers of the court that such behaviour was best postponed until the G.I.s had crossed the German border.

At Le Havre, in March of 1946, I watched my luggage being loaded on to the Liberty Ship that was transporting myself and other American officers home. The temporary longshoremen were SS prisoners. In order to humiliate these arrogant racists, American negro soldiers had been detailed to guard them. I heard one such soldier remark, in friendly fashion, to an SS man that the two of them had something in common: they were both second-class citizens of their respective countries.

Such stories could be, and indeed have been, endlessly multiplied. What they add up to is this: the United States army which entered Germany in 1944 and 1945 was a magnificent fighting machine; it was, however, neither intended nor equipped to be a weapon for moral resurgence among the German people. Soldiers are unreceptive to the rhetoric of politicians and President Roosevelt's sonorous platitudes about the Four Freedoms and heaven knows what else cut precious little ice among the men who actually had to fight the goddamn Krauts. There was considerable hatred against *all* Germans in some units, those which had fought in the Ardennes battle in particular. There was disgusted shock in some others when the concentration camps were liberated. But the basic political causes behind these facts, and indeed behind the war itself, were only dimly understood by American soldiers, whether commissioned or not. How explain to a twenty-year-old lieutenant of the Alabama National Guard, suddenly given authority over a small Bavarian town, that racism was one of the Nazis' supreme crimes? How could a top sergeant whose family still lived in a Boston slum persuade the troglodytes of ruined Frankfurt that he had brought them Freedom from Want, let alone Freedom from Fear? And of course the Germans, fighting a rat-like fight for the most primitive form of survival, soon realized that their American conquerors had not brought a perfect society to Germany nor, apparently, even came from one themselves. Meanwhile the endless official moral exhortations which were poured out by the American and British authorities while the calories-level sank and the raping and looting went on, made the 'average German', if there be such a person, increasingly to doubt anything he heard, even the evilness of his past Nazi masters.

Of course there were many sensitive, educated and even politically educated Americans. Alas, there were not enough, for there never are, at any time, enough sensitive, educated people anywhere. There were certainly not enough in the armies that occupied and administered Germany immediately after the war.

The idea of a G-5, to administer the liberated and occupied territories, was sound from a staff point of view. These men were to take over from the Army's combat troops as soon as possible. But it was equally sound staff policy to assume that combat was what really counted until the war was finally won. One result of this was that G-5, with many honourable exceptions, received the lowest-grade staff officers, or those with only adequate security screening (this included the German refugees, most of whom were Jewish). As an intelligence, or G-2, officer I saw several of my more useless, drunken or unstable colleagues transferred to G-5 and indeed on more than one occasion feared lest this fate befall myself. It was thither that the misfits, with some knowledge of German, were sent. And what they found, when they got there, and particularly if they ended up in the C.I.C. (Counter Intelligence Corps), was an organization dominated by the German refugees. Again, these included a great many honourable men and women whose only interest was to restore their own, first country to decency and morality. Yet when the prime victims of atrocity, the few who have survived at least, are set in judgment over their tormentors and torturers, can anyone be sure that justice will be done? Most Germans assumed that it could not. It is of immense credit both to the American military authorities and to the German refugees that there were so very few vendettas. But from the point of view of the abstract concept of justice, in allegedly total opposition to the violence or *Willkur* of Nazi authority, it is sad that a more acceptable alternative authority could not have been found before ever the war ended. Perhaps the answer is that no such authority could then have been created, and maybe not at any other time either.

Chapter Nine

It had been my intention, when first I planned this book, to include a number of typical or characteristic case histories of Germans who had passed through the process of denazification, some Nazis, some not, some rightly prosecuted, some wrongly so. I also intended to give similar case histories of typical Germans who had sat on the denazification tribunals, with brief biographies of the judges and the judged stretching both backwards and forwards from the actual hearings.

I have abandoned this intention and for these reasons. In the first place the documentation is usually quite inadequate and human memory far too unreliable. When a stenographer was employed, which was seldom save in the most spectacular cases, the stenograms have either been destroyed or are unavailable. Those men and women who were denazified have, in many cases, a very considerable reluctance to discuss an episode, indeed a whole period of their lives. This is hardly surprising. (In about 1956 a friend of mine was compiling a German businessmen's *Who's Who*. He told me that it was astonishing how many prominent men then middle-aged had apparently done nothing whatever between 1933 and 1945, save perhaps military service in war time.) It is hardly surprising and certainly not contemptible that incriminated Nazis should wish to forget the past nor that they should in some measure have succeeded in so doing. What is perhaps less to be expected is that, in many cases, those men who sat on the denazification tribunals are equally anxious to shrug off that episode and to change the subject. This however can be explained by the fact that almost all Germans, of all political views, now regard denazification as a failure, some because it went too far, some because it did not go far enough, all because it *was* a failure, and a failure without past glory nor future promise. Few men care to recall their involvement in such an operation: some have suffered in later years because they were involved: most, like the Nazis, would sooner simply forget.

In the second place even among the scanty documentation and unreliable evidence available it rapidly became apparent that there were no 'typical', no 'characteristic' cases. Quite apart from the different techniques employed within the four zones, there were remarkable variants between the tribunals in each zone, and in time as well. In theory it should be statistically possible to say that a per cent of the bureaucrats earning between b and c thousand marks a year joined the Nazi Party at this date or that: that d per cent were denazified in e, f, g or h zone in year i, j, k and later: that m per cent were found guilty in category n, o, p or q and received sentences on an average of more alphabetical letters: and that so and so many have remained entirely, partly or not at all Nazi in their view of the world. Such a task would be almost fruitless, and such fruit as it might produce would be small and tasteless.

The alternative would be to give several hundred case histories, annotated as to reliability of sources and with explanatory details as to the precise duties of, say, the town clerk of a small Bavarian community in 1933, 1938 and 1945 and who were his personal enemies in 1947 and why. It is no matter of regret to the writer of this book, nor I trust to the reader, that neither the documentation, nor the time, nor the scope of this work, has permitted such a study.

Finally, and perhaps most important of all, the typical man does not exist, save in the abstractions of theoreticians and perhaps in the works of the great artists. We may have an idea, maybe a very clear idea, of what an English eighteenth-century nobleman was like, or a Russian nineteenth-century landowner, or an early twentieth-century American millionaire. We have never met one, and rely on the eyes and ears of those painters and writers of the period whose work has lived through their artistic talent. To produce the true picture of Germans of the denazification period we would need innumerable Boswells, countless Flauberts, a race of Tolstois. Lacking these, it is to be hoped that some equally skilled writer will one day, in fictional or semi-fictional form, produce a novel or play that can preserve, in essence at least, the flavour and tension of what is already an extremely remote period of history.

I have therefore decided to abandon that project, but instead to tell briefly one denazification story.

The story is far from typical. Baron Franz von Papen was once Chancellor of Germany: he was Hitler's Vice-Chancellor: he was one of the few pre-Hitler politicians to play an important if diminishing political rôle throughout the whole history of the Third Reich: and he was one of three among the accused and most prominent Nazi leaders to be found innocent by the International Tribunal which sat at Nuremberg in 1945-1946: he was later tried by a denazification tribunal, and found guilty. Because of his prominence, his case was more fully reported than that of most men who passed through this process. And because he is one of the twentieth century's most skilled 'survivors' he lived to write his memoirs. It must not therefore be imagined that his is in any way a typical case. It does, however, give some indication both of procedure and of atmosphere, and casts some light on the validity of the denazification process.

Franz von Papen was born in 1879 and brought up on a Westphalian estate which, he is reported to have claimed, had been in the possession of his family for nine centuries.[1] His tendency to boast in this fashion about his aristocratic background, even when being interviewed by an American criminal psychologist, was characteristic, as is apparent in his autobiography,[2] and was hardly likely to win him much favour in the U.S. zone during the immediate post-war period. Both in deed and word he appears a very clever, vain and shallow man. He was baptised and remained a Roman Catholic. Educated as a cadet, he was commissioned in the 5th (the Westphalian) Regiment of Uhlans. He belonged to all the best clubs, was a gentleman rider, and bought his clothes in London. In his memoirs he writes: 'I am thankful to have seen the German Empire in all its power and majesty.' In 1913 he became a member of the German General Staff, and at the end of that year was sent to Washington as an unusually young military attaché.

It was in America, in the early years of the First World War, that he won fame or notoriety according to taste. According to the British and, later, the Americans he was not only a master spy but also controlled the German sabotage apparatus in the United States

[1] G. M. Gilbert, *Nuremberg Diary*, London, Eyre & Spottiswoode, 1948.
[2] Franz von Papen, *Memoirs*, London, André Deutsch, 1952.

and was responsible for the blowing-up of factories producing war material for the Allies. He hotly denies this, perhaps with truth, but British propaganda made much of this scandal, involving the loss of American lives in a still neutral United States, and much of the mud stuck. That he was a spy goes without saying, though he maintains that he always carried out these parts of his duties in a most gentlemanly way. If this is true, he cannot have been a very successful spy. On the other hand it is normal practice for military attachés to leave the dirty work to their subordinates. Unfortunately for Papen, one of his subordinates lost a briefcase in the New York subway. It contained many orders and instructions from the German military attaché. The legend of the 'master spy' was created. In late 1915 the United States government asked the German government to recall von Papen as *persona non grata*. Had there been war crimes trials after the First World War it is probable that he would have been in the dock in connection with German sabotage in America: what the verdict would have been it is of course impossible to say.

Back in Europe he commanded a battalion of infantry on the Western Front. According to his memoirs he introduced certain tactical innovations to the combat troops which were of great value to the German army as a whole. These claims do not figure in the military histories of the First World War. Nevertheless he had friends in high places—until 1945 he always had friends in high places—and in 1917 he was transferred to the Middle Eastern front as a staff officer. He spent the rest of the war with the German force supporting the Turks and was interned in Turkey at its end. Early in 1919 he escaped and returned to Germany. He found the Fatherland in a state of revolution, and resigned his commission.

He acquired a small farm in his native Westphalia, but soon entered politics. In 1921 he was elected to the Prussian Landtag, or Provincial Parliament of Prussia, as a representative of the Zentrum Party, an essentially conservative and predominantly Roman Catholic party. He also acquired a controlling interest in that party's newspaper, *Germania*. He was henceforth to make much political capital out of his religious beliefs. Although never a successful parliamentarian, and an object of distrust to many members even of his own party, his social links and personal contacts with army leaders, industrialists, and other politicians of the Right gained him a place of considerable importance in Weimar

Germany. Intrigue is a perfectly legitimate weapon but when it becomes the principal weapon in the armoury—as with General Schleicher, Papen's ally and later his enemy—or almost the only one as with Papen himself, then eyes begin to turn towards men better equipped. By June, 1932, when Papen was appointed Chancellor, German eyes were turning towards Hitler.

His brief Chancellorship, in the worst period of the Depression with approximately one third of the German working population unemployed, was a fiasco. His conservative government suffered an immediate and overwhelming defeat (513-32) in the newly elected Reichstag of which he was not even and never had been a member, and which did not meet again while he was Chancellor. He thus had no parliamentary backing of any sort and governed by presidential decree. In an attempt to obtain non-democratic backing he and Schleicher, technically his Defence Minister actually his puppet-master, tried to inveigle Hitler into the government in a subordinate rôle. Hitler refused, but in order to sweeten the offer Papen had already rescinded his predecessor's ban against the wearing of SA and SS uniform. This gesture was entirely to the advantage of the Nazis and a further blow to the moribund German democracy. Street fighting began again at once between Nazis, Socialists and Communists. He then delivered another and perhaps even more mortal blow to the existing system of government when on July 20th 1932 he deposed the Prussian government on the grounds that it could not preserve order and appointed himself Reich Commissioner for Prussia, Germany's largest and most important province. The importance of this action was less the revelation of Papen's authoritarian and anti-democratic attitude than the proof it provided that the democratic left, which had then ruled Prussia for a dozen years, was impotent to resist aggression even from a man like Papen: there was no general strike and the Social Democrats knuckled under. Papen's Chancellorship was thus of dual benefit to the Nazis.

This did not altogether please the army. Schleicher, who had made Papen, now broke him, and in November became himself the last Chancellor of pre-Hitlerian Germany. As is not unusual in history the kingmaker made no king.[3] Two months later Hitler was Chancellor, in alliance with most of the Right, and he chose as his Vice-Chancellor a man whom he must have regarded as an

[3] John Wheeler Bennett, *The Nemesis of Power*, London, Macmillan, 1953.

utter lightweight devoid of democratic principles, and no threat to his own plans. For some eighteen months Franz von Papen was, in theory, the third figure of the German Reich. He was therefore in some considerable measure responsible for the initial atrocities, for *Gleichschaltung* and for the creation of the Nazi state. He has denied this, and his denial is valid in so far as he was surely not consulted by his new Nazi masters as to their policy of terrorization. On the other hand he did attend Cabinet meetings, and certainly was better informed than most Germans as to what was happening in Dachau, Sachsenhausen, and the streets of the cities. However he was much occupied with arranging a Concordat with the Holy See. For this both his Catholicism and his 'respectability' were of use. The Concordat was of great value to Hitler in that it both gave his government recognition by the most spiritual force in the world and also silenced the German Roman Catholics who might have been expected to disapprove of his methods, some temporarily, most permanently. However by June of 1934 Papen, as a conservative and an aristocrat, was sufficiently worried by Germany's slide into anarchy and by the socialist aspect of National Socialism to protest.

On June 17th 1934 he made a speech at Marburg in which, using moderate but long unheard arguments, he deplored the excesses of the Nazi régime. This was his sole overt act of opposition to the criminal régime which he had helped into office and in which he served throughout its thirteen years of misrule. Even this was done at the request of the dying President von Hindenburg and largely written by three young men of Papen's entourage, Jung, Bose and Klausener.

The speech caused an immense furore both inside and outside Germany. Perhaps the forces of law and order were about to stage a counter-revolution after all with Papen and the generals at its head? Hitler reacted strongly and at once. He had protected his rear by a pact with the army leaders. He now murdered the SA leaders on June 30th and at the same time disposed of some right-wing opponents, notably General von Schleicher but also Jung, Bose and Klausener. Papen's Vice-Chancellery was ransacked by the SS, and he himself kept incommunicado under close house arrest for several days. On the day of his release he attended a Cabinet meeting. A week later he accepted the post of German ambassador in Austria. Thus did he not only fail to protest at the actions of a régime which had murdered his friends and assistants, but he agreed to demotion and to further serve that government in an intensely sensitive post. (The Austrian Chancellor Dollfuss had been murdered by Austrian Nazis, with German connivance, on the day of Papen's appointment, while Papen was fully aware of the German plan for an Anschluss of the two countries, and had even discussed this with Mussolini.) The Roman Catholic gentleman rider lacked not only dignity but even basic humanity in his anxiety to cling on to office, any office, under any German government, even Hitler's, and was perfectly prepared to barter his 'respectability' to retain it.

Hitler had appointed Papen to Vienna as a façade of respectability to appease Mussolini, with whom he was then not yet allied, and to counteract the fears created by Dollfuss's murder. Papen held the job for three and a half years. Just as he had known about, but tried not to be implicated in, strong-arm sabotage in America in 1914 and 1915, so now he was kept or kept himself so far as possible in the dark about Nazi attempts to undermine and overthrow the Austrian state. This suited him and it suited the Nazis too. Only when plans were almost completed was Papen scrapped without ceremony or notice. He was dismissed on February 4th 1938. Eight days later he met the Austrian Chancellor at the German frontier and escorted him to his first meeting with Hitler. Four weeks after this meeting, at which Papen was present, the German army invaded Austria. Papen maintains that he deplored the Anschluss as he claims he deplored all Nazi policy. But once again he had served his masters in the teeth of his own alleged disapproval.

For a year he lived in semi-retirement, but the Nazis still had some use for this emblem of the 'old' Germany. In April of 1939 he went to Turkey as German ambassador. He claims that he insisted that his be a normal, old-fashioned embassy, without the usual increment of Gestapo-led Nazi apparatchiks, yet later admits that his subordinate who dealt with Cicero, the famous spy, was a member of the SD, the espionage and counter-espionage apparatus of the SS.[4] He remained in Turkey, doing his best to help the Nazis win the war until they had lost it. He claims to have been terrified lest he be arrested after the attempt to assassinate Hitler on July 20th 1944, since he knew some of the conspirators and assumes

[4] L. C. Moyzisch, *Operation Cicero*, Wingate, London, 1951, also Papen op. cit.

that they planned to call on him to help form a new government. They had no intention of so doing, nor was he arrested by the Gestapo when he visited Hitler a few days later. He remained in Turkey until very near the end of the war. He then returned to Germany. The Americans picked him up and, to his surprise, kept him under arrest. He was astounded to discover that he must face trial before the International Tribunal as one of the major criminals.

The Nuremberg Trial began on November 20th 1945, and lasted until September 6th 1946. Franz von Papen was not himself cross-questioned until June 14th. The crimes of which he was accused were neither war crimes nor crimes against humanity, but the third, most novel and least defined head of the rather clumsy Act, crimes against peace. The essence of this accusation, however, was stated by the British prosecutor, Sir David Maxwell Fyfe, when he said:

> What I am putting to you is that the only reason that could have kept you in the service of the Nazi Government, when you knew all these crimes, was that you sympathized and wanted to carry on with the Nazis' work. That is what I am putting to you—that you had this express knowledge; you had seen your own friends, your own servants, murdered around you. You had the detailed knowledge of it, and the only reason which could have dominated you, and made you take one job after another from the Nazis was, that you sympathized with their work. That is what I am putting against you, Herr von Papen.[5]

All very fine, but hardly sufficient to send a man to the gallows or even to prison. Disloyalty to one's friends is not a criminal offence. No more were sympathy and assistance to the recent legally appointed government of Germany even with knowledge of its true nature. Or if it were, then most of the German people were guilty, and most of the Germans were not on trial. It was becoming apparent that Papen was being tried because of his prominence, but prominence is also no crime. Since the British and American lawyers were anxious that this strange trial should be as legal as possible in the circumstances, Papen could only be tried as a man, not as a symbol. In his judgment Chief (now Lord) Justice Lawrence was more specific:

> Von Papen was active in 1932 and 1933 in helping Hitler to form the

[5] Franz von Papen, *Memoirs*, London, André Deutsch, 1952, p. 568.

Coalition Cabinet and aided in his appointment as Chancellor on January 30, 1933. As Vice-Chancellor in that Cabinet he participated in the Nazi consolidation of control in 1933. . . . Notwithstanding the murder of his associates, von Papen accepted the position of Minister to Austria on July 26, 1934, the day after Dollfuss had been assassinated. . . . The evidence leaves no doubt that von Papen's primary purpose as Minister to Austria was to undermine the Schuschnigg regime and strengthen the Austrian Nazis for the purpose of bringing about the Anschluss. To carry through this plan he engaged in both intrigue and bullying. But the Charter does not make criminal such offences against political morality, however bad these may be. . . . Under the Charter von Papen can be held guilty only if he was party to the planning of aggressive war . . . but it is not established beyond a reasonable doubt that this was the purpose of his activity.

For earlier in his summing up Chief (now Lord) Justice Lawrence had fixed a date line to the Nazis' planning of aggressive war. Such planning, he laid down, began on November 5th 1937, the date of Hitler's disclosure of his plans to his military leaders and to Foreign Minister Neurath at the meeting reported in the Hossbach Memorandum.[6]

Papen had not attended this meeting and had been dismissed from the Vienna embassy some three months later. Since there was no charge against him for crimes other than against peace, and since there was no evidence that he had committed such crimes in that brief period, the verdict was inevitable: not guilty. So far as the Allies were concerned, he left the court a free man.

But he was not free. The Bavarian authorities were demanding his arrest and re-trial before a denazification court. Papen remained for some time in the prison, while he attempted and failed to obtain permission that he be moved from the American to the French or British zone. When he left the prison he was immediately placed under house arrest by the German authorities first in the house of a friend, later in hospital.

The Denazification Court was presided over by President Camille Sachs of the District Court. Papen states that Dr Sachs was a Jew. The members of the Court included a medical practitioner, a civil engineer, a departmental manager, a police superintendent, and a commercial agent. There were three reserve members: a master plumber, a master decorator, and a trade union official. Prosecuting

[6] See pages 51 e seq.

Counsel was Dr Werner Fiebig, a High Court Judge, Defending Counsel the lawyer Dr Kubuschok, who had defended Papen before the International Tribunal.

The proceedings went on for a month. Both the Prosecution and the Defence provided witnesses who had figured in German political life before and during the Nazi régime. They included General Oskar von Hindenburg, the son of the late President of the Reich, Karl Severing, erstwhile Minister of the Interior both of the Reich and of Prussia, Theodor Düsterberg a co-founder of the *Stahlhelm* organization, Otto Meissner, Secretary of State and head of the Office of the President of the Reich from 1920-1945, and many others. Apart from the usual questions of their personal relationship to the defendant, all witnesses were asked whether they had ever belonged to the NSDAP or its formations. In many cases the Court decided that the oath should not be administered, obviously because there were grave doubts as to the credibility of the witnesses in question.

On February 3rd, 1947, the Court, after deliberations in camera, ordered the immediate arrest of von Papen for which it gave its reasons in the following

Statement:

The Court has hitherto refrained from taking the Defendant into custody. Since, however, both Oskar von Hindenburg and witness von der Schulenburg (Hindenburg's military aide de camp) have made depositions on oath to show that the commendation of Hitler and his Movement in President Hindenburg's Political Testament had been drafted by the Defendant and the latter has repeatedly prevaricated on this point, it has been found necessary to take the Defendant into Custody as, in view of his attitude, there is danger of collusion.

On February 19 both Counsels made their closing speeches. Counsel for the Prosecution demanded a verdict of Guilty, and a penalty of 10 years' penal servitude, confiscation of von Papen's entire fortune and classification as major offender.

On February 24, the Court pronounced its findings.

Judgment

I. The Accused is to be considered a member of the group of major offenders.

II. To expiate his offences,
 (1) he will be sent to a Labour Camp for a term of eight years. In view of his physical disability he will be given special tasks commensurate with his state of health;

One year and five months during which he was under political arrest will be deducted from this term;
(2) all his assets will be confiscated as a contribution to the indemnification of victims. An amount of RM 5,000 will however be left to him for his basic needs;
As far as he is in receipt of income, he will continue to make special contributions to a reparations fund;
(3) he will remain unfit to hold public office, or to act as a lawyer or a notary;
(4) he loses all legal claims to pensions or payments from public funds;
(5) he must neither vote nor stand as a candidate in elections; he must not participate in political activities or belong to a political Party;
(6) he is not allowed to join a trade union or a trade or professional organisation;
(7) for a term of 15 years he will not be allowed to (a) work in a professional capacity, or be responsible for the running of a business or work-shop of any kind, or exercise control and supervision thereof; (b) to be employed in any capacity other than as an ordinary worker; (c) to act as teacher, preacher, editor, author or broadcaster;
(8) his residence and domicile are subject to official permission, he can be called up to take part in public works;
(9) he is deprived of all his degrees, special licences, and entitlements, and of his right to own a motor-car.

III. The costs of these proceedings are to be borne by the Defendant. The value in dispute is RM 416,000. (Note: this is part of German Court procedure to determine the costs arising from a particular law suit.)

The President then announced another Court Decision according to which von Papen was to remain in custody. He added that Defending Counsel had been wrong in stating in his closing speech that von Papen would have been better off before a Court in the British Zone of Occupation. The ruling in that Zone was, on the contrary, that all former government members fell under the provisions of Group II.

The Public Prosecutor appealed against the sentence of eight years to be spent in a Labour Camp, and asked for this to be changed to ten years. Von Papen also appealed on the 3rd April 1947. He asked for a suspension of proceedings against him, or failing this for a new hearing before a lower Court and/or a new classification and a new decision as to the group of Offenders and the punishment imposed.

The Court of Appeal met for the first time on the 18th January, 1949. Its president was J. D. Sauerländer, a former ministerial Counsellor. Other members of the Court were a chief librarian, a businessman, a tool-maker, a school-inspector, a former ambassador and a retired High Court judge. Counsel for the Prosecution was Dr Manfred Frey. Pending the appeal, von Papen stayed at an internment camp outside Nuremberg.

Numerous witnesses were heard during the four days' hearing. The findings of the Court of Appeal were published on the 26th January. They read:

(A) The Public Prosecutor withdraws his Appeal.
(B) Following the appeal by the Defendant, the verdict of the denazification court Nuremberg, Stadtkreis I (Major Cases), dated 24th February 1947, is modified as follows:

I. The accused is considered an offender of the Group II.
II. The term of labour imposed is considered to have been served by the Defendant during his political imprisonment after May 8, 1945.
III. DM 30,000—of his assets are to be forfeited as a contribution to the reparation of wrongs done.
IV. Furthermore the following measures in expiation of his past are imposed:

> (1) He is to be considered indefinitely ineligible for any kind of public office, including that of a notary public or a member of the Bar;
> (2) he is deprived of all rights to claim a pension or annuity from public funds;
> (3) he is deprived of the right to take part in elections either as a voter or a candidate, to indulge in political activities, or to be a member of a political party;
> (4) he must not join a trade-union, or a business or professional organization;
> (5) for a term of five years he is forbidden:
> (a) to work independently in a professional or managerial capacity in in any kind of trade or business, to be a partner, or to control or supervise the activities of such an establishment;
> (b) to be employed in any but a routine capacity;
> (c) to act as a teacher, preacher, editor, author or broadcaster.

(6) his place of residence and domicile are subject to certain restrictions;

(7) he loses all degrees, concessions and entitlements, and the right to own a motor-car.

V. Costs in both proceedings are to borne by the Defendant up to one third, and by the Treasury to the extent of two thirds. The value in dispute is DM 287,000.

In giving the grounds for the decision to modify the findings of the original court, the Court of Appeal mentioned that it had taken into account the depositions made to the lower court and new depositions made during the present trial. 'Von Papen's statements appear thoroughly trustworthy to the Court of Appeal, they are corroborated by the documentary evidence (3 volumes) submitted by the Defence which have been intensively dealt with. Therefore all necessary information was provided, and there was no reason to order a new trial by a lower court.'

Points from the Judgment

LEGAL POINTS

(*1*) *Rule of Terror*. The lower Court stated that the term *rule of terror* as used in the Denazification Law, is not used to constitute a subordinate term under the general concept of National Socialism. Supporters of National Socialism are to be considered supporters of the national socialist rule of terror. The Court of Appeal agrees with this definition. . . . The claim made in the appeal, that a difference has to be made between party members and outsiders, is to be rejected. There were many party members who did not recognize the teachings of the party, and many of them had far less opportunities to see National Socialism for what it was than the non-party member von Papen, and yet all these party members are held responsible. Von Papen admits to have realized on the 30th June 1934 that National Socialism was tantamount to a criminal rule of terror.

(*2*) *Legal responsibility*. The Denazification Law does not define clearly and unequivocally what is meant by individual responsibility. The findings of the lower court on this matter leave room for doubt. They state that even under the denazification law the personal factor would have to be taken into account. Ordinary criminal law presupposes culpable intent, whereas the denazification law has introduced the concept of individual responsibility which goes much further. In one instance it is held that von Papen had a personal responsibility because he omitted to consider in detail the obvious and probably inevitable consequences of his conduct. Under criminal law this would be considered culpable negligence, whereas intent is deliberate.

The legal committee of the *Länderrat* has published an Opinion in which it holds that the Denazification Law is based on the principle that only intent which has led to active manifestations to support the national socialist rule of terror or militarism or to benefit from it can be interpreted as political responsibility. Again we are not told whether intent means criminal or only an ordinary intention.

. . . Everybody seems to agree, however, that there has to be a factual causative action arrived at by a free decision. Nobody can be held responsible for actions under duress. Here, as in criminal law, the privilege of necessity and of self-defence are taken into account. The culpable action must be due to serious intent; people who joined the NSDAP as snoopers in order to be able to fight it more effectively, cannot be held responsible. . . . It is not a defence to state that one was mistaken or deceived about the criminal character of National Socialism. . . . This can be seen from the stipulation that people who joined the NSDAP from idealist motives, believing in its good intentions without realizing that from the start it had aimed at setting up a criminal terror, are to be tried as followers.

Taking into account all these points it is not difficult to apply the law and its concept of legal responsibility to people who were convinced supporters of national socialist terrorism, and even less to a defendant who held a leading position either in the Nazi Party or in a government office, as these could only be held by leading National Socialists or by supporters of the rule of terror. There is no difficulty either in dealing with people who have helped to bring about situations which are regarded by the law as typically Nazi or militaristic. . . . A difficulty only arises with regard to people who were not National Socialists and yet gave essential or even extraordinary help to the rule of terror. We are faced here . . . with the important problem of collaboration in a national socialist state. In spite of grave scruples many public officials who were not party members, or who were often opponents of Nazism, remained in their positions in order to prevent worse things and in order to preserve as much as possible of the achievements of the rule of law. In many individual cases they frustrated national socialist actions, but taken all in all they must be held to have furthered Nazism, because without the cooperation of public officials no Hitlerite government activity would have been possible. The same applies to the workers and to the Army who made and wielded the arms in Hitler's war instead of using their strong arms to stop the wheels and prevent war. All of them, and everybody who carried on with his everyday routine, as was probably unavoidable, have been active in a way which objectively speaking and probably also consciously on their part has furthered National Socialism. All of them ought to be held responsible before the law. . . . The law, however, does not eliminate them from the life of the community, because they do not constitute a danger to the formation of a German democracy, and also because the legislator must take into consideration that the continuity of public and private life was unavoidable, and can therefore not be regarded as active support for the rule of terror.

The argument goes on to say that whilst a public employee must never work against the government employing him because he disagrees with its policy, this only applies to a state under the rule of law. Under a criminal régime 'each and every public official has the right and the duty to mitigate, to prevent, and to actively oppose government actions, and to render as much resistance as is in the power of an individual'. In addition under such a régime a public official is entitled to work for the downfall of the criminal régime and to look for connections in this respect; for public officials in positions where decisions are made, this right becomes a duty. . . . Therefore a public servant who is guided by motives of this kind, does not become guilty by continuing to serve or by accepting a new office. On the other hand, however meretricious the resistance of the holders of high office may have been, it does not justify their official activities unless it was used unequivocally to bring about the downfall of the régime which alone would have saved Germany and with it, probably, the world. Such is the case with von Papen.

CLASSIFICATION

In view of his high position as vice-chancellor and ambassador and in view of the high regard in which von Papen was held by the general public, the political and propaganda support which he gave to the national socialist rule of terror must be considered extraordinary. Therefore he is to be considered a major offender. . . . However a number of new circumstances in his favour have arisen during these hearings. . . .

This Court which seriously finds von Papen a major offender because he did not do justice to the high demands which were made on him, and which holds him responsible under the Denazification Law, finds itself in duty bound to take into account his general attitude and to stress also the points in his favour refuting prejudices and legends which tend to blacken his character.

It is easy to lampoon him as an erstwhile member of the General Staff, as a gentleman rider and as a member of the (feudalist) *Herrenclub*, but as opposed to this we have heard two simple witnesses, mayor Tömmers of Merfeld and the land-agent Schwarz from Wallerfangen, testify to his simplicity, his readiness to help and his fellow-feeling for his humblest neighbour in his home environment. . . . The fact that he set up the Community of German Catholics and the tendency of his speeches on christianity and the church, as well as the attitude of his newspaper *Germania*, refute the accusation that has been made against him to have been the grave-digger of Catholicism. He has been accused of having left his collaborators to their fate, but this is contradicted by the testimony of the survivors among them. . . .

There are a great number of mitigating factors. . . . Von Papen as a member of the government was a centre of opposition. . . . A man who has given such proof of his courage and human compassion . . . cannot be put on a level with criminals and rabid party members. A man who as has been recognized by the lower court risked his life to bring about peace, who dared to criticize as strongly as Papen did in his Marburg speech, who was therefore imprisoned and deprived of his friends, such a man deserves in spite of all the things to his discredit a more lenient treatment.

The Court therefore decided to classify von Papen as an offender of Group II and not as a major offender as had been done by the lower Court. It also decided that von Papen had expiated his culpable responsibility by his long term of imprisonment, first in the Allied prison in Nuremberg and subsequently in the internment camp where for two long years he had been awaiting the verdict of the Court of Appeal. In fixing the amount of the fine to be paid, the Court said that expropriation of some of his landed estate and of his banking account in the Soviet zone had reduced his total assets to DM 267,000, and he had still to provide for his three unmarried daughters.[7]

Needless to say Papen regarded his denazification trial as a gross miscarriage of justice, and the whole concept of denazification as immoral. He wrote, later:

> Nuremberg had one positive result, in that it awakened the conscience of the world and drew its attention to the problem. Perhaps in due course the nations will surrender enough of their national sovereignty to permit a solution. On the other hand, it established the conception of the collective guilt of certain organizations. Under the aegis of the occupying powers this led to the formation of denazification courts, which have probably done more damage to the general conception of law than can yet be appreciated. Millions of people in Germany have been placed under an assumption of guilt which they have had to disprove individually in totally inadequate hearings. This has led to a form of juridical chaos, the moral and political effects of which will weigh on the German people for years to come. The very same methods were employed as those which the Nuremberg Tribunal condemned so roundly in the Third Reich. If the conception of true international law is to be given a firm foundation, respect for the law on a national plane will first have to be re-established.[8]

Once he was finally out of prison and had paid his fine von Papen was free to go and do as he wished. In the nascent German Federal Republic he even seems to have contemplated a return to political activity. Naturally this could only be in a very senior capacity, and he aspired briefly to replace Dr Konrad Adenauer as leader of the Christian Democrat Party. If his reputation as a democrat was impeachable, he had always and vociferously been a Roman Catholic. Had he not signed Hitler's Concordat with Cardinal Pacelli, later Pope Pius XII? but it was rapidly made plain to him that there was no rôle for him to play in German public life.

---

[7] I am indebted to Sir John Wheeler-Bennett and to the Librarian of St. Antony's College, Oxford, for permission to see the record of Papen's denazification trial and appeal, of which the foregoing is a précis.

[8] Franz von Papen, *Memoirs*, London, André Deutsch, 1952, p. 573.

Nevertheless the mere possibility of Papen becoming politically active in the Federal Republic was indicative of a grave danger to that Republic. And for this Karl Jaspers attaches a considerable measure of blame to the denazification process as such.

Our new state cannot thrive unless high-level collaboration with the Nazi absolutely disqualifies a man from political, moral, intellectual participation today. He may have collaborated with the Nazi state by joining in particular wrongful acts, perhaps in death sentences as a judge or prosecutor, or by the literary explanation and vindication of Nazi principles ranging from the race theory and the treatment of Jews to the interpretation of the thesis, 'The Fuehrer's will is the supreme law.' These were not crimes within the meaning of the penal code; but they were acts that showed a man's character to be such as to bar him from positions of prominence in a new state built upon a sense of freedom. The denazification procedure turned out to be the wrong method. However incriminated, the denazified received a paper that spared them any further interrogation or investigation. The piece of paper was regarded as proof. Even against better knowledge, a government agency could appoint an official, citing this paper and feeling relieved of personal responsibility.

The actual choice of the persons now in positions of leadership lies at the root of the obstacles to a free unfoldment of our state. Constructive impulses are paralyzed. Like mildew, a spirit alien and inimical to the task blights the new edifice. If this spirit is not resisted it may ultimately destroy everything.[9]

[9] Karl Jaspers, *The Future of Germany*, 1967, The University of Chicago Press, p. 67.

Chapter Ten

What the Americans were in fact attempting to do in Germany was to impose an artificial revolution, from above, on a prostrate society in a state of temporary disintegration. In this their aims, though not of course their methods or objectives, were closer to those of the Russians than of the French. (The British followed the American lead but modified their technique.) The Nazis and the 'militarists'—an even vaguer and less easily identifiable group of men—were to be stamped into the ground, good democrats stamped out of it. Nor was it only in Germany that this enforced revolution of the old social order was to be carried through. A similar process was envisaged, and partly carried out, in Japan at the same time.

In Japan the American authorities had, in many ways, an easier task.[1] In the first place, although in theory only the representative of the most important of the victorious Allied powers, in fact General Douglas MacArthur was military dictator of almost the entire country. His task there was made much easier by the decision to retain the Japanese Emperor, thus giving the actions of the Americans the appearance of legality and even of continuity in the eyes of the Japanese people, while acceptable Japanese civil servants and officials could be persuaded that they were working for the Mikado through his American Shogun. Secondly, and paradoxically, the very different structure of Japanese society from European and American societies worked against too drastic an attempt at the imposition of the United States model on the defeated, Asiatic enemy. The American-Japanese war could not possibly be understood, nor its solution attempted, in Civil War terms. There were also even fewer Americans who could speak Japanese than could talk German, nor were there Japanese refugees on whom to rely. The 'enforced revolution' was thus, inevitably,

[1] For much of what follows, particularly in regard to Japan, see John D. Montgomery, *Forced to be Free*, The University of Chicago Press, 1957.

reduced in scope and in depth. Finally due to the chronology of the Second World War, General MacArthur's staff had the chance to profit from the lessons learned by General Eisenhower's in Germany: according to Mr Montgomery they took it.

The whole operation was on a much smaller and more manageable scale. The population of Japan in 1945 was 71,996,477. The first census of the U.S. Zone in Germany was carried out in 1946 and showed a population of 16,682,573, or less than one quarter of the Japanese, and it had swollen since May 1945, with a great influx of refugees from the Communist-occupied territories.

At the outset a simpler and more direct process of artificial revolution was adopted, avoiding the complex legalism that had characterized denazification. In Japan the problem was viewed as a purely administrative matter. There were usually no hearings, public or private; no witnesses; no findings of "guilt"; no punishments, and no machinery for prosecution or defense. A shortened questionnaire (23 items) was circulated only among selected leaders, who were either members of political organizations or occupants of important public or private office. These were screened by a national board, 46 prefectural boards, and 118 municipal boards, with the assistance of some 1,000 employees. A total of 2,308,863 cases were screened, as opposed to 3,623,112 in the U.S. Zone of Germany (with less than one-fourth Japan's population).

In Japan only 210,287 persons were removed and excluded from office as opposed to 418,307 in the U.S. Zone of Germany. Thus only 3.2 per cent of the population in Japan were screened, as opposed to 21.7 per cent in the American Zone in Germany; 0.29 per cent of the Japanese were removed or suspended from office, compared to Germany's 2.5 per cent. The volume of the effort in Germany was not only many times greater, it was also performed much less efficiently. In quantitative terms alone, some 16.47 persons were screened by each examiner in the U.S. Zone of Germany, compared with 769.6 in Japan. In addition to the heavy burden of screening in Germany, an enormous effort was required for the mass processing of millions of lengthy questionnaires which were never screened at all. Because of the broadside distribution of the questionnaires to all German adults, only 38.6 per cent of the registered cases were actually screened, and of these only 8.66 per cent were removed and excluded from office. In Japan, where all registered cases were screened, 10.98 per cent were purged.

The differences in the scale of removals in Japan and Germany had no relation to their national social structures. Nearly ten times as many persons were excluded from important public office in Germany as in Japan, proportionately, and nearly seven times as many had to undergo the "screening" process. Yet there is no evidence that the German population was regarded with more suspicion than the Japanese; and it is even more obvious that the German elite group was not larger than the Japanese.[2]

In fact the Japanese operation corresponded, in many ways, more closely to the system in the British zone of Germany, where in general only those persons in positions of authority were screened, than in the U.S. zone, where an attempt was made to sift the entire adult population into Nazis and non-Nazis. (Indeed, perhaps more than the entire population: some thirteen millions of the elaborate American *Fragebogen* were issued to the population which in 1945 can scarcely have been more than some fourteen to fifteen millions: a high proportion of the young men were in prison camps outside the zone: there were certainly many more than two million infants and children in the zone.)

It was in fact a perfectionist's plan. When the operation was at its height the mere reading of the questionnaires required the full-time work of 22,000 Germans. 545 tribunals, or *Spruchkammern*, in the U.S. zone were dealing with as many as 50,000 cases a month. The members of these tribunals, normally three to each, were supposed to include a lawyer, but there were not enough 'denazified' lawyers to go round. The other members of these courts were supposed to be right-thinking, non-Nazi or preferably anti-Nazi Germans, but there were hardly enough of these to go around either, nor was it possible for the Americans always to check on these men's credentials since so many documents had been destroyed either in the bombing or the fighting or deliberately once it was over. Nor did all Germans of impeccably anti-Nazi views, and particularly members of the legal profession, choose to sit on such courts.

There were no full public hearings; no rules of evidence governed the presentation of testimony. All proceedings were "ex parte," offering no opportunity for "prosecution" or "defense." Until a candidate was cleared by these tribunals, he could not occupy any position of importance, and so millions of capable and politically indifferent Germans had to remain idle or engage in "ordinary labour" for an indefinite period. Minor functionaries were often very seriously affected by this procedure, while their frantic employers made appeals to local boards on their behalf so that key staff members and skilled workers could be rehired.

[2] Montgomery, op. cit., pp. 26-27.

Clergymen were busy writing character recommendations for their parishioners and others in order to avoid or mitigate adverse findings (these were sarcastically called "Persil certificates" after a well-known detergent). In the meantime, Nazis whose records had included serious offences followed a policy of watchful waiting while the first fury of denazification reprisals was dissipated on the minor cases that had to be processed first. More active Nazis, who would have been barred from important employment in any case, were content to wait on the sidelines until the fever of revenge (for the motives of denazifiers were not always politically pure) had subsided.[3]

The findings of these tribunals were followed either by a pronouncement of innocence and discharge or by more or less automatic sentences for those found guilty. Major Offenders received from two to ten years of forced labour, confiscation of property, permanent loss of civil rights and of all pensions, restriction as to where they might live, and other punishments. Offenders of the Second Class were given a maximum of five years' forced labour. Minor Offenders received shorter sentences. Followers were, in general, fined. As the Papen denazification process has shown, little attempt was made to judge a man by his 'peers', in this case by men who might be expected to understand the problem with which he had been confronted. Nor were men ruled out as judges who, in Britain and America, would not have been permitted to sit on juries since counsel for the defence would certainly have regarded them as prejudiced. Thus Papen claimed that the court which condemned him in 1947 consisted of one Communist, two Social Democrats, one Liberal and one Christian Democrat.[4] It is to be observed that the court which heard his appeal two years later was drawn from a very different stratum of society. And these were not jurymen but judges.

When the war ended there were very few Germans who were not pleased to see the Nazis disappear, even though they may have regretted the wastage of defeat. They looked at that time to the Americans as liberators. Most of them were probably reconciled to years of future hardship and humiliation, but from all they had been told by the U.S. propagandists they expected at least justice, even if harsh justice, from their conquerors. As a British private soldier is said to have remarked about a famous British general: 'He's a beast, but a just beast.' Instead they had this vast quasi-

[3] Montgomery, op. cit., p. 23.   [4] Papen, op. cit., p. 577.

legal, bureaucratic apparatus clamped down upon them. (It was necessary to fill in a *Fragebogen* in order to obtain a ration card. Thus the alternative was starvation.) Armies of occupation are always beasts in the eyes of the occupied. Denazification made the Germans doubt that the Americans were just.

There was a joke current in Berlin towards the end of the war: 'Which would be the worse, to lose the war or to keep the Nazis?' And the answer was: 'The worst would be to lose the war and still have the Nazis.' To some Germans the bungled, incompetent and legally dubious proceedings of the denazification programme seemed to have produced something not unlike this appalling solution, particularly as so many of the little Nazis were tried and punished while the big ones were not.

No planned sequence of cases from major to minor offenders was revealed in the statistics released by the Office of the Military Governor (see Table 1). On the contrary, the actual denazification findings were relatively constant. Almost the same percentage of the 11,268 cases considered by July, 1946, were found to be "incriminated" (that is, as Major Offenders, Offenders, and Lesser Offenders), as among the entire 947,000 cases reported as of June, 1949. Within the guilt categories themselves the percentages of Major Offender findings declined during this period, while that of Lesser Offenders increased: but these dimensions suggest a haphazard order of processing rather than the reverse, especially since greater leniency was displayed toward a number of important cases that were considered late in the program. The stability of the statistics over a three-year period suggests that the boards were exerting their efforts in the direction of uniformity of findings rather than an absolute standard of justice and helps to explain the almost universal criticism throughout Germany that denazification

Table 1
TRENDS IN DENAZIFICATION FINDINGS, 1946-49 (U.S. ZONE)

Date	Total Cases Processed	Per Cent Major Offenders	Per Cent Offenders	Per Cent Lesser Offenders	Total Per Cent 'Incrimin.'
July, 1946	11,268	0.67	4.23	8.53	13.43
Jan., 1947	183,836	.36	2.32	8.58	11.26
July, 1947	396,796	.17	2.24	9.80	11.41
Jan., 1948	657,050	.15	2.19	11.00	13.34
July, 1948	900,802	.15	2.18	11.05	13.38
Jan., 1949	934,900	.17	2.28	11.24	13.69
June, 1949	947,000	0.15	2.32	11.21	13.70

concentrated its fire on minor Nazis while allowing bigger quarry to escape.⁵

In Ernst von Salomon's autobiography he describes his own arrest, and that of his Jewish mistress, by the Americans. He was beaten up, starved and insulted by the bureaucratic apparatus. His attempt to equate the internment camp, in which he spent a little over a year before his release, with the Nazi concentration camps is, to this writer at least, totally unconvincing. And he does admit that the ignorance of his American captors was the root cause of the cruelties and indignities to which he and 'Ille' were subjected. The whole passage⁶ is far too long to be quoted here, but it is highly relevant to anyone interested in this subject. The book became a German best-seller in the immediate post-denazification period not merely because of its great literary skill and intrinsic historical interest, but also because it damned the whole American idea of how to deal with the Nazis. Although he cannot, and indeed does not expect to be, accepted as a fully reliable witness, this most sensitive artist does reflect in his writing feelings shared by many of his contemporaries. And these are summed up in his descriptions of the men he had met in Nattenberg Camp in 1945 and early 1946. These, in his opinion, were the men who were the object of denazification.

> The Americans meant more or less nothing to me. To be objective about them implied inevitably defending them, and I felt that they were quite men enough to do this job for themselves.
>
> I was far more interested in the National-Socialists. It was true—and it became apparent at the moment of collapse—that despite the 99 per cent plebiscites and the pompous facade of national unity, there had really been two distinct worlds face to face in our country, worlds that knew nothing of each other save, in the one case, what was to be read in the police files and, in the other, what was gossiped in back rooms. The few National-Socialists whom I had known personally could almost be counted on the fingers of two hands, and their company had never interested me, for they talked in their official jargon. In the camp I had got to know them intimately, and luckily for me they no longer spoke in any jargon.
>
> True enough, the choice had been extremely difficult. When the Americans decided to pass the contents of the pot—in which everything had been stewed up together—through the sieve, they found in their

---

⁵ Montgomery, op. cit., pp. 23-24.
⁶ Salomon, op. cit., pp. 430-546.

sieve as many categories of man as there had been in that other pot, the Jewish one. It was the second greatest crime of the *terribles simplificateurs* that they had not attempted to pass the contents of the Jewish pot through the sieve, their greatest being that they had simply destroyed the whole brew.

There was the large, fairly homogeneous group of district leaders, but everyone must admit that to occupy oneself with this group for the purpose of producing any fruitful results would have been a fairly hopeless undertaking. There was the group, almost as large and even more homogeneous, that had been the Waffen-SS; to occupy oneself with it would be an extremely fruitful undertaking but one I dared not tackle. These men grew increasingly hardened beneath the constantly growing pressure of a monstrous slander, until at last they had nothing left on which they could fall back save their honour as soldiers. I might have told them that military honour was no longer so easily defined, since women and girls had stood on rooftops throwing incendiaries and tins of burning phosphorus into courtyards between the waves of bombers—but I could not say this, for I had never seen an incendiary. However, I could tell them that this hardening process was in danger of producing nothing more than the metamorphosis of the 'front-line spirit' as it existed in the First World War into the *Stahlhelm* attitude —a change that was not necessarily fruitful. The large and by no means homogeneous group of senior civil servants—well, that was not likely to intimidate anyone. There could be no doubt that unless some new concept of the state were to crystallise, these skilful, sensible men must certainly, by reason of their solid, expert, professional knowledge, very soon once again become the cadre of the bureaucracy—a fact of which well nigh all of them were quietly and confidently aware—for a bureaucracy has always provided the ideal substitute for a state. And then there was the small group of early Party members who had later risen to high positions within the Party hierarchy. They had had personal, direct contact with their leader, and with his death their lives had lost their meaning.

But among all these groups there were individuals—not many, considerably less than a hundred—who never for a moment attempted to deny that they were really and truly National-Socialists. These were both old men and young, whose lives were conditioned by the phenomenon of National-Socialism, and who had consciously tried to live accordingly. These too were the people who always refrained from joining in the endless discussions that took place in the camp and which almost invariably revolved about the idea of guilt, a guilt that each man searched for—and quite quickly found—in his neighbour. It is not surprising that a very high proportion of this guilt was ascribed to those men who had remained convinced National-Socialists. They seemed to accept it quite calmly, which might have meant nothing but callous insensitivity on their part had not they been specifically intelligent and highly educated men, astonishingly open-minded towards all the problems of life, whose genuine patriotism was not open to dispute and whose behaviour in all matters was in general above reproach. If anyone could give the information wanted, then it must be they: information about the burning questions of the time, questions of recent history, questions of responsibility towards one's own standards, and, last but not least, questions concerning the nature and reality of that force which had proved capable of changing the order of the world and which in some form or other must continue to exert its influence if—and this too remained to be discovered—if this were a force of a spiritual nature.[7]

He goes on to qualify this descriptive catalogue at great length, and the whole passage is of interest, but this short passage shows how alien the concept of 'collective guilt' was to one German and his many readers, and how repulsive American bureaucratic methods made the democratic proselytization to millions of Germans. Luckily, from the American as well as from the German point of view, this strange, ideological enterprise did not go on for long. But it is indeed to be hoped that if ever similar circumstances should arise, and the Government of the United States finds itself in a position to exercise its will upon the citizens of another defeated totalitarian state, the same blueprint will not be produced once again. If the Americans were lucky in Germany, and on the whole they were, this was due to Russian frightfulness, which made the Western Germans prefer the lesser of the two evils in a Cold War which certainly most Americans did not anticipate in 1945. Should such a situation ever arise again, they would be well advised to remember MacArthur in Japan rather than Eisenhower in Germany.

[7] Salomon, op. cit., pp. 514-516.

Chapter Eleven

It is when we try to discuss what was in fact achieved by denazification, that we are perhaps on the most slippery ground of all. This problem can be best divided into three: punishment, administrative cleansing, and re-education or moral reformation.

As a punitive measure, it was not an unqualified success, either in the short term or the long. As General Clay recognized, too many 'little' Nazis were punished at once, too few 'big' Nazis. Furthermore, the whole question of legality was never satisfactorily solved. Retroactive laws enforced by occupying armies are in some ways even less acceptable than drumhead courts martial, since these are understandable as part of the horrors of war. Few Germans felt or feel any humiliation at having been convicted by an American-run denazification court for the crime of having been Nazis at a time when to be so was not only legal, but normal and, as many thought, patriotic. This rejection of the denazification process produced results which were, almost without exception, unfortunate.

If to have been a small Nazi was adjudged a crime, though no criminal act as such has been proven according to the old German criminal code, then those who had committed such crimes could pretend that their punishment was less for their crime or crimes than for their political allegiance or even their nationality. And this gave great persuasive value to the criminals who pleaded 'superior orders': as German Nazis they had obeyed and *therefore* it was as German Nazis that they faced trial. Denazification thus invalidated, for many years, the whole concept of justice in Germany. For some ten years after the creation of the German Federal Republic, this denial of guilt prevailed, both in the public and the private sectors. In the public, the new German authorities very rapidly amnestied convicted German nationals. On occasion, they went even further. When 'Panzer' Meyer, the SS general, who had been convicted by an American court for the murder of Canadian prisoners-of-war, was released from prison by the German authorities long before his sentence had been served, he was treated as a hero, a returned prisoner-of-war, with a torchlight procession and a telegram of congratulation from the Head of State. He became a prominent spokesman for former members of the SS. In 1945 it was hard to find a German who admitted that he had been a devout Nazi: in 1955, it was equally hard to find one who would admit that he had served on a denazification court, for many who had were socially ostracized or economically penalized in their own communities. And some anti-Nazis who had attempted to purge their country of the guilty men now found that emigration was the best answer. This, of course, was Germany's loss, and a permanent one.

Denazification was also intended to purge the new German administration of former Nazis. Here it was more successful in some fields than in others. Since the Nazi régime had only lasted for twelve years, it was not too difficult in 1945 to find politicians of some, sometimes of great, experience who had withdrawn, or been driven, from public life during this period and who were willing or even eager to return. Adenauer and Schumacher were the most outstanding, but there were others. With younger men, it was more difficult. Some anti-Nazis had survived, almost miraculously, at home, such as Herr Gerstenmaier, others abroad, such as Herr Brandt, but there was a noticeable reluctance among men born between, say, 1910 and 1925, to take any part in politics. This was the *Ohne Mich* spirit which wanted to opt out of a country, and indeed of a world, where politics had become incomprehensible and, at times, lethal. German political life suffered, and still suffers to some extent, from this generation's cynicism. Karl Jaspers has analysed this with his usual subtlety:

> When the republic was founded, the unincriminated—that half-million or so of Germans who had never wavered—did not, or could not, take command. Was it an insoluble task? A majority of our people was seriously incriminated, though in varying measure and in varying ways. Now we were to form a new state and repudiate the old one as criminal, but the people, for the time being, remained the same. The mass prevailed; the minority kept silent and inactive. For a time the others were glad to have individual figures from this minority represent the new Germany before the victors, serving, as it were, to shield

the majority. The incriminated benefited by the tolerance of the unincriminated, whether it was due to magnanimity or to opportunism. The unincriminated in turn failed to realize how radical a change was needed. They played a cozy, comfortable kind of politics and held their high offices with the consent of the incriminated, being not truly serious about the liberal demands but content with rhetoric. They were wanted as long as the new state with the old mentality had not yet won independent power. Once it had that power, once it began to look less and less like a new state, they became superfluous.

But the half-million or so who had kept their heads clear throughout and remained unincriminated were subsequently sidetracked or forced to see their libertarian idea tacitly thwarted rather than put into practice.[1]

The purging of the administrative apparatus was even more difficult. The German civil service—the *Beamtentum*—had previously enjoyed a very high esteem both in the eyes of its members and of their compatriots. It had therefore been a primary target for Hitler's *Gleichschaltung*. Together with the Nazi Party's administrative apparatus and the armed forces, it had provided the pillars on which the Nazi state rested and the organization which largely implemented that state's policies, criminal and otherwise. Almost every single German civil servant, apart from the handful of active resisters and deliberate saboteurs, was a direct accomplice in Crimes against Humanity and in Crimes against Peace. The genocide of the Jews alone had ramifications throughout almost the entire administrative apparatus, from the railroad officials who organized the trains, through the various ministries responsible for building the death camps, to the bank officials who stowed away the gold fillings torn from the mouths of the dead.

And not only were the civil servants, in the British and American sense, almost without exception incriminated. There were other large and highly sensitive sectors of public life where it was extremely difficult to find an innocent man. The law, the police, the teachers . . . the list is almost endless. In order to satisfy the purists and perfectionists, particularly among the Americans who had devised the concept of denazification, all these men, or at least some 90% of them, should have been excluded from public life forever. And this applied to most big and many medium-sized businesses as well.

[1] Jaspers, op. cit., p. 65.

It could obviously not be done. Any modern state, even in defeat and occupied by foreign armies, needs a huge administrative apparatus. The men who run that apparatus cannot simply be created. Therefore, the old administrators, judges, school teachers and so on were generally denazified, sometimes punished, and usually retained in their old or similar jobs. In general, the major offenders and men convicted of specific crimes in a court of law were dismissed—though many slipped through—but save in so far as the denazification courts unearthed some of these criminals, those courts had very little effect on German public life.

What about the effect of denazification on the Germans, that is to say, its educational influences as an instrument for moral reform and for democratization? Professor Guenther Roth and Professor Kurt H. Wolff, two distinguished American sociologists, studied this problem in the field. Professor Wolff was in charge of a team of experts who interviewed the Germans. He has described the men and women who were interviewed as follows:

> The reactions come from 188 Germans who were interviewed in ten small and middle-sized communities in the three occupation zones (four in the American, three each in the French and British) in the summer of 1953. They were selected so as to reflect, presumably, different reactions: they included those who had undergone denazification (roughly 65 per cent), those who had done the denazifying (10 per cent), and "non-chargeables" (25 per cent), that is, those who on the basis of the questionnaire they had filled out were exempted from denazification—this last category contained many who had been picked for background information on their communities. At the end of the war, every third of the interviewees had been in military service, a fifth had had a party function, 16 per cent each had been in business and public services, 11 per cent in the professions, and 4 per cent had been workers. At the time of the interview, on the other hand, a third were in public and private services, 28 per cent each in business and the professions, and 11 per cent in manual work. They thus were more on the "knowledgeable" side of affairs and also, and heavily, on the side of higher age: nine out of ten were over 40, seven out of ten over 50, and almost four out of ten over 60. In general, therefore, it is probably right to assume that this population was more articulate in reacting to denazification than a less bureaucratic, academic, and old group would have been.

In the following year, he and Professor Roth wrote a paper

entitled *The American Denazification of Germany: A Historical Survey and an Appraisal*, privately printed by the Department of Sociology and Anthropology, Ohio State University. They have kindly given me their permission that I quote from this most learned treatise, but though my conclusions almost always coincide with theirs, they are my own.

By 1953, denazification was a thing of the past. What is of particular interest in this scientific appraisal—I shall spare the reader the scientific terms employed by the sociologists—is the memories it had left behind. The first was of injustice. The second, an aping of Nazi methods: [2]

> MG had instituted five classes into which chargeable cases had to be divided: Major Offenders, Offenders, Minor Offenders, Followers, and Persons Exonerated. The tribunals' procedure was to place the defendant, chiefly on the basis of his questionnaire, into one of the five categories. It was *his* task to prove that he had the right to a lower placement. In consequence of this practice, the tribunals were flooded by what may be called exculpation certificates, soon known as *Persilscheine*, whitewash slips, after *Persil*, a brand of soap flakes. Furthermore, many persons were reluctant to testify against a defendant because they feared public opinion, which disapproved likewise. Secret denunciations and false accusations, however, were not rare. They reached their peak during the first year, when they caused the defendant to lose his job or to be confined to an internment camp without his knowing why or having any opportunity for rehabilitating himself.

The reversal of the burden of proof involved in this procedure has been severely criticized. Yet the tribunals could not possibly have investigated the behavior of every individual prior to finding on him: this would have delayed their work so as to defeat one of the intentions of the Law, the defendant's speedy return to normal life. While the legal and moral objection to the reversed burden of proof is very serious, the volume of cases made another procedure practically impossible. The situation could have been saved only if the Law had applied to a much smaller number of persons in the first place.

All who filled out a questionnaire or deposed other written documents before the tribunals had to testify in lieu of oath to the correctness of their statements. Critics of denazification have claimed that this and the many *Persilscheine* amounted to a ridiculous devaluation of the oath and its dignity. Here, as in regard to other aspects of denazification, the legal and moral concerns which emerge are even more properly applicable to Nazi phenomena. The significance of the oath had become

[2] Roth and Wolff, op. cit., pp. 16-17.

doubtful at the latest over a decade before, when the *Führer* and Blomberg, then Commander of the Reichswehr, on the occasion of the death of President Hindenburg and a few weeks after the murders of June 30, 1934, hurriedly had the army swear to the person of Adolf Hitler, a step which came close to being a *coup d'état*. But if one were to "balance" the two devaluations of the oath, or of the word, one would be victimized by the morality of the balance sheet. Both must be condemned.

Indeed, the whole procedure, which was intended to 'democratize' the Germans, itself took on an increasingly undemocratic hue, at least in German eyes:[3]

When in 1945 American public opinion pressed for a more severe denazification policy, in Germany there was no public opinion. Its bases, the free development and competition of thought, had not existed under Nazism, which had only an official view, manufactured by Goebbels. Opposition had gone underground or exploded in political jokes, although the regime tried to manipulate even them. Nor could public opinion crystallize immediately after the collapse, because the political, even the technical facilities for it were lacking. Months passed without there being any political parties, and hardly a communication system, including newspapers, regular train service, or mail. Military government had to rule by decree, as the Nazis had done. Political jokes, therefore, continued until democratic institutions, especially political parties, were established, beginning toward the end of 1945. Then public opinion started to develop, and the disappearance of the jokes was striking.

For the new parties, denazification became an ever worse nightmare because public opinion grew increasingly antagonistic toward it. The Communists left the tribunals as early as '47, justifying their move with the argument that the 'little' Nazis were being persecuted too severely. (The hoped-for increase in votes, however, did not materialize.) A little later, the Christian Democrats and the Free Democrats withdrew many of their tribunal officials so that in the end often the Social Democrats alone hung on.

With the establishment of tribunals, denazification became the only part of Allied and German politics that could be influenced directly by individuals, rather than indirectly through press and parliament. The tribunals, which existed in every town of any size, were exposed to the influence of both public opinion and particular persons. In the American Zone it was as common to write "purification certificates" or put pressure on tribunal personnel as it is in America to send letters

[3] Roth and Wolff, op. cit., pp. 21-22.

to newspaper editors and congressmen. The importance of this direct contact became evident in the discussion of German rearmament some years later. This issue was discussed as violently as denazification had been, and was rejected with a resentment which in part derived from the denazification experience. But public opinion did not manage to influence the development of remilitarization as it had that of denazification. The reason was not only the fact that the rearmament problem was a matter of political negotiations which did not yet have a great impact on the lives of large numbers of people, but also that the special circumstances which permitted a direct influence on denazification did not exist.

The Soviets amnestied—at least in theory—all nominal Nazis in August, 1947, thus bringing to an end their version of denazification. The Americans ground on with their process for two more years. And more and more it seemed to the Germans that what they were watching, and were being subjected to, was less a process of 'democratization' than a sort of *Gleichschaltung* in reverse, the substitution of an ideology based on sterile and unfair legalism, for another also based upon a sterile and murderous racism, both with the basic revolutionary intent of supplanting one governing class by another. K. H. Knappstein, then Deputy Minister for Political Liberation, wrote at this time:[4]

> At least since the defeat of Stalingrad, a revolution was due in Germany, which never materialized, however. . . . Revolution was by-passed by Capitulation. . . . After the capitulation, an understandable fusion of parallel forces inside and outside emerged: when German democrats and Allied victors met, they found they had one aim in common: the elimination and permanent removal of the past ruling class . . . from all positions in government, economy, and culture. It is the intrinsic aim of every revolution which is a genuine transformation to deprive the former elite of its power and to elevate a new elite into the key position. In Germany, however, this "natural means" was lacking. Hence the attempt at achieving by rational means, laws and legal institutions, what appeared to have been missed by the failure of a spontaneous social "natural catastrophe" to take place. An artificial revolution was organized, as it were: denazification. It probably is the first time in history that an attempt was made at bringing about legally, through organization and legislation, not revolution itself, but the most important product of revolution, the removal of the elite. Such

---

[4] Karl Heinrich Knappstein, *Die Versaeumte Revolution*, 'Die Wandlung', Vol. 2, 1947, p. 664, quoted by Roth and Wolff, op. cit., p. 26.

an artificial solution of the problem may well be possible, may even be affirmed, but one must be clear that at bottom it *is* a revolutionary act, even if it proceeds in more civilized and rational forms than a "wild" revolution does. But one also must see the danger that the ambition to remain "legal" and stay within the framework of "peace and order" can only too easily limit and even destroy the effect of the whole action, that is, the real transformation of the elite. For there are no arguments against the revolution which has "broken out", whereas the artificial revolution can be choked to death on its own rational plane by arguments and reports . . . The fathers of the artificial revolution of denazification did not know or did not heed this elementary empirical law of revolutions.

In 1953, Professors Roth and Wolff concluded, in parts, as follows:[5]

Whereas most measures connected with denazification gave democratic forces a real chance, the mass purge did not, was unnecessary, and made for strong resentment which ought to have been avoided. The prohibition of Nazi organizations had eliminated most functionaries, and governmental administration had collapsed. Key positions in the communities could have been occupied by new people; other persons could have been left where they were. Few were thinking of obstructing Allied efforts and policies, not only for fear of losing their jobs but because of a genuine readiness for loyal cooperation. The situation was chaotic and could have been structured in ways other than it was. The somewhat static conception of the "Nazi" and later the fivefold classifications did not help much in the appraisal of individuals. When was a person "really" a Nazi? In 1933? In the war? What does he think now? Differences and distinctions became clear, if at all, too late. In the beginning, denazification was dominated by the notion of the Nazi monolith made up of the German people. It did not exist; and the blows designed to shatter it hit the most heterogeneous persons.

If denazification had not been so broad, it could have focussed on people who could reasonably be supposed to have committed crimes or who would be likely to sabotage efforts to reconstruct Germany. This would have saved personnel, the need for accepting incompetent and unreliable employees, and graft. In the popular image of the denazification tribunals, they consisted overwhelmingly of good-for-nothings and corruptible opportunists.

While the mass purge hit people too indiscriminately, the later attempts at dispensing individual justice once more suffered from the large number of cases. For reasons of both propriety and expediency,

[5] Roth and Wolff, op. cit., pp. 33-37.

their volume made it necessary to dispose of the lighter cases first, because prior to the findings by the tribunal, a person could only do ordinary labor. The long period of waiting was a hardship for many among the less incriminated. Since denazification became ever milder, those fared relatively worse than did the more serious offenders who had had every reason to delay their trials as long as possible. The well-known case of the former secretary of state of Goebbels, Werner Naumann, is in point. He had not been denazified when he was arrested in January '53 by the British police on the charge of conspiracy against the British Occupation authority and the Federal Republic . . .

The great mistake of denazification thus was the mass purge, which was based on erroneous assumptions and on neglect of available information. By a stroke of irony, it created a pathetic "community of fate" ("*Schicksalsgemeinschaft*") between small and big Nazis, the persiflage of the glorious "community of fate" which Nazi propaganda had tried to make of the whole German people. For the mass purge cancelled the differences between the high Nazi functionaries and the common members of the numerous Nazi organizations. It also necessitated a tremendous administrative machinery, facilitated the morality of the balance sheet, and permitted a crude quantification and even commercialization of guilt and responsibility. Guilt and responsibility, however, cannot be shoved off to particular groups, neither to 100,000 internees, nor to three million charges, nor can it be determined by administrative fiat or atoned for by administrative ritual. The ambivalent character of denazification as mass purge and punishment and the blurring of guilt, responsibility, and liability led to its moral, political, and organizational failure.

But it is not only the proponents of a "hard policy" toward Germany who are responsible for this mass purge, even though their influence on the design of denazification was decisive. American public opinion affirmed measures bound to lead to purge and punishment *en masse*, and pressed for such measures. This affirmation and pressure spring from the traditional American tendency to have a moralistic and legalistic perspective on one's wars and one's enemies. Since the United States had been threatened in both World Wars I and II, participation in them was widely interpreted as the launching of a crusade or punitive expedition which, moreover, was to end war for all times. With isolationism weakened and Germany an enemy for the second time in 25 years, the fight had to be total and it had to end in the foe's unconditional surrender, which would be followed by a complete revamping of conditions in the enemy country. Thus in 1945, a public opinion which had followed such a train of ideas and events considered a total purge a necessity. While the planners of denazification adopted this technique from the totalitarian system, oddly enough, they made membership in totalitarian organizations the criterion for applying the technique. But membership in organizations is another means of the totalitarian state, which lures and forces people into their fold in order the better to control them.

The moralistic and legalistic attitude which contributed so much to the attempt at a total purge, in the end prevented it from becoming total altogether. In a totalitarian regime, the purged individual usually is lost. He cannot appeal to any authority, and neither the public nor particular persons can intervene on his behalf. Denazification, by contrast, had a second phase when the attempt was made to do justice to the individual. But this second phase, too, failed, because of legal complications and contradictions, and thus completed the abortion of the whole undertaking.

By 1953, of course, both the international and the internal German situations were utterly different from what they had been eight years earlier. The Korean War was nearing its conclusion, nor had it been fought with any remarkable gentleness by the Americans and their allies: no more were French attempts to pacify Indochina and Algeria carried out with kid glove treatment: but the Cold War, above all, and the resultant publicity given to the Stalinist terror in Russia and Eastern Europe, had deprived the moralizers of their principal argument. Even the best Germans, and those who most sincerely deplored Hitlerite crime, now found it increasingly hard to accept the idea of collective guilt with its corollary that the German people were somehow imbued with a higher degree of original sin than their former enemies. The worst, and stupidest, went far beyond this. The Russians were evil, weren't they? Therefore Hitler had been right to attack them, hadn't he? And as for the Jews, well, a mistake perhaps, but then you can't make an omelette without breaking eggs, can you? This was the period when the Nazis were re-emerging more and more openly. The Socialist Reich Party, led by the man who, as a soldier, had put down the 20 July, 1944, putsch, was openly Nazi. (It was later declared illegal: its leader fled abroad.) Associations of former SS men met openly and boasted about their past bravery in the field (though not, at least in public, about their achievements in the camps.) The League of the Homeless and the Expelled, Germans from the lost Eastern territories, became a fairly potent political force, with a definite Nazi tinge. Other associations of the same kind came into existence, including the Victims of Denazification, numbering some 30,000 members in 1954, who were hardly anti-Nazi in their views. In rebuilding the German state, Adenauer was prepared to give high office to men such as Globke and Oberlaender with a very bad political record, while he evinced a marked distaste for the few surviving men of 20 July; he, too, liked authority, and distrusted those who opposed it.

In western liberal circles, and particularly in Britain, many people began to fear the worst. The Germans, it was felt, were incorrigible: Nazism was just around the corner once again. The war had been fought, and won, in vain.

But for the mass of the German population, all this was of very little importance. The currency reforms and the creation of the Federal Republic in the late 1940s had permitted a vast economic expansion. In retrospect, the 'Economic Miracle' seems less impressive than it did in the early 1950s, but there can be no doubt that, in those days, the *enrichissez-vous* philosophy of the Bonn government offered a most attractive alternative to political brooding about the past. Most Germans were only too happy to stop thinking about Nazis, anti-Nazis and denazifiers. The fact that the Americans had executed one of the great *renversements d'alliances* and were now allied with the Germans against the Russians gave an air of political respectability to this denial of the past. While for those who worried about the future of their country, the 'European ideal', essentially a French concept invented by Jean Monnet, was a new departure which promised the Germans an opportunity for dumping a lot of unwanted political baggage. This made a particular appeal to the young, to the post-war generation that was beginning to emerge. For their compromised seniors, the defence of European freedom through European unity provided, in a way, an ex post facto justification. Indeed, the cynics of the time said in Germany that any man who spoke of peace was a Communist, while the Nazis talked only of freedom. During the 1950s, it might be said that the unformulated policy of most Germans, both in private and in public, was to forget that there had ever been a Nazi government.

The Allensbach Institute for Demoscopy, a sort of Gallup Poll organization, carried out a poll in May, 1954. Of those questioned, 47% had a poor opinion of Hitler, 24% a good one, with the very high proportion of 29% 'don't know'. In November of that year, the same Institute carried out a poll among young people born between 1936 and 1940. Most of these knew nothing about the Nazi régime, or so the poll reports. Indeed, the subject was not in the school curricula (it is now, in most *Laender*) for a sort of conspiracy of silence had descended both upon the teachers—almost all ex-Nazis at that time—and upon the parents too.

Former Nazi officials and SS generals now received pensions (Law 131). With the establishment of the Federal Republic, even the trial of criminals, for crimes against the Nazis' chosen enemies, ceased until 1954. By then the process was in some measure in reverse in West Germany, while in Berlin active measures against the Nazis continued. Indeed, in May of that year, Berlin's Social Democrat chairman, Franz Neumann, declared: 'The greatest scandal threatening post-war democracy in Germany is the renazification of the public administration'.[6]

However, not all Germans were prepared to accept these compromised men, let alone the real criminals. According to a stoutly anti-Nazi periodical issued by the German Trade Unions,[7] it was the return from Russian captivity of many criminal Nazis, a repatriation which really began in 1955, that led to a severe questioning of the Bonn régime's permissive attitude. It would seem probable that much attention was devoted to these men for fear lest there be communist agents among them. But to quote the article in question, it was soon found that 'there were lice in the pelt' again. A group of politicians of all parties took the line that a true German enquiry into past Nazi crimes was overdue. And the trials began again.

One of the major administrative reforms carried out under the Allied Control Commission, and intended to weaken the powers for evil of the German state, had been the decentralization of the German police force. In the early days of the Nazi régime, Edgar J. Hoover, head of the United States Federal Bureau of Investigation, had described the German police force as the most efficient in the world in the detection of crime. Unfortunately it was also the most efficient in other, less admirable, activities. It was therefore deliberately broken up, as part of the denazification policy, so that each *Land* had its own police force, and the liaison between these forces was kept to a low level. This applied and applies, though to a lesser extent, among the departments of the various

---

[6] *American Jewish Year Book*, 1954, Vol. 55, p. 243.
[7] *Für die Demokratie*, Vol. 6, No. 2, March 1965, p. 2.

public prosecutors of the *Laender*. (In England, each county has its own constabulary, in the United States, each state its own police. In Britain, they are well co-ordinated, and it does a criminal little good to cross a county border. In the United States the crossing of a state line gives minor criminals, and some major ones, a measure of relief. The F.B.I. is a very modern invention, which only intervenes reluctantly and in serious cases, and then almost always, except where federal offences are concerned, at the request of the individual state's or states' police forces. Like so much in Federal Germany, the democratic police force followed the American model.) One result of this has been that the German police, unless *gleichgeschaltet*, would be a cumbrous instrument for enforcing any new totalitarian rule. Another is that undetected common crime has, according to *Time Magazine*, December 5th, 1967, increased by some 47% in the past fifteen years. But a third, and to this book relevant, result—and certainly one not wished for by the Allied powers—is that it became very easy for Nazi criminals to move on and escape prosecution.

Indeed, this became, to German anti-Nazis during the period of Nazi tolerance in the 1950s, so scandalous a state of affairs, that a Central Agency for the Investigation of Nazi Crimes was created at Ludwigsburg in 1958. This was a Federal office, which has done much in bringing many criminals before the German courts. The prime mover in creating this admirable and highly efficient bureau —it was responsible for the Auschwitz Trial among others—was Herr Eugen Kogon, author of *Der SS Staat*, which is the greatest personal documentation on Nazi atrocities so far published. Unfortunately, the usual sequel of farce to tragedy took place. It was discovered that the first head of the Agency was himself an ex-Nazi. . . . Nevertheless, it has continued to do good work in bringing criminals to justice. And, perhaps more important, it was a German foundation intent, at a most difficult period, on bringing German criminals to trial in German courts. In this admirable aim it has undoubtedly achieved great success, and has alerted the young to some of the dangers under which many of their parents succumbed.

How many Nazis are there left in Germany? I refer the reader to Appendix 2, which seems to this writer an excellent, if rather long-winded, summary. Anything of a later date must take on the nature of contemporary polemic, which is not the purpose of this book. That there are many men and women tainted to a greater or less degree with Nazi ideas is inevitable, but those guilty of criminal acts can scarcely be less than fifty years old. That some of the young will have acquired those ideas is also inevitable. The evidence is, at present, that they are few, despite some recent *Land* elections. There was some synagogue daubing and other Nazi unpleasantness by young hooligans in the winter of 1959-60. The world immediately feared the worst, but the nastiness rapidly subsided. The German Federal Government published a white paper on the subject. Dr Gerhard Schröder, then Minister of the Interior, made a speech in the Bundestag which served as introduction to this white paper, and sums up admirably the whole problem of neo-Nazism as it existed in 1960. It is quoted in Appendix 2. Since that date, little has changed. There are ideas abroad which are far more attractive to those who hate our society, with its democratic basis, than an outmoded form of totalitarianism which, above all, failed. And, what is perhaps more important, a democracy as fair as any in the world today has, in 1968, survived through close upon twenty years of German sovereignty. Few would have believed this possible in 1945. For all its faults and follies, denazification may have helped to achieve this admirable end. But in history, there is no end. . . .

Appendix 1

Extracts from: The Answers of Ernst von Salomon to the 131 Questions in the Allied Military Government 'Fragebogen'. London: Putnam, 1954 (*Der Fragebogen* first published in Germany, 1951.)

MILITARY GOVERNMENT OF GERMANY FRAGEBOGEN

WARNING: Read the entire Fragebogen carefully before you start to fill it out. The English language will prevail if discrepancies exist between it and the German translation. Answers must be typewritten or printed clearly in block letters. Every question must be answered precisely and conscientiously and no space is to be left blank. If a question is to be answered by either 'yes' or 'no' print the word 'yes' or 'no' in the appropriate space. If the question is inapplicable, so indicate by some appropriate word or phrase such as 'none' or 'not applicable'. Add supplementary sheets if there is not enough space in the questionnaire. Omissions or false or incomplete statements are offences against Military Government and will result in prosecution and punishment.

A. PERSONAL

1. List position for which you are under consideration (include agency of firm)
2. Name:
Surname: Fore Names:
3. Other names which you have used or by which you have been known
4. Date of birth
5. Place of Birth
6. Height
7. Weight
8. Colour of Hair
9. Colour of Eyes

10. Scars, marks or deformities
    (a)
    (b)
    (c)
11. Present address (City, street and house number)
12. Permanent address (City, street and house number)
13. Identity card, type and number
14. Wehrpass No.
15. Passport No.
16. Nationality
17. If a naturalized citizen, give date and place of naturalization
18. List any titles of nobility ever held by you or your wife or by the parents or grandparents of either of you
19. Religion
20. With what church are you affiliated?
21. Have you ever severed your connection with any church, officially or unofficially?
22. If so, give particulars and reasons
23. What religious preference did you give in the census of 1933?
24. List any crimes of which you have been convicted, giving dates, location and nature of the crimes

B. SECONDARY AND HIGHER EDUCATION

Name and Type of School (If a special Nazi school or military academy, so specify)	Location	Dates of Attendance	Certificate, Diploma or Degree	Did Abitur Permit University Matriculation?	Date

25. List any German University Student Corps to which you have ever belonged
26. List (giving locations and dates) any Adolf Hitler school, Nazi Leaders College or military academy in which you have ever been a teacher
27. Have any of your children ever attended any such schools? Which ones, where and when?

28. List (giving location and dates) any school in which you have ever been a Vertrauenslehrer (formerly Jugendwalter)

C. PROFESSIONAL OR TRADE EXAMINATIONS

Name of Examination	Place Taken	Result	Date

D. CHRONOLOGICAL RECORD OF FULL TIME EMPLOYMENT AND MILITARY SERVICE

29. Give a chronological history of your employment and military service beginning with 1st of January 1931, accounting for all promotions or demotions, transfers, periods of unemployment, attendance at educational institutions (other than those covered in

From	To	Employer and Address or Military Unit	Name and Title of Immediate Superior or C.O.	Position or Rank	Duties and Responsibilities
					Reason for Change of Status or Cessation of Service

Section B) or training schools and full-time service with para military organizations. (Part time employment is to be recorded in Section F.) Use a separate line for each change in your position or rank or to indicate periods of unemployment or attendance at training schools or transfer from one military or para military organisation to another

30. Were you deferred from Military Service?
31. If so, explain circumstances completely
32. Have you ever been a member of the General Staff Corps?
33. When?
34. Have you ever been a Nazi Military Leadership Officer?
35. When and in what unit?
36. Did you serve as part of the Military Government or Wehrkreis-administration in any country occupied by Germany including Austria and Sudetenland?
37. If so, give particulars of offices held, duties performed, location and period of service

38. Do you have any military orders or military honours?

39. If so, state what was awarded you, the date, reasons and occasions for its bestowal

E. MEMBERSHIP IN ORGANISATIONS

40. Indicate on the following chart whether or not you were a member of and any offices you have held in the organizations listed below. Use lines 96 to 98 to specify any other associations, society, fraternity, union, syndicate, chamber, institute, group, corporation, club or other organisation of any kind, whether social, political, professional, educational, cultural, industrial, commercial or honorary, with which you have ever been connected or associated.

Column 1: Insert either 'yes' or 'no' on each line to indicate whether or not you have ever been a member of the organization listed. If you were a candidate, disregard the columns and write in the word 'candidate' followed by the date of your application for membership.

Column 2: Insert date on which you joined.

Column 3: Insert date your membership ceased if you are no longer a member. Insert the word 'Date' if you are still a member.

Column 4: Insert your membership number in the organization.

Column 5: Insert the highest office rank or other post of authority which you have held at any time. If you have never held an office, rank or post of authority, insert the word 'none' in Columns 5 and 6.

Column 6: Insert date of your appointment to the office, rank or post of authority listed in Column 5.

	Yes or No	*From*	*To*	*Number*	*Highest Office Rank Held*	*Date Appointed*
41. National-Socialist Party						
42. General SS						
43. Armed SS						
44. SS Security Service						
45. SA						
46. Hitler Youth League German Maidens						

	Yes or No	From	To	Number	Highest Office Rank Held	Date Appointed
47. NSD St B						
48. NS Do B						
49. NS Women's Org.						
50. NS Motor Corps						
51. NS Flying Corps						
52. Off. German officials						
53. DAF						
54. Strength through Joy						
55. NS Welfare						
56. NS Nurses' League						
57. NSKOV						
58. NS Tech. League						
59. NS Med. League						
60. NS Reach. League						
61. NS Leg. League						
62. Germ. Women's Union						
63. Germ. Family League						
64. NS Phys. Cult. L.						
65. NS Vet. League						
66. Germ. Stud. Org.						
67. Germ. Parish Org.						
68. NS War Vet. League						
69. State Prof. Union						
70. State Culture Chamber						
71. Ch. Germ. Writing						
72. Ch. Germ. Press						
73. Ch. Germ. Radio						
74. Ch. Germ. Theatre						
75. Ch. Germ. Music						

	Yes or No	From	To	Number	Highest Office Rank Held	Date Appointed
76. Ch. Germ. Art						
77. Ch. Germ. Film						
78. American Inst.						
79. Germ. Acad. Munich						
80. Germ. Foreign Inst.						
81. Germ. Christ. Movement						
82. Germ. Faith Movement						
83. Germ. Fichte League						
84. Germ. Hunters' League						
85. Germ. Red Cross						
86. Span. Amer. Inst.						
87. Inst. Jewish Question						
88. Comrades League USA						
89. East Eur. Inst.						
90. Nat. Lab. Serv.						
91. Nat. Col. League						
92. Nat. Air Def. League						
93. State Acad. Racial and Health Service						
94. Union Germans Abroad						
95. Advis. Off. Germ. Econ.						

Others (Specify)
96.
97.
98.

99. Have you ever sworn an oath of secrecy to any organization?
100. If so, list the organizations and give particulars
101. Have you any relatives who have held office, rank or post of authority in any of the organisations listed from 41 to 95 above?
102. If so, give their names and addresses, their relationship to you and a description of the position and organization
103. With the exception of minor contributions to the Winterhilfe and regular membership dues, list and give details of any contributions of money or property which you have made directly or indirectly to the NSDAP or any of the other organizations listed above, including any contributions made by any natural or juridical person or legal entity through your solicitation of influence
104. Have you ever been the recipient of any titles, ranks, medals, testimonials or other honours from any of the above organizations?
105. If so state the nature of the honour, the date conferred, and the reason and occasion for its bestowal
106. Were you a member of a political party before 1933?
107. If so, which one?
108. For what political party did you vote in the election of November 1932?
109. In March 1933?
110. Have you ever been a member of any anti-Nazi underground party or groups since 1933?
111. Which one?
112. Since when?
113. Have you ever been a member of any trade union or professional or business organization which was dissolved or forbidden since 1933?
114. Have you ever been dismissed from the civil service, the teaching profession or ecclesiastical positions or any other employment for active or passive resistance to the Nazis or their ideology?
115. Have you ever been imprisoned, or have restrictions of movement, residence or freedom to practise your trade or profession been imposed on you for racial or religious reasons or because of active or passive resistance to the Nazis?
116. If you answered yes to any of the questions from 110 to 115, give particulars and the names and addresses of two persons who can confirm the truth of your statements

F. PART TIME SERVICE WITH ORGANISATIONS

117. With the exception of those you have specially mentioned in Sections D and E above, list: (a) Any part time, unpaid or honorary position of authority or trust you have held as a representative of any Reich Ministry or the Office of the Four Year Plan or similar central control agency; (b) Any office, rank or post of authority you have held with any economic self-administration organization such as the Reich Food Estate, the Bauernschaften, the Central Marketing Associations, the Reichswirtschaftskammer, the Gauwirtschaftskammer, the Reichsgruppen, the Wirtschaftsgruppen, the Verkehrsgruppen, the Reichsvereinigung, the Hauptausschüsse, the Industrieringe and similar organizations, as well as their subordinate or affiliated organizations and field offices; (c) Any service of any kind you have rendered in any military, paramilitary, police, law enforcement, protection, intelligence or civil defence organizations such as Organization Todt, Technische Nothilfe, Stosstruppen, Werkscharen, Bahnschutz, Funkschutz, Werkschutz, Land-und-Stadtwacht, Abwehr, SD, Gestapo and similar organizations.

From	To	Name and Type of Organisation	Highest Office or Rank you Held	Date of Your Appointment	Duties

G. WRITINGS AND SPEECHES

118. List on a separate sheet the titles and publishers of all publications from 1923 to the present which were written in whole or in part, or compiled or edited by you, and all public addresses made by you, giving subject, date and circulation or audience. If they were sponsored by any organization, give its name. If no speeches or publications, write 'none' in this space.

H. INCOME AND ASSETS

119. Show the sources and amount of your annual income from January 1 1931 to date. If records are not available, give approximate amounts.

Year	Source of Income	Amount

120. List any land or buildings owned by you or any immediate members of your family, giving locations, dates of acquisition, from whom acquired, nature and description of buildings, the number of hectares and the use to which the property is commonly put.
121. Have you or any immediate members of your family ever acquired property which had been seized from others for political, religious or racial reasons or expropriated from others in the course of occupation of foreign countries or in furtherance of the settling of Germans or Volksdeutsche in countries occupied by Germany?
122. If so, give particulars, including dates and locations, and the names and whereabouts of the original title holders.
123. Have you ever acted as an administrator or trustee of Jewish property in furtherance of Aryanization decrees or of ordinances?
124. If so, give particulars

I. TRAVEL OR RESIDENCE ABROAD

125. List all journeys or residence outside of Germany including military campaigns
126. Was the journey made at your expense?
127. If not, at whose expense was the journey made?
128. Persons or organizations visited
129. Did you ever serve in any capacity as part of the civil administration of any territory annexed to or occupied by the Reich?
130. If so, give particulars of office held, duties performed, location and period of service
131. List foreign languages you speak indicating degree of fluency

REMARKS

The statements on this form are true and I understand that any omissions or false or incomplete statements are offences against Military Government and will subject me to prosecution and punishment.

Signed   *Date*

CERTIFICATION OF IMMEDIATE SUPERIOR

(Verify that the above is the true name and signature of the individual concerned and that, with the exceptions noted below, the answers made on the questionnaire are true to the best of my knowledge and belief and the information available to me. Exceptions—if no exceptions, write 'none')

   Signed   *Official Position*
      Date

Appendix 2

Antisemitic and Nazistic Incidents

Dr Gerhard Schröder,
Federal Minister of the Interior

made the following statement in the Bundestag, when the White Book of the Federal Government *Antisemitic and Nazistic Incidents* was debated on the 18th February 1960:

'Yesterday the Federal Government submitted to this House and to the general public a survey of the antisemitic and nazistic incidents which took place in the Federal Republic between the 25th December, 1959 and the 28th January, 1960. In making this statement, I am assuming that all members of the House are acquainted with the contents of the White Book, and that they are probably anxious to learn what developments have taken place in the period between the 28th January and the 15th February. Perhaps I may briefly state the facts:

Since that date, a further 148 incidents have been investigated, though most of these actually occurred before January 28th. Among them, there were again some 31 scribblings by children.

The incidents described in the White Book were spread throughout the Federal Republic. A breakdown of their occurrence in the various Länder did not lead to any significant result. In my view, the frequency of incidents in Berlin—123 out of 685 up to 28th January, and 160 out of 833 up to 15th February—is probably explained by the fact that in Berlin instigators from the Soviet Zone have been able to be rather more active than elsewhere. The age-groups of the perpetrators—321 of whom are at present known—are the same as in previous investigations.

A breakdown of the occupations and motives of the perpetrators did not lead to any startling results either.

The Federal Government intends to publish more facts, as soon as a more or less definite survey of the situation becomes possible. Further light on Communist participation in these events is thrown by one particular incident which has not been mentioned in the White Book. At the end of January 1960, a building at Tennenbronn near St. Georgen in the Black Forest was daubed with swastikas by a group of people two of whom had only last year been in a camp of the FDJ (*Free German Youth*) in the Soviet Zone. A search of their homes led to the discovery of copies of the newspaper *Neues Deutschland* which in its edition of 5th January 1960 printed a cartoon showing the Federal Government adorned with swastikas.

Having explained all this, I should now like to try and answer some of the questions raised both in Germany and abroad, and to point to some of the conclusions which have been reached by the Federal Government.

First of all, I should like to repeat that the population of the Federal Republic showed indignation and disgust at the first news of the swastika daubings. Wherever possible, people gave help to the police investigations. There was general contempt for the culprits among their fellow-citizens. No attempts were made to explain these deeds away, the general public was unanimous in its condemnation, and the perpetrators found themselves in moral isolation. This attitude expressed itself in public meetings, in letters to the press, in private conversations and in many individual actions. The German people does not dismiss these daubings as the vile work of a few incorrigible fanatics or as mainly gutter politics only concerning the police and the courts. It looks upon them rather as an evil violation of its desire—a desire which has expressed itself in deeds—for restitution, reconciliation and general tolerance.

What education has so far been given?

The sensation caused by these incidents all over the world was exploited by a Communist propaganda campaign which tried to blacken the Federal Government by calling it fascist, militarist and thirsting for revenge. The White Book goes into this matter in greater detail. I shall therefore not deal here with these attempts to blacken the Federal Government, but rather with the questions raised out of grief and apprehension on the one hand and out of reawakened distrust on the other, whether the majority of these incidents stemmed from a fertile political soil whose layers originated far back in the Nazi past. Looking at the guilty juveniles, we have to ask ourselves: *What went wrong in teaching German youth about the guilt and the fate of the Third Reich? What do these young people know about Hitler and about the Jews? What has so far been done to enlighten them?* These questions are justified, since they are raised abroad and at home by all those responsible, by governments and political parties, schools and churches, trade unions and other organizations. Rowdies—and most of the culprits are rowdies—are, it is true, not deterred from their horseplay by teaching them the facts of politics and contemporary history. I shall have to go into this later. Their deeds however have led to such questions being asked, questions which we have asked ourselves and which world opinion has asked us.

Let me first explain what the Federal Republic has done to spread enlightenment. It cannot influence schools and educational institutions direct, but through the *Federal Centre for Service to the Homeland* and the *Institute of Contemporary History* it gives valuable assistance to all those working in the field of political education.

The work of the Federal Centre

The Federal Centre for Service to the Homeland has since its inception done intensive work in fighting antisemitism and in spreading information about the persecution of the Jews. Its work was based largely on the results of two conferences in 1952 and 1953 attended by historians, sociologists, theologians and psychologists. The Federal Centre has since promoted a great number of study circles, courses of lectures and seminaries at the Evangelical Academies, the Roman Catholic social institutes and other educational centres. At the same time it has sponsored a considerable number of popular and scholarly publications on antisemitism and on the extreme right-wing parties. The following may be quoted as examples of publications for the masses:

Special supplements—particularly in business house journals and sports papers—on the history of the Jews. Circulation at about one million.

Full pages in the *Katholischer Lesebogen* and *Neue Bildpost* with circulations up to 500,000.

Publications for reading circles on *Prejudice*. Circulation up to 300,000.

Publishing and distributing the pamphlet on the subject of the *Reichskristallnacht* edited by the *Friedrich-Ebert-Stiftung* in 50,000 copies.

I should like to mention only two of the many books financed by the Federal Centre: Reitlinger's *The Final Solution* and Eva Reichmann's *Hostages of Civilization*. It may well be said that practically all important books in the field could not have been published but for the active support of the Federal authorities.

The supplements of the weekly *Das Parlament* which has a circulation of 80,000 copies and which is distributed in schools of all kinds, contain documents about Jewish policy of the Third Reich, eye-witness reports by former concentration camp inmates and other relevant information. These articles also appeared in the series of pamphlets published by the Federal Centre *Schriftenreihe der Bundeszentrale für Heimatdienst*, again with a very wide circulation.

Films were also enlisted to spread information. More than 100 copies of the documentaries *Night and Fog* and *Concentration camp Henchmen*—the latter a report on the Sorge-Schubert trial—were distributed. Among the feature films available free for non-commercial distribution I may mention *In those days*. This film contains a long sequence which tells the story of an elderly couple where the wife is Jewish, who are driven to suicide by the *Kristallnacht*, the boycott of their business and other measures of the Third Reich. The documentary *The people and country of Israel* serves as an antidote to the distorted picture propagated by antisemitism.

The wall calendar for schools, of which 65,000 copies were sent out, and the great Christmas competition for schools, in which more than 40,000 school classes participate every year, were used to spread information. The Federal Government and the Länder Centres for Service to the Homeland paid special attention to schools in this respect. A few months ago, to quote only one example, copies of the Hitler biography by Alan Bullock, the Oxford historian, were sent to the history masters of all secondary schools.

Report on the Work of the Institute of Contemporary History

In this context I should like to refer to the work of the Institute of Contemporary History in Munich which is supported by the Federal Government and the Länder Governments. During the ten years of its existence it has become the research centre for the study of National Socialism. Within this framework it also participates in spreading information and enlightenment about modern antisemitism. This is done by the study and portrayal of the nationalsocialist Jewish policy, its intellectual premises, its methods and its results. So far the Institute has published some 25 monographs mainly concerned with national socialist persecution in the Reich and in the occupied territories. Its studies and publications include a fundamental investigation of the incidents during the pogrom of 9th November 1938 which has become known as the *Reichskristallnacht*, documentary evidence of the mass gassings in the East, including the recently published diaries of camp commander Höss on life at Auschwitz. Further publications, both popular and scientific, are being prepared on the persecution of the Jews, the fate of Jewish communities in Germany and the organization of deportations. An interim pamphlet on the number of Jewish victims of National Socialism has already been published, and at the moment investigations are being undertaken to make it a sound basis for research by establishing the exact figures.

By providing the necessary data, the Institute for Contemporary History not only serves the purposes of historic research, but also directly and indirectly influences the work of political education. In close and constant cooperation with institutions such as the Federal Centre and the Länder Centres for Service to the Homeland, suitable publications are made available to a wide circle of readers. The Institute assists all those teaching civics in schools and institutes of further education by providing information, checking manuscripts, promoting exhibitions, supplying visual aids, advising educational publishers and school broadcasters. The members of the Institute take a greater share in the spread of information about the national socialist period by giving lectures at courses sponsored by Länder centres, polytechnics, teacher training colleges, Protestant and Roman Catholic academies and at conferences of the Institute itself. In the practical field members of the Institute are increasingly enlisted to give their expert opinion. During the last few years the Institute has supplied information and expert opinion on the question of the persecution of Jews to public authorities and courts in more than 1,000 civil and restitution cases. The more important of these opinions have since appeared in print.

Success?

Having given this report on the work which certainly bears witness of much serious endeavour, the question remains, how far this work of spreading information has been successful. It will not do to question the success of the enterprise by referring to the answers which young people between 10 and 20 years of age have given in television interviews and Gallup polls. They are supposed to have said that all they knew of Hitler was that he built the Autobahns and did away with unemployment, that all they knew of the Weimar Republic was how long it had lasted, and to have given fumbling and halting answers to the questions: *How do we vote nowadays?* and *Who makes our laws?* (A disappointing result indeed!)

I think, however, that it is quite wrong to deduce from this that in general the work of spreading information has failed and to accuse all schools of having seriously neglected this part of their task, or even of having intentionally and in a spirit of animosity neglected the teaching of contemporary history. Not to mince words, it is wrong and unjust to say so. There is no-one who can claim to have interviewed what might be called a representative cross-section of our young people. Those who accuse the schools and their teachers wholesale, are relying on random samples, and furthermore believe their interviewees when they tell them: *We have not yet done this at school. We have not got that far in our history lessons. We know far more about the events of earlier centuries.*

Little historical knowledge

What about the knowledge of the history of earlier centuries? The *Frankfurter Allgemeine Zeitung* in its edition of May 9th 1959 published the results of the interviewing of primary and secondary school children and of sixth-formers by experts. The material which the newspapers published does not claim to be indisputably representative, but to me it seems valuable because of its samples taken from all the regions and the uniform interpretation of the results. The results which are of interest to us in this context are as follows:

Students of all types of school were quite competent in answering questions referring to measurements and technical subjects. Their knowledge of geography was rather more restricted. The meagreness of their knowledge when historical questions were asked, however, was striking, and this applies to all age-groups and school-types, though there may have been differences in the degree of the lapses, It must not be assumed—we read in this article— that all sixth-formers know about Caesar as a matter of course. Whole groups of other school-leavers referred to Luther as an evangelist, to Kant as a poet, and fifth-form school-leavers placed the apostle Paul in the third century and Frederick the Great in the year 1300, while Napoleon was thought to have been a Roman emperor.

From the results of these tests we must not conclude that earlier periods are as neglected in the teaching of history as is contemporary history. The gaps in the knowledge of our young people only point to the conclusion that in our days, as is generally known, technical matters arouse greater interest than history, the humanities and contemporary history. This impoverishment of interests is, however, quite obviously not peculiar to Germany.

Wall of Silence—Wall of Ignorance

To quote only the British, they too, have their grievances as far as the teaching of contemporary history is concerned as may be seen from an article in the *Manchester Guardian*. I am quoting this article to throw some light on the situation in other countries, rather than to exonerate German students by referring to the shortcomings of their British counterparts. That newspaper wrote a few weeks ago:

"Where the Germans are said to have their *wall of silence*, we seem to have our ramparts of ignorance. . . . Most of the boys and girls who leave our schools know least about the period of history which, to them, is likely to matter most. So it is not surprising that sixth-form pupils should know nothing about the Battle of Britain except that it is some kind of an anniversary. . . . Belsen and Buchenwald mean no more to them than to the average German child, although,—in a different way perhaps—that knowledge is equally important to both."

I should like to add that to our young people this knowledge is not only important, but rather a moral duty and a political necessity. Many of them are aware of it. We are told that there are teachers who devote themselves to this task passionately. Whilst only too often students and teachers are nowadays disparaged, it is often overlooked that the vast majority of young voters have closed their ears to extreme slogans during the Federal and Länder elections, that our young people opened their hearts to the fate of Anne Frank, as can be seen from the number of copies of the book printed and circulated and from the size of the theatre audiences who saw the play, and that there are many more gratifying examples of their open-mindedness. The schools and the informatory work of our public institutions may well claim their share in bringing this about. I feel these few remarks to be necessary to correct the general picture.

History Teaching today

I do not wish to deny that to raise the question of history teaching and of political education both as a subject on the school curriculum and as a matter of principle, does indeed touch on a sensitive point. The difficulties with which this kind of instruction is beset on various levels, seem, however, to be widely ignored. I shall not have time enough today to go fully into all the problems involved, and I shall restrict myself to enumerating just some of the difficulties.
(1) There is no generally valid concept of German history. There is no accepted yardstick to guide the teachers, and for this reason the teacher's own sense of insecurity in this field will often become apparent.
(2) There is no generally valid guiding principle in education. This fact leads to great insecurity in present-day German teaching, particularly in its effect on the teaching of history and politics. In view of what on the face of it looks like superiority of the Eastern Zone, which opposes the diversity of the West with a single order of life and existence, allegedly based on scientific fact, many a teacher asks himself anxiously: *What is the aim of education in the West? Have we no ideological system to compete with theirs?* We have to tell these teachers that the process of differentiation which has become manifest ever since the 15th century, has led not to weakness, but rather to an abundance of ideas which enrich our lives.
(3) The demand made on teachers by the political tasks imposed on them, are very great. The critical assessment of Hitler as well as of

the guilt and fall of the Third Reich has not progressed far enough to enable the results to be passed on during lessons with the desired clarity—to give one example I should like to mention the Reichstag Fire—however much historical research has been endeavouring to draw up at least the broad outlines of the historical and political background.

The subject *political education*, also called education in citizenship, social studies, or social science, must moreover contend with three more complications. Firstly, political education in the Federal Republic cannot take place in a vacuum. It must start from the existing German state. German democracy has twice had to face the same extraordinary difficulty of originating at a time of defeat. In the Anglo-Saxon countries, and above all in the U.S., the culmination of their national history has coincided with the culmination of democratic life. In the Weimar Republic, in spite of the efforts of outstanding individuals, German democracy was unfortunately unable to acquire a convincing identity. Historical research has done little so far to show why the seeds of democracy have failed to come to fruition in German history.

The second factor to be reckoned with is the fact that political education, like all other educational subjects, depends on the age of a child. In accordance with the age of the pupil, a start must be made by conveying concrete facts and only at a later stage it is possible to proceed to explain in the abstract the workings of administration and government. As long as we have a primary school with an 8 years' curriculum, only during the last few years will it be possible to teach the bare rudiments of political education. The third factor is that educating young people for democracy is education for one of the most complicated, though also one of the noblest of political concepts. It means education for freedom and tolerance, for truth and justice, but to make the concept of liberty, even of civic liberty, come alive in lessons, is unfortunately more than difficult.

I have mentioned some of the difficulties, but I shall have to refer to another two presently.

Political knowledge does not ensure political insight

Realizing these difficulties, we should abstain from making demands on education which are impossible to fulfil. It is obviously desirable to teach contemporary history and political education as thoroughly as possible. It is equally desirable that they should be absorbed by the children, so that untruths and the even more dangerous half-truths should soon disappear from their concept of history. It must, however, not be forgotten that political knowledge does not ensure political insight. The teaching of history and contemporary history can only create the conditions for the formulation of political judgment. To protect young people from the seductive appeal emanating from the intolerance, political excesses and inhumanity of Nazi and Communist totalitarianism, the formative powers of religious and ethical teaching are necessary. This job does not rest with the schools, even if only because young people are not merely students, but also apprentices in factories, in craftsmen's workshops and in offices.

The Schools do not bear the sole responsibility

The German Committee for Education and Training was therefore right when it declared in its recent public statement:

The teaching profession will not be prepared to accept a sole responsibility which in fact it shares with the school administration, representatives of public opinion and churches, but above all with parents and the politicians.

Of course this statement is not meant to be an excuse for those schools and those teachers who have in fact neglected the task imposed on them. It quotes several possible reasons for such neglect: inertia, lack of courage and lack of insight, secret sympathy with National Socialism, and a questionable *objectivity*. The Ministers of Education of the Länder who have for many years stressed the urgency of political education in all kinds of schools will doubtlessly intervene ruthlessly wherever failure is due to sabotage of these aims.

The Problem of the Home

The Statement of the Committee goes on to say:

Many teachers are under the influence of parents who do not desire their children to learn the truth about National Socialism.

This is one of the most difficult problems, and in this connection two things seem important to me: the opposition many parents put up against the alleged appeal by the school to the children to sit pitilessly in judgment on their fathers, and the desire of the

older generation to suppress and forget unpleasant facts—not only the chapter entitled *The Third Reich*, incidentally, but history altogether. Friedrich Sieburg once pointedly expressed this in an epigram:
Since the whole past seemed tainted, the Germans decided never to have had a past.
The resistance of many parents leads—in the words of one teacher of history—to the dismantling at home of any results reached in the contemporary history lesson at school.

A thorough Study of history

We see today how one event revives the memory of the past. We should make use of this moment in time. The historian Hans Rothfels of Tübingen University once said that *the wish to forget and suppress . . . has never yet paved the way for recovery. We cannot desert from contemporary history, if we wish to understand ourselves and to establish a vantage point from which to view the future. To achieve this we must work through history in a disciplined search for the truth* though not with *a neutral attitude in questions which concern us essentially and which lead to human decisions.* Historical research totally committed to the spirit of truthfulness, can contribute to the re-emergence of a well-balanced national consciousness by an incorruptible though judicious assessment of the historical self-knowledge of the German people.

At the end of last year when she was awarded the Lessing prize of the city of Hamburg, Hannah Arendt, the Jewish emigrant, conspicuous equally for her intellectual achievements and for her years of personal suffering, mentioned the tendency so frequently found in Germany to pretend that the years between 1933 and 1945 had not existed at all and said:

"Behind all this there is probably far less of that ill-will so often suspected abroad and far more genuine perplexity. This perplexity may well be an inheritance from the so-called inner emigration; it certainly is a direct consequence of the Nazi régime, that is to say of that organized guilt in which the Nazis managed to involve everybody living on German territory, inner emigrants no less than fellow-travellers and party-members. We also find here the roots for that total inability—so startling to the outsider—to take part in a discussion of the problems of the past. The widely-held belief that the past has not been overcome and that a start will have to be made to overcome it, seems to indicate how difficult it must be to find a way out of this dilemma. It is probably never possible to overcome one's past and it is certainly not possible to overcome this particular past. The best thing to strive for is to get to know the past for what it has been, learn to live with this knowledge and to try and build up from there."

A commission of educationalists, theologians and historians

To show a way out of this situation is difficult. Nobody is bold enough to point nonchalantly in this or that direction and to set the pace. We are therefore considering an Advisory Commission to be composed of educationalists and theologians, historians, philosophers and political scientists. The Federal Government intends to set up such a commission as soon as the necessary preparations have been made. It is intended to enlist a few eminent men for this job. We expect advice from them—taking into account our recent past—on the salient points on which best to concentrate political education and what methods appear to be most suitable. Two subjects will in any case be included: the proper dissemination of knowledge about the persecution of the Jews and about the totalitarian abuse of power in the Third Reich. As there seem to be fairly narrow limits within which the knowledge and experience of contemporary history can be transmitted or absorbed, an expert is needed to pick out the most essential subject-matter and the best method of committing it to the students' memory.

The focal point of the task before us is in the field of education in citizenship and political teaching. To be sure, a large part of this task will have to be performed by the schools, but an even more important one may perhaps fall upon the parents. This programme can only be carried out successfully, if all the channels of public opinion and all those who help to form public opinion, play their part in it. Obviously the politicians, too, bear a special responsibility.

Repressive Measures

Perhaps you are going to ask me what is done to suppress such happenings. In this context I may refer to the prompt action of the police and of the public prosecutors. We know that in some cases it has been said that it had taken too long to try the culprits, since sentences pronounced without delay are the most efficacious. It seems to me, however, that there are cases and circumstances which, for reasons of court-procedure or on other important grounds, require a more thorough investigation and therefore take more time. In my view, it can be said that the offences have met with a swift and adequate retribution while over-harshness which might possibly have had a contrary effect, has been avoided. We may expect the maximum effect from sentences which seem fair and adequate to the general public. The Federal Government has already stated in public that the co-operation between the Federal and the Länder authorities in dealing with these incidents has been excellent. The Federal Government is convinced that the cases still pending will be dealt with in the same way, and that the search for culprits who have not yet been apprehended, continues relentlessly. This House surely realizes that the main burden of police investigations and court cases falls on the Länder, but we have no doubt that they look at the position in the same way as we do here.

Banning Parties and Associations

In this context the question has obviously been raised whether there are still organizations or even parties which ought to be prohibited. I should like to refer to the two main tenets of our constitution. We must distinguish between a ban on organizations and a ban on political parties. According to Art. 9 of the Basic Law

Associations the objects or activities of which conflict with the criminal laws or which are directed against the constitutional order or the concept of international understanding, shall be prohibited.

The law says: these organizations shall be prohibited. That means that the police can dissolve them on the spot if and when these conditions apply. This is a matter for the Länder to decide upon and, as you know, several Länder have already used this procedure. According to Art. 21 of the Basic Law the problem of prohibiting a political party is more complicated. I should like to quote the relevant regulations:

Parties which according to their aims and the behaviour of their members seek to impair or abolish the free and democratic basic order or to jeopardize the existence of the Federal Republic of Germany, shall be unconstitutional. The Federal Constitutional Court shall decide on the question of unconstitutionality.

No Opportunism

Political parties therefore enjoy the privilege of being able to act until the Federal Constitutional Court has decided whether they are unconstitutional. You know that this has so far happened twice: in the findings against the *Sozialistische Reichspartei* in 1952 and in that against the Communist party in 1956. In both cases, incidentally, the application had been made almost simultaneously in 1951. This House is equally aware that the Federal Government opines that a procedure of this kind should not be initiated just because it may appear opportune, and that it feels itself in duty bound to apply for a prohibition if and when the conditions in Art. 21 para 2 apply. We do not think it right—and I have good reasons to emphasize this point once more—to distinguish between the dissolution of organizations and the prohibition of political parties for opportunistic reasons. This would be a grave contravention of the spirit of the rule of law. Under different legal systems and in different constitutional areas it might be debated whether the provisions of the Basic Law which I have quoted, serve a useful purpose. As we have to start from the provisions of the Basic Law, however, we do not feel justified in being guided by considerations of expediency in these matters, though much to our amazement we have been repeatedly urged to do so. Obviously no government will be prepared to jeopardize its authority by starting prosecutions which depend on the availability of a vast amount of evidence. Let me say, however, that it would be quite wrong to deduce from this that existing political parties which might possibly be liable to prohibition, should feel secure. The potential enemy of the state lives under the constant threat of the sword of Damocles. The Federal Government cannot, however, be expected to issue a statement every few days as to whether it considers a particular group of people liable to prohibition, and what its intentions are in this respect. Proceedings of this kind are always held in public, though it is by no means necessary to conduct the preliminary government deliberations in public.

Vigilance for publications of the extreme right

I now turn to a different chapter. In recent years there have been frequent complaints from different quarters about a certain kind of extreme right-wing publication. In two cases we have, with the help of Federal lawyers, obtained a ruling by the Federal Court on anti-semitic pamphlets (I am referring to the Lenz and Nieland cases). I agree with members of this House that there are a number of publications especially some from rather unimportant publishing-houses which we all consider highly undesirable. Close study of such publications will confirm that they are entirely undesirable, but leaves a justified doubt as to whether this is in fact unconstitutional literature which ought to be prohibited. We shall—together with the Länder governments—see to it that these publications are and will remain under constant vigilance. I am sure that we all agree on the principle that in our country there must be no freedom for the enemies of freedom. In spite of this, weeds are obviously still allowed to thrive in this our liberal State. It seems to me that the only way to combat these weeds is to deprive them of the fertile soil in which they can grow. In practical terms, this means that everything must be done to keep both the production and the consumption of this product within narrow limits. To achieve this we must not draw undue attention to them, and I greatly regret that publications which had hitherto been completely unknown, are given gratuitous publicity by over-zealous clamour. Again I want to make it quite clear that publications which ought to be proscribed will not be tolerated just because of their lack of importance, but will be dealt with swiftly and noiselessly. Furthermore, we shall again examine in this context how far the *Federal Examination Board for the Protection of the Young from Corrupting Literature* can be further enlisted to help in keeping these things out of the hands at least of our young people.

Summary

I should now like to summarize what I have been saying. The Cologne incident and its repercussions at home and abroad have made us all sit up and consider whether we have fully recognized the tasks which face us today, and whether the measures we have taken are adequate to carry out this task. We are fully aware of the Communist background of part of these incidents. It is palpably true that the concentrated attack launched by Communism on the Federal Republic as the sanctuary of freedom in Germany and the only hope for the liberty of all Germans, tries to make capital out of the events which followed that Christmas night in Cologne. Of course it perfidiously endeavours to hide its own involvement in these events and to raise feelings of fear and disgust against the Federal Republic all over the world. It is equally obvious that it has met with many accomplices who for various reasons assist it in this endeavour. This subject, important though it may be, cannot be discussed further today.

We ask ourselves seriously whether we can continue on the road we took after 1945 and especially after the setting up of the Federal Republic in 1949. We are fully aware of the fact that we can only do this if we untiringly explain the necessity, the meaning and the goal of this road to the whole of our people and enlist their support. It is a most unusual task to start a new chapter of German history following a devastating rule of terror—comparatively short though its duration may have been—and a complete collapse and unconditional surrender. Twenty-seven years have elapsed since the 30th January 1933, and nearly 15 years since the debacle of 1945. Fifteen years is already three years more than the duration of the so-called Thousand Year Reich. It seems to me that the time has come to take a more balanced view of the past. It is not as if we were today faced with the kind of personal decisions we had to take between 1933 and 1945; we have deliberately walked in a different direction for the last 15 years. There still remains the question how we can continue in this direction tomorrow and the day after in view of the mortal threat of Communism which still holds 17 millions of our fellow-countrymen under its sway. We must not quibble about whether people actually or allegedly failed to resist totalitarian National Socialism which after all forced everybody under its yoke; we must judge people by their firm determination to continue unperturbed on the road which we have taken these last 15 years. If we are to achieve the aims which we have set ourselves, four principles will have to be adhered to:

1. Unconditional respect for the constitution and the laws

2. Ruthless disclosure of the crimes of the past régime
3. Prompt retribution for all crimes of that period which have not yet been tried
4. Complete legal protection for all supporters of the constitution and rehabilitation of our country.

We need reconciliation and tolerance not only towards our Jewish fellow-citizens, but amongst all of us. We need the co-operation of the whole of the German people to defend and protect the rule of law.

To summarize: we have listened carefully to the voices from abroad during the last few weeks. Many things that have been said and written abroad have shown that in spite of all the writings about the Third Reich and in spite of the totalitarian reality in today's Communist-controlled countries many people still have no idea of what it means to have to live under a totalitarian régime. On the other hand we have heard expressions of understanding for the problems we have to deal with at the moment. Among them is an article by the Archbishop of Canterbury which we shall remember. In conclusion I should like to quote his words from *The Times* of 20th January 1960:

' "I always feel very conscious of sympathy with the German authorities, because they are not faced with the simple problem of combating anti-semitism, they are also faced at the same time with the problem of restoring the self-respect of a nation that has suffered humiliating defeat in war, and the two things get confused in our minds as well as in other minds. I have noticed a tendency here and elsewhere to take this exhibition of anti-semitism into a kind of spirit of anti-Germanism, and that is the one fatal thing we should not do. We must appreciate, acknowledge and admire the efforts made by Dr. Adenauer to stifle and destroy this evil thing which they know is evil as well as we do." '

Index

Index

Aachen, 87-91
Aachen, Bishop of, 88, 89
Abwehr, see under German Army
Act of Indemnity and Oblivion (Charles II), 24
Adenauer, Konrad, 103, 172, 181
Administration: difficulties in establishing alternative to Nazi, 126-7
Algeria, 180
Allen, W. S., *The Nazi Seizure of Power,* 39
Allensbach Institute for Demoscopy, 181
American Civil War, 19-20, 26-9
    disfranchisement of participants, 28
    Reconstruction, 27-9
    break-up of Southern aristocracy, 29
    of democracy, 28-9
    similarity of post-war conditions with Germany after World War II, 26
American influence in post-war Europe, 106
American Jewish Year Book, 1954, 182n.
American Zone:
    denazification, 75-7, 87-97, 129-38, 161-8, 175-6
    Military Government, 87-94, 131, 144
        lack of German speaking officers, 88
Amnesties, 140
Anti-Nazi movements, 54-5
Anti-Nazism: dangers of, 67

Antisemitic and Nazistic Incidents: statement by Gerhard Schröder, 184, 195-211
Anti-semitism, 33, 44, 57-64
    fight against, 197-8
Arendt, Hannah *The Burden of Our Time,* 48-50
Arnim, General von, 98
Artificial revolution, 177-8
Atrocities, 12
    guilt placards, 96-7
Auschwitz, 64
Autocracy, 34, 35
Ayer, Fred, *Before the Colours Fade,* 93n.

Bad Nauheim, 96-7
Batty, Peter, *The House of Krupp,* 127n.
Beck, General Ludwig, 42-3, 53-4
Bedford, Sybille, *A Legacy,* 108n.
Bennett, John Wheeler, *The Nemesis of Power,* 149n.
Biscarlet, Alfred, 106
Blacas, 14
Blomberg, General von, 54
Bose, 150
Brandt, Willi, 172
Brauchitsch, General von, 54
Brecht, Berthold, 11
Brett-Smith, Richard, *Berlin '45,* 86, 87
Breuer, Buergermeister, 90
British attitudes to Germans, 115-8
British influence in post-war Europe, 106
British Zone:
    denazification, 85-7, 119-26

British Zone—*cont.*
  German government in, 122
  Military Government, 87, 118-28
Bunyan, John, 25

Carnot, General, 15
Central Agency for the Investigation of Nazi crimes, 183
Chamberlain, Neville, 63
Charles I, *King of England*, 21
Charles II, *King of England*, 22, 23, 24, 25
Charles X, *King of France*, 15
Churchill, Winston S., 9, 72, 73-4, 82
  The American Civil War, 27
  Closing the Ring, 73n., 74n.
  Triumph and Tragedy, 74n.
Civil wars, 18
Clarendon, Lord, 23, 25
Clarke, Governor of Mississippi, 25-7
Clay, General Lucius D., *The Present State of Denazification*, 129-38
Cold War, 82, 180
Collective guilt, 11, 95-9, 161, 169-70, 180
  incompatible with denazification, 99
  meaningless to Germans, 99
  precedents, 98
Communism, 35
Communism, Soviet: danger to Western Europe, 127
Communist Party, German, *see* German Communist Party
Concentration camps, 46-50, 64
Control Council, 69, 119
  denazification programme, 77-9
  Directive 24 'Removal from office . . .', 130
  Directive 38 'Arrest and Punishment . . .', 108-13, 130
  Directives: responsibility for implementation, 130
  Law 10 '*Punishment* . . .', 69-71, 74, 140
Cot, Pierre, 106
Crimes against humanity, 70, 71-2, 173
Crimes against peace, 69, 71-2, 152, 173

Cromwell's government, illegality of, 21-2
'Crystal Night', 57-61, 63

Davis, Jefferson, 27
Déat, 103
'Decromwellization', 24-6
Demilitarization, 77
Democratic government, British, 19, 24
Democratization, 12-13, 138, 184
Denazification:
  achievements, 171-84
  American public opinion, 179-80
  American Zone, 75-7, 87-97, 129-38, 161-8, 175-6
  amnesties, 132
  artificial revolution, 163, 177-8
  British difficulties, 127-8
  British doubts of legality, 126
  British Zone, 85-7, 119-26
  and Civil Service, 173
  classification of offenders, 131
  Control Council's Programme, 77-9
  criticisms, 135-7, 178-80
  divergence of methods and policies between zones, 108, 115, 139
  duration of operation, 138-9
  educational aspects, 102, 174
  elimination of Nazis from public life, 76, 78, 82, 87-94, 108, 172-4
  employment of former Nazis, 103
  escape of some guilty persons, 134
  French Zone, 102-103, 107-108, 114, 139
  German 'Law for Liberation from National Socialism and Militarism', 131-3
  German participation, 131
  German view, 145, 168-70, 171-2, 176
  ineffectiveness of, 128
  mass purge, 178-80
  objective, 130
  paper by General Clay, 129-38
  penalty variations, 135-6, 140-41
  precedents, 13-30
  prohibition of Nazi organizations, 178

Denazification—*cont.*
  questionnaires, 164-5
  Russian Zone, 100-101, 130-140, 177
  screening, 164-5
  statistics, 133-4, 167
  termination, 134-5
  trial complexities, 140-41
  trial delays, 135
  tribunals, 131-3, 139, 165-6, 175-6
  U.S. Joint Chiefs of Staff directive, 75-7
Dictatorship, 35
Diethelm, André, 105
Disarmament, 77
Divine Kingship, 21
Doernberg, Stefan, *Die Gebert eines Neuen Deutschland 1945-1949*, 100
Dolfuss, 151
Doriot, 103
Dunning, W. A., *Essays on the Civil War and Reconstruction*, 29*n*.

Education, 78
Eichmann, 66
  trial, 81
Eicke, 4, 47
Eisenhower, General Dwight D., 98, 119
Enabling Act (Hitler's 1933), 39
English Civil War, 19, 21-6, *see also* Restoration of Charles II
Ernst, 44
'European ideal', 181
Extermination camps, 64

Faust, Buergermeister, 90
Federal Centre for Service to the Homeland, 197
Federal German Republic, *see under* Germany
Ferrard, 16
FitzGibbon, Constantine *The Blitz*, 115*n*.
Fouché, 14, 16
Frankfurter Allgemeine Zeitung, 200
Fraternization, *see* Non-fraternization
Freedom (of speech, etc), 79

French Army: 'Vichyism', 105-6
French attitude to denazification, 102, 108
French 'collaborators', 103, 105-6
French influence in post-war Europe, 106-8
French political divisions, 103-6
French Revolutionary War, 14-17
French Zone:
  denazification, 102-3, 107-8, 114, 139
  Military Government, 104-8
Fritsch, General von, 54
Für die Demokratie, 182*n*.
Fyfe, Sir David Maxwell, 152

Galen, Cardinal, 54
Garner, J. W., *Reconstruction in Mississippi*, 26-7
Genocide, 64
German Army, 34, 42, 51
  Abwehr, 54
  arrest of officers for joining Nazi Party, 42
  attitudes to Nazis, 43
  conscription and its effects, 52
  conspiracies against Hitler, 1938-44, 54-5
  exemption from *Gleichschaltung*, 53
  Hitler's consideration for, 52-3
  oath of allegiance to Hitler, 44
  political aloofness, 42, 52, 55
  rearmament, 53
  and SS, 65
German Committee for Education and Training, 204
German Communist Party, 32, 38
  members seek safety in Nazi Party, 40-1
German National People's Party, 31, 38
German public opinion, development of, 176-7
German resistance, *see* Anti-Nazi movements
German State Secretariat of South Wurtemburg: *Ordinance for Public Cleansing*, 108

Germany:
  condition in defeat, 9
  emergence of public opinion in 1945, 176-7
  Federal German Republic, 129
    allied trust, 138
    economic expansion, 181
    trial of Nazi criminals, 182
  pastoralization proposals, 9-10
  post-war economic situation, 123-5
  post-war food situation, 85-6, 122, 125
  undesirability of partition, 101-102
Gerstenmaier, 172
G-5, 144
Gilbert, G. M., *Nuremberg Diary*, 147n.
Globke, 181
Goebbels, Josef, 9, 32, 44, 56, 57
Goerdeler, 55
Gollancz, Sir Victor, 118
Göring, Hermann, 32, 36, 44, 81
Government decentralization, 78-9
Grumbach, Salomon, 106
Guderian, Heinz *Panzer Leader*, 53
Guilt, collective, *see* Collective guilt

Hague Convention of 1907, 126
Hammerstein, General von, 43
Hassell, 55
Heines, 44
Helldorf, 55
Herwaith, 120
Hess, 81
Heydrich, Reinhard, 57
Himmler, Heinrich, 32, 44, 45, 50
Hindenburg, 52
Hipt, Op de, Buergermeister, 90
History:
  teaching in Britain, 201
  teaching in Federal Germany, 198-206
Hitler, Adolf, 31, 34, 37, 38-9, 44, 45, 149, 150, 151
  appointed Chancellor, 39
  breaks Munich Treaty, 63
  Enabling Act, 1933, 39
  and German Army, 52-3
  opinion poll on, 1954, 181
  skill in manipulating followers, 34-5
  territorial claims, 51
  lack of public approval of war, 56
Hoess, Rudolph, 46
  Commandant of Auschwitz, 46-8
Hoover, Edgar J., 182
Horne, Alastair, 103
Hugenberg, Alfred, 38

Indochina, 180
Industry, break up of, 127
Institute of Contemporary History, 198
International Military Tribunal, 69, 132

Japan: artificial revolution, 163-5
Jaspers, Karl, *The Future of Germany*, 55, 162n., 172-3
Jews, non-German: attitudes to Germans, 118
Johnson, President Andrew, 28
Judicial system, reform of, 78, 79-81
Jung, 150

Keitel, 81
Kersten, Felix, *The Kersten Memoirs*, 50n., 64n.
Kesselring, *Memoirs*, 53
Kiesinger, 99-100
Klausener, 150
Knappstein, Karl Heinrich, *Die Versaeumte Revolution*, 177n.
Koch, 47
Koenig, General, 119
Koestung, General, 120
Kogon, Eugen, 183
Korean War, 180

Lafayette, Marquis de, 15
'Law for Liberation from National Socialism and Militarism', 131-3
Lawrence, Chief (Lord) Justice, 152, 153
Leber, 55
Leuschner, 55
Liddell Hart, Captain Sir Basil, 91

Lincoln, Abraham, 27
Lindemann, Professor (Lord Cherwell), 117, 118
Looting, 11-12, 142
Loritz, 47
Louis XVIII, *King of France*, 14, 16

Maginot Line, 53
Maistre, de, 17
Maitland, F., *Constitutional History of England*, 22
Manchester Guardian, 201
Marxism, 32
Meredith, George, 27-8
Meyer, 'Panzer', 65, 171-2
Mies, Buergermeister, 90
Military courts, 81
Milton, John, 25
Mitchell, Margaret, *Gone with the Wind*, 20
Moltke, 55
Montgomery, Field-Marshal Bernard, 118-20
  Memoirs, 119, 120-26
Montgomery, John D., *Forced to be Free*, 163-8
Morgenthau, Henry, 9
Moyzisch, L. C., *Operation Cicero*, 151n.
Munich Treaty, 63
Müssnazi, see under Nazis
Mussolini, Benito, 34, 151

Namier, Sir Lewis, 117, 118
Napoleon, 14, 15-16
Napoleonic Wars, 14-17
  Act of Amnesty, 16
  White Terror, 16
Napoleon's Hundred Days, 16
Nazi: synonymous with German, 57
Nazi crimes, 64-5
Nazi criminals, 64-7
  accomplices, 67-8
  ease of escape in Federal Germany, 183
  exoneration claims, 66, 67
  murder not confined to Jews, 66
  refusal not punishable by death, 66-7

  see also War criminals
Nazi government: illegality of, 22
Nazi laws: abolition, 78
Nazi officials: pensions, 182
Nazi Party:
  abolition by Occupying Powers, 130
  dissolution, 75, 78
  governing class acceptance, 44-5
  increase in support in 1931-2, 38
  increase in support after Hitler became Chancellor, 39
  lack of homogeneity, 38, 45
  murders of 1934, 43-4
  political prisoners, 46
  professional organizations, 40
  property, 70, 76
  records, etc, 76
  tensions of 1934, 43-4
Nazi plebiscites, 45, 55
Nazi regime:
  illegality of, 75
  opinion poll on, 1954, 181-2
Nazi-Soviet Pact 1939, 56, 63
Nazi supporters (non-Party members), 41-2
Nazi terror, 40-1, 44, 45-6
Nazis, 36-7
  elimination from public life, 76, 78, 82, 87-94, 108, 172-4
  Control Council Directive 38, 108-13
  difficulties, 88-91
  Ordinance for Public Cleansing, 108
  motives for becoming Party members, 37-8, 39-40
  Müssnazis, 41, 55
  re-emergence of, 130, 180-1
  re-employment in public life, 103, 136-7
  Russian attitude and treatment, 83, 100
  types, 37-8
Nazism, 31-6, 50-1
  anti-semitism, 33, 44
  appeal, 35-6
  attitude to culture, 36
  criminal nature, 64

Nazism—*cont.*
 destructive policies, 32, 33-4
 economic policies, 33, 44
 Gleichschaltung, 33, 34, 40, 44, 45
 lack of opposition by 1938, 51
 'leadership principle', 34-5, 36-7
 and Marxism, 32
 paradoxes of, 31-2
 responsibility of non-Party members, 157-9
 study and teaching in Federal Germany, 199
Neumann, Franz, 182
Ney, Marshal, 16
Niemoeller, Pastor, 41
Night of the Long Knives, 43-4
Non-fraternization, 11, 83-7
 abolition, 119
Nuremberg Trials, 12, 81

Oberlaender, 181
Occupation :
 allied responsibility, 77
 American, 82
 purposes, 11
 Russian, 82
 Zones, 75
Oppen, B. Ruhm von, *Documents on Germany under Occupation 1945-1954*, 71*n*., 81*n*.
Oppenhoff, Franz, 88-90
Ordinance for Public Cleansing, 108
Organizations, prohibition of, 207

Padover, Saul K., *Psychologist in Germany*, 83-5, 89-91
Papen, Baron Franz von, 41, 44, 147-62
 denazification trial, 153-4
 court of appeal, 156-7
 judgement, 154-5, 157-61
 Memoirs, 147*n*., 152*n*., 161*n*.
 Nuremberg trial, 152-3
Pastoralization proposals, 9-10, 74
Patriotism, 56
Patton, General George S., 91-4
Peace Settlement of 1919, 10
'Persil certificates', 166, 175
Police, 182-3

Political apathy, 55-6
Political education, 203, 206
Political parties, prohibition of, 207-209
Political reconstruction, 78
Potsdam Conference, 75, 77, 82
Propaganda leaflets, British, 56-7
Public opinion in post-war Germany, 176-7
Punishment, 70
 collective, 11
 individual, 12

Questionnaires, 140, 185-94

RFK, 37, 40
Rathenau, Walter, 41
Red Choir (Anti-Nazi Communist Group), 54
Re-education, 12
Reitlinger, Gerald, *The Final Solution*, 64
Restoration of Charles II, 22-6
 'decromwellization', 24-6
 property, 23-4
 punishment of Cromwellians, 22-3
 restoration of legal system, 26
 treatment of clergy, 24-5
 treatment of enemies of the Crown, 23
 treatment of writers, 25
Revolutionary war, 18
Rhodes, James F., *Lectures on the American Civil War*, 27*n*.
Richelieu, Duc de, 14, 16-17
Roehm, Ernst, 32, 37, 43, 44, 45, 53
Rommel, Field-Marshal, 120
Roosevelt, Franklin D., 9, 72, 73
Rotfrontkämpfer (Red Front Fighters) *see* RFK
Roth, Guenther, and Wolff, Kurt H., *The American Denazification of Germany*, 174-180
Russell of Liverpool, Lord, *The Scourge of the Swastika*, 64
Russian attitude to denazification, 10
Russian attitude towards Germans, 74, 75

221

Russian exploitation of defeated Germany, 10
Russian influence in post-war Europe, 106
Russian Zone:
  communization, 130
  continued occupation, 11
  denazification, 100-101, 139-40, 177
  political incorporation of East Germany, 101

SA, 37, 38, 40-41
  murders of 1934, 43-4
SD, 64, 66
SHAEF, 118-19
SS, 43-4, 45, 49, 50, 51, 57, 64, 65-6
  hate indoctrination towards prisoners, 46-7
SS generals: pensions, 182
Sack, Dr Carl, 42, 55
Salomon, Ernst von, 41-2, 168-70, 185
  The Answers, 57-63
Save Europe Now movement, 118
Schacht, Dr, 38
Scheele, Godfrey, *The Weimer Republic*, 127n.
Schefer, Buergermeister, 90
Schleicher, General von, 44, 149, 150
Schmid, Carlo, 103
Schröder, Gerhard, 184
Schulenberg, 55
Schumacher, 172
Schützstaffeln (Protection Squads), see SS
Shirer, William, *The Rise and Fall of the Third Reich*, 51n
Sicherheitsdienst (Security Service), see SD
Siegfried Line, 53
Social Democrat Party, 31-2, 38
Soult, Marshal, 14
Soviet Control Commission: orders dissolution of forced labour camps, 101
Soviet Military Administration: order on denazification, 100
Sozialistische Reichspartei, 208
Stalin, Joseph, 72, 73
  advocates pastoralization, 74
  attitude to war criminals, 74, 75
Stathelm (Steel Helmet), 37
Stauffenberg, Colonel von, 43
Stern, James, *The Hidden Damage*, 95-7
Strasser brothers, 32
Sturmabteilungen (Storm Battalions), see SA
Swastika daubings, 184
  communist exploitation, 196, 210
  German reaction, 196
  investigation, 206-7

Tabert, Paul, 105
Talleyrand, 14, 16
Torture, 48-9
Treskow, Henning von, 68
Trott, 55
Truman, Harry S., 82

Ulbricht, 10
Ultras, 15, 16
United States Army: Counter Intelligence Corps, 89
United States Joint Chiefs of Staff: directive on denazification, 75-7

Vane, Sir Harry, 23
Vansittart, Lord, 117, 118
Versailles Treaty, 10

Waffen SS, 65-6
War, aims of, 13
War crimes: definitions, 69-70
  see also Crimes against humanity, Crimes against peace, Nazi crimes
War criminals, 69, 78
  accomplices, 70
  categories and definitions, 70, 109-13
  complexities of trials, 140-41
  Control Council Law 10, 69-71, 74
  limitation of immunity, 71
  punishment, 70
    allied decision on, 72-4
    Moscow Declaration 1943, 74
    warning by allies, 73
  responsibility, 66, 70-71

War Criminals—*cont.*
  Stalin's attitude, 74, 75
  trials, 81-2
War criminals, *see also* Nazi criminals
Weber, Max, 126
Wedgwood, C. V., *The Trial of Charles I*, 21
Weissberg, Alex, *Advocate for the Dead*, 66*n*.
Wellington, Duke of, 14, 16
Westphalia, Treaty of, 13
Whig Party, 24
White Rose (Anti-Nazi Group), 54

Wilkie, Wendell, 20
Willis, F. Roy, *The French in Germany 1945-1949*, 104*n*.-6
World War I, 17
World War II:
  British aim to restore law and order, 26
  seen as civil war by U.S. and Britain, 20, 29-30
Wurm, Bishop, 54

Yalta Conference, 75

Zhukov, Marshal, 119